The SOCCER COACHING Handbook

Martin Bidzinski

The Crowood Press

First published in 1996 by
The Crowood Press Ltd
Ramsbury, Marlborough
Wiltshire SN8 2HR

British Library Cataloguing-in-Publication Data
A catalogue record for this book is available from the British
Library

ISBN 1 85223 973 5

Picture Credits
All photographs by Lewis Walsh and Martin Bidzinski
Line drawings by Martin Bidzinski

Printed and bound by J W Arrowsmith Ltd, Bristol

CONTENTS

INTRODUCTION

If you are a teacher, parent, coach, manager, trainer or player and you care about what happens to the talent in your charge, or to yourself, then take this opportunity to develop a constructive approach to soccer training. This approach can change your playing potential. Forget the mythology which some believe, that players are born and not made because even the greatest players in the world have worked hard to improve their skills. The back streets of Argentina and the beaches of Brazil are no strangers to the game of soccer. What people do not realize is that many of our children in the Western world do not venture out on to the streets to play soccer-type games. There are housing estates that only provide children with warning signs of 'No Ball Games'! So it is little wonder that many children have been discouraged from taking up sporting activities.

The recent changes in the laws of the game will have enormous consequences for local children. The notion that your child does not need coaching will prove to be incorrect in the future. In the past the skills element came second to mental and physical toughness, and most players were chosen for their tackling ability and strength in running. Astonishingly, there are people today who still do not believe in soccer coaching, thinking it unnecessary. How many times have you heard it said that players are over-coached? This is a refusal to face facts, and its effect on the game has been to deprive thousands of children of the opportunity to play the game professionally.

Just take a look at the playing conditions for most players and you will see how many have lost out because of this attitude. Many facilities are poor and date back to Victorian times; for example, there are often no shower facilities. Many people still play on fields that resemble patches of wasteland, allocated for soccer only because of their uselessness for other purposes. The men who spend millions of pounds building a super club should take time out to look over their shoulder and see the many children that go without. Perhaps it is time to consider the whole structure of the game from top to bottom, and not just build isolated fortresses that could become just that in the end. Does it make sense to disregard local talent, and spend millions of pounds buying in talent from elsewhere? I know my answer to this question.

Playing the game at any level requires putting in some effort and thought regarding the work that involves the team. The easy option is always to do nothing, but this attitude is harmful to the players. Ill-prepared teams suffer the indignity of constantly having to experience losing matches. Confidence is not built in such an environment, and anyway it is wholly unnecessary. With the right approach to training everyone can share in the feeling of being a winner.

WHAT IS WRONG WITH THE ENGLISH GAME?

The future standards of play and the long-term prospects of the game of soccer depend on a new and modern approach to training. It is vital to understand that the acquisition of skills for the modern game comes from special training exercises, which are concerned with working with the ball in a specific way. Acquiring skills therefore depends on the way the player practises. In the past, many of the training sessions were in fact detrimental to the skills side of the player's abilities because they were based purely on fitness routines that catered for an aggressive approach to play. The emphasis on running exercises has enormous consequences for the future prospect of any player, because when your work is dominated by running formats you are in danger of actively reducing the player's potential through an incorrect development of his body shape.

What do I mean by that? Well, when you concentrate on nothing but hard running and playing five-a-side soccer the legs develop the so-called short hamstring syndrome; this type of leg is then restricted in its ability to perform the range of movements required to reach higher levels of skill.

Furthermore, because of the changes currently being implemented in the game of soccer, it is more vital than ever to train players properly, or

they will not make the top grade of professional soccer. Players brought up in an incorrect training environment may be selected to play in league/national sides because they are better than most, but when it comes to the international standards of play, they will not make the grade under the present circumstances. There are still far too many people who think that the answer lies in such concepts as two-touch play formats, where the first touch receives the ball and the second plays it to the designated target. They do not appreciate the significance of the first touch, or the importance of other skills in play. These are not practised in isolation as they should be, but are simply taken for granted.

My approach to training has evolved as a result of my own experience abroad and after a great deal of time spent studying the English working system. This study has taken a number of years and has involved watching training sessions in dozens of clubs up and down the country. The results of my work are put together here to create a new approach to improving skills, one which recognizes that these skills are not brought into being by simply letting the player loose with the ball on the practice ground. I have watched how well-intentioned, skilful players show everyone what they can do, expecting others to emulate their work. But this approach does not work, as the skills involved are too complex to be transmitted in such a fashion. The solution was to develop exercises and work routines which would transfer skills from coach to player as effectively as possible.

It is simply not possible to achieve high standards of play in conventional training sessions. Look at the facts. If your players go out and perform a warm-up routine for thirty minutes, then come in and continue training in a keep possession format, working in a group environment, for a further thirty minutes, that is an hour or so into the training session already, and the players have hardly kicked the ball. When such working sessions are rounded off with the players playing a full game conditioned to the two-touch play format, I can assure anyone with common sense that this type of training programme is regressive in the long run. The players may have worked hard, but many skills have not been dealt with at all in their practice session. The actual volume of work with the ball is minimal, and the only (questionable) benefit to the player is to his fitness. Players will lose out as a result of this type of training session because in the long run they will be lacking in skills.

The training routines in this book are about the practice of skills. These include natural soccer fitness movements and effects built into the working formats, but fitness is put in a proper context in relation to skills: this time the cart is not put before the horse. Fitness should be used as a supplement to the practice of skills, and not the other way round. The exercises in this book make use of cones as training aids, and are designed to give the player the best chance ever of acquiring skills with the ball. Helped by the cone formations you can simulate the required movements in play, and in this way can develop your game to world-class standard.

The first part of this book deals with conventional fitness, explaining how to develop your body in a way that does not restrict proper growth of the limbs. The variations in training routines enable the body to develop an all-round fitness. The soccer training routines subsequently develop the player's technical side, and they complement each other to produce the right type of player for the modern game of soccer.

Training routines must simulate game conditions: there is no point in sticking to convention and the square format mentality if it means that players become less skilful with the ball. The training programme must also include all aspects of play. There are skills beyond the two-touch format, and these can only be brought out through appropriate training routines. Each skill has to be worked on separately – there is no point working on game formats that do not distinguish between the different ball-play skills.

The whole secret to improving skills lies in repetition formats. These allow the player to practise different skills without wasting time. There is a misconception that the only way to practise soccer is to play the actual game. Nothing could be further from the truth. If you rely on one, or possibly two games per week, to improve your playing skills, it is most unlikely that you will achieve the standards required to play professional soccer. If you want to play professionally, you need to start young and be prepared to spend most of your free time working out to repetition skills-training exercises, as well as playing soccer. When you are much older, you may be able to achieve high enough standards to be considered.

One thing is for sure, if you do not practise you will never find your true playing potential. If you have this book to hand, there will be few excuses left for not acquiring skills; and some of the exercises described are so simple to organize – all you need is a partner and a ball. Remember that practice does improve your skills, and that these will come in handy when you actually do come to play a game.

There are three very important skills which are considered fundamental to playing requirement. The first is getting the ball under control. To achieve this skill, use the exercises described in Chapter 5; these will make you proficient when you first touch the ball. Relate this skill format to the more advanced ball-control formats in Chapter 6 and later chapters. The second essential skill is the ability to keep possession of the ball; and the third is the skill of passing, which is also practised as an end product to many of the working formats. On issues concerning passing, take a look at the two- and three-man formats explained in Chapter 6, and relate these to the more advanced passing options described later.

I feel that it is time for everyone to be honest about the future prospects of many (especially children) who participate in the hope of becoming professional soccer players. I have already mentioned that the two-touch formats are doing damage to the English game. If this were the only problem then it could be changed overnight, and in time the skills would improve, of that there is no doubt. However, there are more serious issues at stake, such as the misguided notion that reducing the number of young players in a team to eight will solve the problems of how to improve ball-play skills. This will only serve to make the game even more exclusive, and could mean that soccer becomes a purely middle-class sport. This would be a disaster for soccer, which in order to evolve properly needs to be open to everyone.

The solution to the problem of skills development does not lie in reducing the number of participants in soccer; after all, we have already lost thousands of young people to the computer industry. It would be far better to use money from the National Lottery to pay for proper training and facilities for young people. The answer lies in building proper-sized soccer fields with the right surface and playing conditions, so the players have more room to play the ball and can develop their ball skills effectively. With good facilities and the right approach to training there is no reason why many young players cannot develop their skill potential to take up the game professionally. It is sheer nonsense to suggest that there is no room at the top – players cannot last forever, and in fact there is a current shortage of talent, which means there are not enough quality players out there to satisfy the needs of the top clubs. The dearth of proper coaching and appreciation of what coaching is about, together with such limited investment in playing and training facilities, have all contributed to this lack of skills and developed talent today.

FITNESS

Players: before you start implementing

the training programme, get some advice from your doctor regarding your well-being. Check over your heart rate, blood pressure, weight and so on. If the results are good, start the initial training period of three weeks. Use the heart-rate assessor formula to help you to set your fitness level, and working with this information, formulate your work-load heart-table to establish the correct pace for your work within the relevant parts of the training programme (*see* page 14).

There are very important physical considerations that need to be taken into account prior to commencing fitness training. It is vital to be honest with yourself and find out just how fit you really are. The tests described in Chapter 1 can help you with this task, but even a simple mirror assessment can tell you if your body needs some attention. The easiest way to assess fitness is by looking at the amount of fat around your waistline. This area of the body is the first to show signs of deterioration in your general state of fitness. You do not need to be a scientist to know if you have problems in this direction. Try the simple test of tying up your shoelaces: if you are becoming fat you will find it difficult to bend down without your stomach pressing on your diaphragm, making it difficult for you to breath. The remedy lies in such actions as changing your diet – which, if you are honest with yourself, usually means cutting back on things such as chocolates and fry-ups – and exercising. If you like the occasional beer, this could also contribute to your fitness problems. None of the products mentioned are bad for you as such, and a

glass of beer when you are older is even advisable to help your digestive system and blood circulation. The real problem lies in the quantity consumed on any given day.

Other problems include a legacy of keeping to regular habits, instilled in you for a lifetime, which means that you usually eat at regular intervals, rather than when you are hungry. These problems are further compounded by our modern indoor lifestyle, which often leads to snacks between meals; and people are especially at risk of over-eating when watching television. Certain media advertisements depict food and drink, and this can induce a feeling of hunger; moreover some people cannot resist these temptations, and will get up to make the tea, with which they will almost certainly eat something. The worst time for this type of habitual advertisement-induced over-eating is in the evenings and at the weekends. Excess carbohydrates are stored as fat for use at a later time, but of course repeating the same eating and lifestyle habits day after day leaves the stored fat intact. Therefore the most important consideration in getting back to fitness is *you*: being strict with what you eat and drink goes hand in hand with this fitness programme.

The only way to become fit is to get out and about, to get out of that arm-chair and to find something really pleasurable to do. The following fitness plan has this in mind and is set to bring you back to fitness in a gradual way. The first stage of the structured plan is as follows: in weeks 1, 2 and 3 concentrate on your general fitness activity or activities, for example swimming, fell walking, or bicycle riding, which are all recommended for building up general fitness. Combine this type of activity with a reduction in your intake of extra top-up snacks such as biscuits and sweets, and soon you should be able to proceed with the next fitness level stage – interval training. Once you reach weeks 7 and 8 of the fitness programme, you are well on your way to regaining fitness. If you are already fit and play soccer, you will find that fitness is sustained thereafter by the various specialized training exercises. The outline of the programme is explained in detail in the following chapters.

Every individual is different, and what is good for one may well be harmful for another, yet most players train in a group environment where no consideration is given to individual players. No assessment of their physical condition takes place before training begins, although this should be standard procedure. I have taken part in training sessions where the coach has almost run the group into the ground in order to get them fit. That initial approach to fitness was incorrect and the coach was

very fortunate to get away with it. It is important to stick to time schedules and to build up the workload gradually and in stages so that you can become fit safely. This will also mean that your fitness will be sustained for longer periods of time, and you do not have to spend weeks recovering from a pre-season injury, which is often the case when you try to force the pace of training early on, or when you try to cram your pre-season training into just five weeks.

Soccer is very demanding on the human body. When watching players in action, you see them constantly having to stop, sprint, jog, walk, run, jump, stop again, and this type of movement variation is emulated in training exercises. The coach should be able to create training routines that reflect real game situations, especially when the topic is fitness, keeping in mind that everyone is different.

FOOTWEAR
(Figs 1 & 2)

It is important to understand how to avoid long-term injuries and how to minimize the effect of wear and tear on

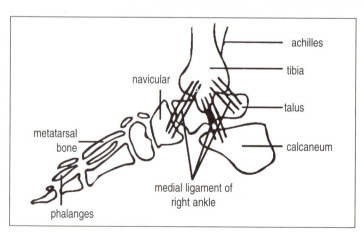

achilles

tibia

navicular

talus

metatarsal
bone

calcaneum

medial ligament of
right ankle

phalanges

Fig 1 The ankle joint has very little in the way of shock absorbers. As you can see there is not much substance between the talus and the calcaneum. All the more reason for proper footwear. The achilles tendon is just visible attached to the back of the tibia; this region should also be protected from blows, kicks and cuts.

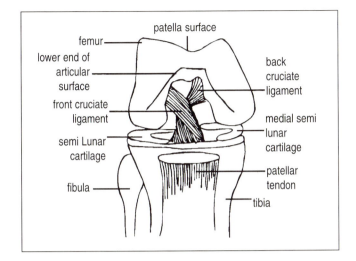

Fig 2 The knee joint has the semi lunar cartilage and the medial semi lunar cartilage. These are the main shock absorbers between the femur and the tibia, and can suffer wear and tear through bad management of your body.

your joints. The legs, heart and lungs are the player's main tools of the trade in soccer. Throughout my younger days I was not concerned with any part of my body; I shrugged all injuries off with resignation and accepted them without question, thinking that they were unavoidable and that beause I loved soccer so much I was willing to pay any price just as long as I was able to play. This attitude is common among young people, but as adults we are responsible for guidance and setting good examples. This applies particularly to choice of footwear. It is true that in the 1960s footwear technology was primitive and it was common to perform exercises in plimsolls, which offered no foot or leg support. There is no excuse today, and no teacher worth his salt should permit physical training to take place on hard surfaces using this type of footwear. It should be common knowledge that to protect your leg joints you need some kind of shock absorption at the base of your feet.

Parents do have priorities, however, and it is a fact that most household economies are budgeted to the limit and that sadly the price of shoes today is off-putting to say the least. However, providing proper footwear should be a priority, considering the damage that can occur to young joints and bone structures otherwise.

In England soccer is played during the autumn and winter months, when wet and hard grounds and windy conditions are commonplace. No one seems to be aware of the vital need for grass, or to understand its function in sport. Grass is dormant in the winter, and has simply no shock absorption value whatsoever. It is very important for young children to play on grass: grass protects the joints because it absorbs and cushions the leg on impact with the ground. Thus it would be better for young people to play soccer in two separate seasons, early summer and early winter, because this would avoid playing in appalling ground conditions which are detrimental to the development of skills. Better playing surfaces would

11

greatly reduce long-term health problems such as arthritis and other more serious conditions, such as diseased hips, in later years.

If you do have to play in hard conditions, try to protect your feet by avoiding footwear with a limited number of studs. Make sure that the stud configuration keeps your feet from slipping in any direction. Remember that running forwards has a pulling grip motion, and that trying to stop has a pushing motion; your studs should be able to cope with both. I once sustained a very bad injury to the base of my spine because I did not suspect that the grip configuration on my boots was faulty. Most injuries occur as a result of bad grip configuration and a lack of consideration given to the type of grip necessary for the surface you are about to use. Perhaps shoe manufacturers should consider an all-purpose shoe, which would greatly help youngsters to avoid injuries because it is common practice to buy one type of footwear and use it come what may.

PREPARING FOR FITNESS TRAINING 1

THE NEED FOR FITNESS

The training programme introduces the player to a gradual escalation of difficulty in physical training, a process which allows his body to adjust to ever-greater needs. The heart becomes stronger and the muscles firm up in response to training. The most important point in this approach to training is that the initial energy requirements come from the fat cell reserves around your body. Reducing the fat content of your body helps your lungs and heart to work more easily, because there is less resistance to blood and oxygen flow.

Oxygen debt is a common occurrence in athletic activities; for example, in soccer it happens when a player competes for the ball, but cannot perform the task of breathing properly while having to sprint or turn or jump for the ball in competition with his opponent. In these circumstances all the player's efforts go into performing one given task such as sprinting (rather than breathing), thus causing a reduction of oxygen in the working cells. We need oxygen in order to transform food into energy. Food and oxygen are transported to the cells by the blood (oxygenation), and the blood is forced around the body by the heart. The more energy you need, the more oxygen and food the cells need in order to give you that energy. Insufficient oxygen causes a breakdown in the energy process, and the cells, instead of giving energy, produce toxic substances known commonly as lactic acid. The build-up of toxic waste products causes a loss of energy. The speed of recovery depends on your lung and heart capacity: the bigger the capacity, the quicker the recovery of oxygen to these cells. Hence the need to develop the right amount of muscle cells and sufficient heart and lung capacity to deal with the energy and recovery requirements of soccer.

ASSESSING YOUR FITNESS

Players who are doubtful about their fitness can go through the tests described below to establish just how unfit they are. The tests require you to have access to a beam, or failing that, a similar stout bar that can be fixed at a suitable height above the ground. The results of the fitness tests should be a guide to the starting point of your training programme. It could be that your fitness level is good enough to allow you to come in at the interval training stage (weeks 4 and 5) of the fitness program. If the results are poor, however, then obviously you need to come in at the beginning of the programme.

There are two types of fitness test: one to test your cardio-vascular fitness, and the other to test your physical fitness. If you have been inactive for some time the tests are there for your initial fitness assessment. These tests will give you information about which parts of your body are at their weakest and which parts do not need as much attention. This is very important, as you do not want to work on strengthening muscles which are already strong and could be affecting other muscles in an adverse way. If you did, your body could become deformed with time, causing you pain and problems in later years. Once you have achieved at least the pass mark on all the tests, then you can assume that all your muscles are on equal terms of fitness, and you must maintain a balanced training programme.

The Cardio-Vascular Test

This cardio-vascular test is quite common and is suitable for anyone who can run. It is safe to assume that if you can perform to fairly high standards in most of the tests here, there should be no problems in your taking up work in relation to soccer. Check your pulse rate before you start by counting the number of beats in 15 seconds and multiplying by four – this gives you your resting heart rate. Jog for a period of 4 minutes (this uses 60 per cent of your maximum running power), stop and take your pulse again.

This tells you how your heart is performing and on this result you adjust your pace of training. For example, if your target is 130 beats per minute (bpm), and your pulse showed a rate of 160bpm, you should slow down; if your pulse showed 120bpm, you should increase training intensity. Take your pulse again after 10 minutes of resting to see how quickly it returns to your normal resting rate: the fitter you are, the quicker you will recover. For example, if after jogging for 4 minutes your heart-rate pulse was around 112bpm

and after 10 minutes of inactivity it was still 80bpm, and your normal resting rate was 70bpm, you would be in obvious need of fitness training.

Very fit athletes may have a resting heart rate of as low as 58bpm. Such fitness levels can be found in tennis players and short distance sprinters. Soccer players have slightly higher rates set at around 60 in general terms. Normal heart rates are set at an average of around 70bpm, while unfit people (ones who are overweight or inactive) are logged at around 90 resting heart rate bpm. The heart has a working range of anything up to 200-plus bpm when under severe exertion so it is vital to determine your fitness starting point in relation to the training programme.

If you are fit, but have not trained for a long time, you should still proceed cautiously because fit or otherwise it is a mistake to begin training without a gradual build-up to fitness. Follow the stage-by-stage guidelines in the programme. If you are totally unfit, the simple solution is to extend the general fitness part of the programme and give yourself more time to reach the next level of fitness.

The Physical Fitness Tests

Balance (Figs 3 & 4)

The three semicircular canals and the vestibule parts of the ear are responsible for balance. It is possible to walk on pavements without noticing a particular balance problem; but if there is anything wrong with your balance, then attempting a steady walk along the beam with arms outstretched will bring the problem to light.

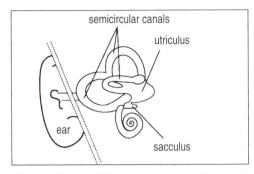

Fig 3   The semicircular canals are filled with a special fluid. The balance of the player is adjusted when the canals are tilted and the fluid touches specially located balance sensory receptacles.

Upper Body (Figs 5 & 6)

The second test involves the suprasinatus, the deltoid and the pectoralis major muscles and the scapula (shoulder blade). This part of your body must be able to cope with the impact of a fall. The hands are positioned differently on the beam according to which muscle group you wish to strengthen. Fig 5 shows the underarm hand grip which exercises the biceps, while Fig 6 shows an alternative hand grip targeting both the biceps and the deltoid muscle groups across your upper back. To assess how strong you are, hang from the beam (Fig 5) and try to pull yourself up to touch the beam with your chest (Fig 6) ten times. The pass mark for this test is seven.

Abdominal Strength (Figs 5 & 7)

This test is very good for training stomach and back muscles safely, because the body position on the beam utilizes the natural weight of the body without putting pressure on the spine – in fact

the spine is flexed. Fig 5 shows the starting position. Pulling with the hand while curling the body up will bring the body up into the required position as shown in Fig 7. Repeat as many times as you can. The fitness of the stomach muscles can be assessed as follows:

4 or fewer curl-ups	=	Poor fitness
6 curl-ups	=	Pass mark
8 curl-ups	=	Above average
10 curl-ups	=	Excellent fitness

Fig 4   The beam walk.

Fig 5   The underarm pull-up.

Fig 6   The under- and overarm pull-up.

Fig 7   The abdominal curl.

The Rope Climb (Fig 8)

Rope climbing was part of a test for fitness in the British army. It is good for developing strong muscles, feet and arm co-ordination in movement, and tests both the lower and upper body parts. The climbing technique can be adapted to concentrate on specific muscles; for example, a pulling action whilst climbing will concentrate on strengthening the upper part of the shoulders, while pushing with your feet only will concentrate on the lower parts of the body, the thigh muscles.

This test must be properly supervised, and you need soft protection material under the apparatus in case

Fig 8   The rope climb.

you fall. The height of the rope can be varied according to age groups. For the general fitness test, climb a 6m (16ft) rope up and down three times if you can. The pass mark is two – three climbs are excellent.

Legs
The simplest form of endurance test possible requires the tested player to jump repeatedly to a point marked on a wall 20cm (8in) above the fingertips of either hand when he stands beside the wall with arms raised above his head. Time the player's jumps to that mark on the wall. He should be able to jump up and down at least twenty-five times in the 35-second time span allocated; a suitable height for adult players would be 7ft (2.3m), although naturally this can be adjusted as required.

Stamina
To test stamina, you could organize a 6km (3¾ mile) road walk. A fit person should be able to walk the distance in 62 minutes, giving an average speed of 10.2 minutes for every kilometre walked.

The Weight Factor
(Figs 9 & 10)
Players tend to put on weight during the closed season, because the reduction in activity is not compensated for by a reduction in food intake. It is a contributory factor to unfitness that if you are overweight your heart has to work harder because of the extra cells that it has to

Height (cm)	Medium body frame (kg)	Large body frame (kg)
154	45.5–52.3	54.5–59.0
167	50.0–59.0	56.8–65.9
175	54.5–63.6	63.6–65.9
183	61.3–67.8	68.0–75.0

Fig 9   Correct weight for different heights and builds.

Name	Bed-time Weight Monday	Tuesday	Wednesday	Thursday	Friday	Saturday	Sunday
Week 1							
Week 2							
Week 3							
Week 4							
Week 5							
Week 6							
Week 7							
Week 8							

Fig 10   Keep a record of your weight as you work through the fitness programme.

service. At the start of your training programme and as part of your fitness test you should record the weight of each player and monitor this throughout the training programme. After the first three weeks the weight should initially show a downward trend before settling to hold at a steady average determined by height and build. Monitor weight at pre-determined stages of training. A fit player will have the correct bodyweight for his size and build.

In practical terms the only way to find out a player's unfit weight is to weigh him after a period of inactivity (such as a holiday). Write his weight down prior to starting training. Keep a record of his weight over a period of time, on a monitor sheet such as the one in Fig 10, and as he becomes fitter you can build up a picture of how his fit weight and his unfit weight compare.

WARMING UP 2

It is vital to prepare for each training session systematically, no matter what activity you are doing. Most people know about the importance of warming up before training (and warming down afterwards), but you will also get more out of your activity if you are careful about what you eat beforehand.

Some people suspect that the process of providing your muscles with oxygen can be affected by the type of food we eat. Meat products eaten before training can adversely affect the process of oxygenation, as oxygen is diverted from the cells because it is needed to transform food into energy. It is therefore advisable to eat food products which apparently do not affect this process, that is, carbohydrates such as pasta, bread, potatoes and rice.

Before (and after) you begin any training or play a match you will also need to warm up.

THE WARM-UP ROUTINE
(Fig 11)
There are no exceptions to the correct approach to training. There is a definite working sequence, and there are important physiological reasons for adhering to it. To prepare your body to perform any exercise, you should warm up, whatever the type of activity you are about to undertake.

The reason is very simple, and is best explained by looking at an analogy from the world around us. If you stop to look at electricity pylons in mid-summer you will see that the wire between the pylons sags towards the ground,

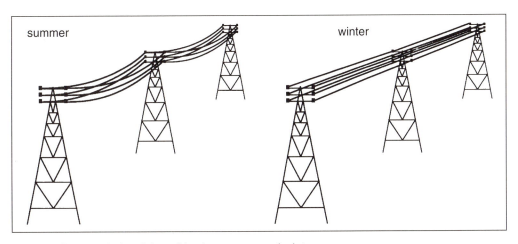

Fig 11 Overhead electricity cables in summer and winter.

19

rather than being stretched taut. It is the warmer summer temperatures which make this possible – higher temperatures unlock the molecules which make up the wire, so the length of wire is actually extended. In winter the low temperatures shrink the molecules and cause a shortening of the length of wire. In extreme cold, the wires could actually snap.

Your body tendons and muscles respond to temperature changes in the same way. When you are cold every part of your body is tight and the molecules of your tendons and muscles are locked firmly together, so their length is shortened and any sudden stretch could strain or even tear them. Warm muscles on the other hand have the flexibility to cope with any sudden physical demands. The whole point of a warm-up is to prepare the body for physical activity: it raises the body temperature, loosening up muscles and tendons, in turn making it possible for the athlete to cope with sudden bursts of energy without any serious consequences.

The importance of the warm-up cannot be overstated, especially as it is also fundamental to correct body shape development. There are three separate sections to work on: the arms, trunk and abdomen. When warming up, it is best to start with the upper body and work downwards; the following examples show the correct sequence of work. These exercises do not need to be elaborate. Figs 12 to 15 show a typical hand routine, followed by a ground routine concentrating on the groin region (Fig 16); this position is also useful for other dorsal ground exercises. In this groundwork position you can concentrate your

efforts on the inner or outer dorsal groups of muscles/tendons. The abdominal example is one that I can never forget, as it is intense and sometimes horrible to work with. Fig 17 shows the boys straining. I always preferred sit-ups, to this lift and hold feet torture.

A word of warning about warming up. Our spine and hip joints have moving parts which can trap nerves, the best known of which is the sciatica nerve. When you are doing any bending, whether to the side, forwards or while circling, do it very gently; the groin exercises in particular can be dangerous. Thus for example when you lift one of your legs off the ground and bring it up bending the leg at the knee, then force it sideways at 90 degrees, it can actually jump out of the hip socket for a fraction of a second; when it returns it can trap the sciatica nerve. So take care when doing this exercise and never overdo it. The easiest and safest way to exercise the groin is to lie on your back, legs raised and bent at the knees. Get a partner to place one hand on the inside of each knee, then try to stop him from forcing your legs apart (without using excessive strength). This exercise can also be performed by yourself in the weight training room where specialized equipment can be used to strengthen your adductor muscles, paying particular attention to the (so-called) hamstring, which in fact consists of many groups of specialized muscles at the back of your leg (knee upwards), such as the gluteus maximus, biceps femoris, and vastus lateralis.

Whatever you do, do not warm up with vigorous kicking exercises; such movements put great and sudden strain on your muscles and tendons, and should not be practised until you have warmed up thoroughly.

Further warm-up examples are given in the training session planners throughout the book.

Lateral Exercises
(Figs 12–15)

Always begin with an arm exercise, for example, circling your arms (together or one at a time), pumping your arms up and down, or arms touching shoulders

Fig 12   Arms horizontally in front of you.

Fig 13   Straight up.

Fig 14   To the side.

Fig 15   Both arms slightly to rear and down.

and straightening out above the head, to the front or sides. The illustrations show a backwards and forwards movement of the arms; this movement is simple to perform but has the desired effect of getting the blood circulation moving, warming up the upper part of the body. The movement can also be reversed to go the other way.

Dorsal Exercises
(Fig 16)
Stand up straight, arms by your sides, legs apart. Lean to the right as far as you can go, come up, then lean to the left. Repeat in a rhythmical manner, alternating sides.

For a lower body alternative, lie on your side on the floor using your hands to support yourself. Raise your top leg then lower it, and repeat as often as you wish. Turn onto the other side and do the same.

To work on the dorsal/trunk part of the body, simply raise your hips and lower them back on to the ground. Repeat this move several times. When you raise your hips, use one hand to support the body on the ground, and extend the free hand over your head, reaching out as far as you can.

Fig 16   Leg raise and lower.

Abdominal Exercises
Stand with your legs apart and stretch out your arms in front of you. Bend at the waist and touch the ground. Come back up to a standing position and repeat several times. Stand with your legs apart and stretch out your arms in front of you. Circle your arms and upper body to the left then to the right.

Fig 17   Abdominal stretches lying down. The legs are raised and lowered slowly a few inches off the ground.

The Skipping Rope
(Fig 18)
One of the finest exercises for a soccer player is using a skipping rope, as the use of the rope on a regular basis promotes elasticity of the leg muscles. It also has a positive effect on the development of your heart and lungs, but make sure that the rope is long enough and heavy enough for you to use it properly.

When skipping, vary the leg movements:

- Skip on one leg
- Skip with both feet together
- Skip hurdle, one leg in front of the other

- Skip, legs together, from side to side
- Skip, kick
- Skip, straddle, legs together

This is a very enjoyable and positive warming up exercise and should be more widely used.

Fig 18   Using the skipping rope is a good general exercise routine.

BEFORE A MATCH

Players should prepare for the actual game at least one hour before kick-off. It is not fair on any player to try to cram in all sorts of things at this time. Team talks and other such business should have been taken care of earlier; this is a time for encouragement, for preparing body and mind. Players have all sorts of ways of getting themselves psyched up for playing soccer, and some even warm up by standing in hot water; well, this works and at least is not as drastic as someone throwing a bucket of cold water over a player; this type of warm-up should in fact carry a health warning.

It is possible to arrive late for a game and be ill prepared. If you find yourself in this situation, you may still be able to do some form of stretching exercises en route. Perhaps there is room on the coach/bus or train to work out on; if not, perhaps you can stop somewhere and have the players take a brisk walk. If you are on a coach the players can certainly change into their playing strip and arrive prepared in this way; it may then be possible to fit in a quick warm-up on the field of play. You should aim to work out to a mixture of stretching exercises and keep-possession-of-the-ball formats. This should achieve your warm-up quickly and safely, providing you follow the correct working procedure. Whatever you do, do not let anyone panic, as this can sap vital nervous energy, which in turn will affect physical energy; stay calm and go about your business methodically.

The Procedure
(Fig 19)

The players go out on the field and work at passing the ball to each other in a fairly small area. This short pass sequence should cause no problems in terms of injuries; do not be tempted to practise kicking the ball long, as is

Fig 19 Warm-up – short pass and stretch.

often seen. While some players are thus working with the ball, others stand still and do stretching exercises, in the order of lateral, dorsal, abdominal muscles. The players alternate between stretching and playing throughout the workout, which should last for 10 to 15 minutes. This should be sufficient in short-notice circumstances. In all other cases, the players should prepare in their usual pre-planned way for at least an hour, combining gentle aerobic exercises with stretches.

AFTER EXERCISE

After any vigorous activity such as playing soccer or training, you need to stretch again and then detoxify the body. Poisonous gases are easily removed by warmer temperatures. There is nothing simpler than to stand under a warm shower, which warms up your body and allows the gases to escape through your lungs. A massage also helps in this process, but make sure that the body is massaged with strokes towards the heart, and not backwards and forwards as is sometimes done. Be careful with hot water if you are injured, as it could actually make matters worse; in this case seek medical advice.

THE TRAINING PROGRAMME 3

Once you have established how fit you are and have set reasonable fitness targets for yourself, you are ready to begin the fitness training programme.

The working plan is divided up into sections in order to cover all the working topics that are necessary to prepare the player for the soccer season. In reality, most soccer players are fit enough to skip the first three weeks and come into work on the fourth week of training, without too many problems. Injured players, however, do need to start the process of recovering fitness at the beginning of the working programme. Young players also need to work on all aspects of the programme; they require the general fitness activities in order to develop their full range of body shape, fitness and skill potential.

General fitness activities are an essential part of training. The choice of activities has been largely left up to the individual, and the warm-up routine is also considered personal; one can only give advice on this issue. The tests described in Chapter 1 can be used to assess how fit you are so you can set realistic targets.

The programme can be divided up as follows: (1) initial training period – general fitness, weeks 1 to 3; (2) interval training, weeks 4 and 5; (3) endurance and speed work, week 6; (4) final preparation work, weeks 7 and 8. You should endeavour to keep to this training sequence. The four separate stages of the programme are pre-planned, because the coach has to set training objectives that have to be met within specified time limits.

In soccer it is important to co-ordinate physical fitness with soccer skills; the two have to be developed together. As time goes on in your training programme you will realize that fitness does improve the quality of a player's passing and running off the ball. Of course training has to go on throughout the year, but Fig 20 shows the initial eight-week training period only because once the season starts you will have two other important considerations when planning your programme: the league/cup timetable, and the need to reassess training after each league game, as strengths and weaknesses are exposed.

FORMULATING A TRAINING CHART
(Fig 20)

In this book you will find many exercises you can use to build up your training programme. The following list of abbreviations will help you to formulate your own chart, which can go beyond the eight-week training schedule. It is not necessary to use activities from all the categories when filling in your chart, as one abbreviation can cover several types of exercise; for example, ST (Speed

week	0	1	2	3	4	5	6	7	8	9	10	11	12	13	14	15	etc
		initial training period			two weeks interval training		endurance & speed work	final preparation work		start of the season							
day: coach:										new season							
Monday		GF	GF	GF	IT	IT	ET TT	TT T	PT TT	LM							
Tuesday					IT	IT	ET WT	ST TI	TI ST								
Wednesday			your own programme		IT	IT	ST TiR	TT TI	ST PT		programme according to needs during season						
Thursday					IT	IT	ST TiR	TI SF	SF TI								
Friday					IT	IT	DO	ST TT	SF								
Saturday					IT	IT	ST ST	RT MO	DO								
Sunday					DO	DO	DO	DO	DO								

Fig 20   *The eight-week programme shows a professional approach to planning training sessions for the coming weeks, using some of the abbreviations listed. Adapt this training chart to your needs.*

Training) can cover An (Anaerobic Work). The abbreviations will become a part of your training language and with constant use they will become familiar to you and can help you to plan your daily programme chart. With time you will know exactly what abbreviations to use and for which exercises, bearing in mind that most soccer exercises are not as simple as they look, and incorporate several skill and fitness elements.

The complete list is given here, and some of the key training elements are defined below.

IT   Interval Training
PT   Pressure Training (Physical and Reaction Training)
ST   Speed Training
TT   Technical Training

AW   Awareness
ET   Endurance Training
TI   Tactical Instruction
T   Theory of the Game
WT   Weight Training
SF   Soccer Friendlies
DO   Day Off
An   Anaerobic Work
A   Aerobic Work
GF   General Fitness
Km   Kilometre Run
LM   League Match
AO   Afternoon Off
MO   Morning Off
RT   Reaction Training
TiR   Technique in Running

Pressure Training (PT)

When fatigue sets in during the later stages of a game, mistakes can be made which may result in giving away goals. Pressure training helps the player to cope with being tired, when he must make a concerted effort to make proper use of the ball. He learns to be more accurate in passing and make an extra effort when tired to ensure the quality of pass.

Speed Training (ST)

A player has to be very quick in most ball-play situations. Speed training gives him an understanding of the power needed to run short distances efficiently, and to time his run correctly.

Technical Training (TT)

You can tell how good a player is when you look at his performance under pressure. When he is tired, he shows his true qualities. Technical training helps the player to perform and practise his technical skills under pressure, thus raising the level of his performance.

Endurance Training (ET)

Endurance training is as much psychological as it is physical. It develops discipline of thought and the ability to keep going – the determination to get to one more ball.

Anaerobic Training (An)

Any work over short distances will have a certain physiological benefit: it will develop the player's ability to perform well above the levels of lactic acid tolerance, and will strengthen the heart. The result is a speedy recovery rate during the intervals between a player's involvement in play. These gaps are generally sufficiently frequent throughout the game for him to be able to continue playing without the need to stop.

Reaction Training (RT)

Very often it is the speed of thought that decides who gets to the ball first. Reaction training forces the player to concentrate on the job at hand, by varying the tasks he has to carry out in an unpredictable way. Serving the ball to the player as late as possible in the exercises will speed up his reaction time, making him quicker all round.

PLANNING THE TRAINING SESSION

You cannot just jump in and start practising a training routine, whatever its subject, without any form of preparation. The warm-up sequence is lateral, dorsal, abdominal, in that order. The same principle applies to your skill training exercises. There are four distinct stages in a training session: warm-up, individual practice, introducing opponents and a team work format.

The overall subject is chosen and appropriate exercises are then selected for each stage of the training session. It is best to plan out your selection of topics in the correct working sequence. I would advise you at this stage to go on and read the whole book, before constructing your own working planner based on your own requirements.

Stage 1 – Warm-up This is in accordance with the standard procedure explained in Chapter 2.

Stage 2 – Individual practice The second stage of the working planner introduces the player to the coaching theme of the working session and begins with exercises in which he practises the skills required by the coaching topic.

Stage 3 – Introducing opponents
The introduction of an opponent at this stage of the practice enables the player to start working with his newly acquired skill in simulated game conditions. However, although there is opposition, the working format is still designed to concentrate on the individual. Some training routines have special area size requirements, which deliberately bring out the coaching theme of the working format. This stage should guarantee each player a fair share of practice time.

Stage 4 – Conditioned game format
These exercises are very closely related to the proper game. There are differences, but these are in the way the exercises are used. The game is played according to certain imposed conditions, which practise the skills being concentrated on that day. The coach can stop the flow of the game if he thinks that the players have not carried out his requests or achieved his coaching objectives. He can also recreate movements from standing positions. Once he is satisfied that his players understand what is required, he may allow the rest of the game session to continue without interruption.

THE INITIAL TRAINING PERIOD

If the fitness assessment shows that you are unfit, you must start the training programme at the beginning, with general fitness training. The key is to pick at least two physical activities you enjoy, and start doing them regularly. The heart rate of work in that case must be kept down to approximately 130 beats per minute, because it would be harmful at this initial stage of training to set unrealistic targets. It is very important that your introduction to physical training should be without pressure and that you should enjoy it. Follow these rules for the first three weeks of your general fitness activities:

1. Do not keep to just one chosen activity, but alternate your chosen activities from day to day.

2. Only have two days off a week.

3. Your choice of activities must allow you to stay within your pre-set heart rate and you should keep to the set target of heart beats per minute.

4. Any chosen activity should have a time limit of up to 1½ hours, but not less than one hour on any given day.

It is best to select aerobic activities such as brisk walking, swimming – although too much swimming can develop the wrong muscle shape for soccer – ice-skating, canoeing, cycling or orienteering; these all keep the body in motion for long periods at a stretch, thus improving your cardio-vascular fitness. Anaerobic activities, such as squash, tennis and most team sports, involve a lot of stopping and starting, and so are not suitable for your initial general fitness training.

Running is acceptable as long as you keep to a steady jog and do not include flat-out sprinting. Sprinting should only be practised in special, soccer-oriented training exercises, and because it works the heart far harder than is appropriate for general fitness activities, it is best not tackled until the interval training stage of the fitness programme.

Weight training is useful to develop leg, arm and stomach muscles in soccer training if you concentrate on endurance-type routines, where the emphasis is on repetition work, rather than strength of lift. Using excessive weights is counter-productive – you do not want to develop excessive muscle bulk as this will not be helpful in mobility, agility or acrobatic movement. There is also a risk of developing shorter muscle lengths and heavy-set legs and arms if the weights are too heavy. Heavy-set legs may be strong in the tackle and good for short bursts of activity, but they may result in the player being unable to keep up with the technical requirements of the modern game.

It is safer to use no weights other than your own bodyweight. You will go a long way to find more constructive, positive stomach and arm training routines than the ones shown in Figs 5, 6 and 7, using the beam. The reason is simple enough: lifting the weight of your own body guarantees the correct weight ratio to your own strength capability.

With all activities, make sure that when you finalize your plans you check on the opening and closing times of your chosen facilities. There is nothing worse than turning up and finding the place closed for the day. Many of the activities, such as fell walking, can be enjoyed collectively, and if you are a member of a soccer club it will be up to the coaches to deal with the many organizational problems in planning and implementing sporting activities for the weeks ahead.

INTERVAL TRAINING

The aim of interval training is to prepare the heart and lungs to work with oxygen debt.

This important part of the programme is designed to link the initial training for general fitness (aerobic work) with the anaerobic phase of the eight-week training period. It incorporates important physiological changes which have to take place in the body in order to prepare the player for heavier demands on his heart and lungs. Up to the point of interval training, the training routines should have been selected for enjoyment rather than effort – although they should still have been sufficient to prepare the player for the next stage of the programme.

For the next two weeks the player concentrates on preparing the heart for sudden changes in the demand for oxygen in order to achieve quicker recovery rates and the ability to work with higher levels of lactic acid in muscle cells. This will enable him to pass to the anaerobic exercises safely. Interval training will cause greater fluctuations in the blood supply because of oxygen debt occurring. It is vital, therefore, that when carrying out these exercises you constantly refer to the pre-set target of the working heart rate, which should be set to peak at 140bpm during the running stages of this part of the programme. The first training routines allow for longer recovery periods, but these will decrease towards the end of this two-week phase.

The varied exercises described in this section are also designed to give the player the training which begins to mirror the soccer game itself. Think again of the game and how it is played: stop, start, sprint, run, jog, and so on. This is exactly how interval training is conducted, but before I go on to explain this in more detail I feel that the word 'sprint' needs some clarification. The sprinting sections of interval training are vital to the player's physical fitness because they are also an introduction to this essential (for soccer) form of physical training.

Preparation for Interval Training

Only you know how fast you can run at top speed, and only you can assess your body's reaction while sprinting. No one can predetermine whether at full speed your heart will work at 179bpm or not.

It is important to get to know how your heart is performing at different speeds, and the simplest way to do this is to formulate your own workload heart rate table. This will help you to recognize the different stages of effort required to get yourself fit, and it will make sure that you are not overdoing things in training by keeping you to a progressive fitness target. A table showing your heart rate at different running speeds may look like this:

Pace over 100m	Beats per minute
Flat out	179
Three-quarter pace	160
Half pace	120
Quarter pace	100
Jog	85

Of course your own heart rates may vary from those shown, but only you can find out what they are by taking your own pulse. In interval training the sprinting sections of your work should be set to a standard heart rate of 140bpm. By forming your own table by taking your own pulse at the end of a sprint you will learn to judge how fast you must go to achieve a certain heart rate for the sprinting section.

Remember that the aim of interval training is to introduce your heart to rapid changes. Some of you may not have the right type of heart muscle for this type of work. Constant long-distance runners have hearts with thin walls, the heart being developed according to the blood supply required. In soccer, rapid changes of pace dictate the need for a different type of heart. The long-distance runners would have to change their training routines, as soccer requires a thick-walled heart that can only be developed through sprinting short distances. Interval training introduces you safely to sprinting short distances because you only sprint according to set instructions and according to your planned route. This type of training begins to develop the right type of heart muscle for soccer.

Week 4
(Fig 21a)

For interval training follow the basic guidelines set out below.

1. During the sprinting sections of your work do not exceed a heart rate of 140bpm. Check your pulse immediately after a sprint and adjust your speed for the next sprinting section of the working

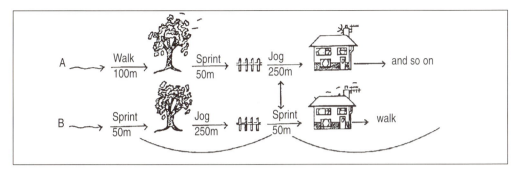

Fig 21   Planning your route for interval training.

route accordingly.

2. Plan a working route of up to 4km in distance, which has plenty of natural waymarks such as fences, trees, bushes, and so on, and a fairly even surface with few gradients.

3. In the fourth week do no more than 200m of sprinting in any one kilometre. The 200m of sprinting distance can be split up into four portions of 50m each. Do this for each kilometre of the 4km route.

4. Alternate planned and spontaneous sessions. On some days go out and improvise, doing sprints and running only when you feel you want to, along the whole 4km route.

There should be no surprises along the route, because having chosen it yourself, you will know where the best places are to sprint (do not exceed the pace of work set at this stage) and where you can walk. It is all the more fun if the route is picturesque. Keep up the momentum of your training and do not make unnecessary stops along the way. A sample route plan might be as follows:

1.   Start with stretching exercises to warm up the muscles in the following order: lateral (arms), dorsal (side of body) and abdominal (stomach).
2. Walk for 350m.
3. Sprint for 50m.
4.   Stretching exercises involving the hamstring, calf muscles and Achilles tendon.
5. Sprint for 50m.
6. Walk for 150m.
7. Sprint for 50m.
8. Walk for 100m.
9. Sprint for 50m.
10. Walk for 200m.

Total 1,000m. Repeat three times.

Week 5
(Fig 21b)
When you are planning your training for the fifth week, you must introduce more and more sprinting. For every alternate 1,000m worked, the overall sprinting distance must be at least 400m. This

must be split up into sections of not more than 50m in length, which cannot be consecutive.

In the fifth week you can extend the training distance to 6km and introduce more variety of work and sprinting sections into every alternate 1,000m worked; the fitter you feel the more sprinting sections you should have, so that your route plan looks similar to Fig 21b. In sprinting every second or third section your heart will be alternating between your pre-set targets of 140bpm and 80–60bpm. You can see how this type of training begins to emulate the soccer game itself – sprinting, jogging and walking are all things that you will have to do during a game.

For groups of younger players, simply adjust the distance worked and select appropriate activities.

ENDURANCE TRAINING

A building, if it is to remain standing, needs strong foundations. It is the same with our bodies. The preparatory work of the first three weeks followed by the two weeks of interval training will have provided you with a foundation to build on over the remaining three weeks of the training programme. While you have had many opportunities to have fun and enjoy yourself, you now have to adopt a more serious approach. The nature of your training will change dramatically as you approach the start of the soccer season. It is not an unpleasant change as you will begin to learn more about the game itself and will no longer be concentrating solely on the physical aspects of training. This part of the training programme is, however, the ultimate in physical and technical

endeavour because you will work on exercises which cause oxygen debt and as a result you will acquire greater tolerance to lactic acid. You will develop very quick recovery rates and improve your soccer skills by paying attention to every detail.

With such a demanding physical and technical content, it is most important to adopt the correct attitude. Discipline comes as a result of doing things right, and because you will be working at the ultimate in physical exertion levels, it is highly advisable to work under supervision. The nature of the work – sprinting short distances at very high speeds, high levels of effort sustained for 30–40 seconds at a time – will cause greater oxygen debt in your body. This physiological process causes your heart to return oxygen to your body system at a rate which is determined by your fitness. It is not unusual to find working rates of 179bpm.

Preparing for Speed Work

From now on, fitness is built into the soccer working exercises, and all the training formats are soccer-related so that we emulate more closely the type of movements that occur in the game. After endurance work, speed training becomes part of everyday training. For the remaining three weeks and the whole of the soccer season the coach will plan his work for any given day according to match requirements: thus he may wish to concentrate solely on technical skill training, but then again he may wish to vary the training session and include tactical training. In a professional soccer club the coach can but spend as much time on any subject

Attacking Play (Positive)

Attacking play is about the creation of movement through the use of different types of skill. The skills of the individual are harnessed to those of the other players to create playing options, which have two major functions: to retain possession of the ball, and then to make use of this possession in order to create a goal-scoring opportunity.

Defensive Play (Negative)

This part of the game is concerned with using different methods to stop creative movements by the opposing side, therefore affecting play options and possession of the ball.

as he wishes; if you are short of time you can choose one specific topic to work with. Begin the first two days of week 6 with endurance running.

This forms the basis for speed work, helping players to experience the sustained effort of running 200m. Although the heart does not experience fluctuations in its beat rate (which happens in speed training) it does work to high levels of exertion. Allocate plenty of training time for this session, which can last up to three hours, because you should have a 7-minute break between your 200m runs. The coach will set the running targets and recovery times: an example session might be fifteen sets of 200m runs with a 7-minute rest period in between each set, the speed of work being at three-quarter pace sustained for the full length of the run.

SPEED TRAINING

The Skills of Turning
(Figs 22–24)

The first approach to speed training teaches the player the correct turning

techniques. Soccer is said to be a game of opposites, for example, an attacking player wants to score a goal, while his opponent wants to stop him doing so. At first sight this might be rather obvious, but the implications for the game of soccer are rather less so. Attacking principles lean towards the creative, positive side of any player, whereas defending principles adhere to the negative aspects of play. You should bear in mind, however, that a successful defence is an essential part of a successful team. The difference between the two major components of the game lies in the huge array of skills on both sides. When attacking, the running patterns can take any shape or form; when defending, they need to conserve space and energy, and they must be specific in order to close down space or opponents quickly. This topic is a coaching priority because it teaches the player what he is trying to achieve with his running and working angles in relation to the ball and his opponent.

Prior to any soccer activity, the player should be introduced to the

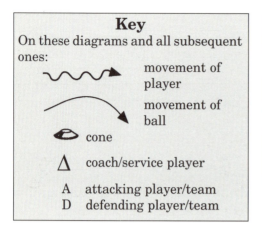

Key

On these diagrams and all subsequent ones:

~~~~~➤ movement of player

⌒➤ movement of ball

🔘 cone

△ coach/service player

A attacking player/team
D defending player/team

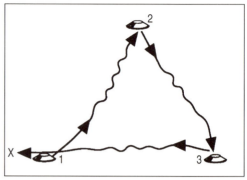

Fig 22   Correct running angles.

working soccer angles. The sharpness of his turns, and how economically he runs, depends on a clear understanding of this topic. Thus, straight lines are used to reduce the time it takes to cut across attacking runs. The team shape is affected by angles, so knowing how to use angles effectively is vital for good defensive play. There are many occasions when understanding angles helps the player to play the game properly.

Turning round quickly to face in another direction is not as simple as you might think, and you will have to learn the correct technique for turning

at a sharp angle.

Fig 22 uses a triangle to show how to practise the correct turning technique. The player has to run round all three corners of a triangle (marked by cones) at speed, the aim being to combine speed of thought with the correct turning technique. Good practice results in getting to know the angles, and knowing the right angle to turn at helps you to get to the opponent or ball by the shortest possible route. How you should position your body in different playing circumstances will become clearer as you work through the exercises. For

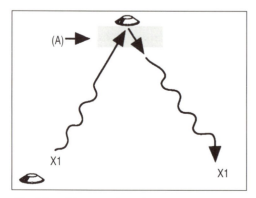

Fig 23a   Very good turning.

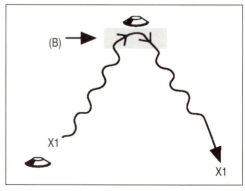

Fig 23b   Bad turning technique.

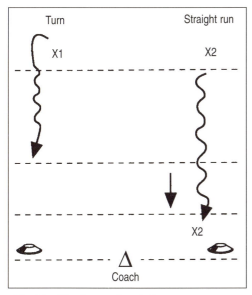

Fig 24   Turning and sprinting.

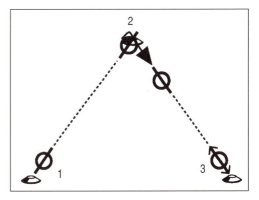

Fig 25   Triangular working format.

now, just bear in mind that the angle on turning must be sharp. It should be clear from Fig 23 that a sharp turning angle (Fig 23a) will get you to the ball faster than a sloppy one (Fig 23b). If your work is sloppy and you develop bad turning angles as shown in Fig 23b you will always be struggling against any of your opponents.

You can introduce a competitive element to sharpen up your turning technique. Fig 24 shows an exercise where two players compete to reach the coach first; they start the same distance away from him, but one starts facing the coach, while the other has his back to him, and is therefore at a disadvantage. Both players take turns to face away from the coach.

The Triangle Exercise (Fig 25)
Changing direction is a matter of using the upper part of the body and feet cor-

rectly and the player needs to follow certain rules. The play scenarios nearly always relate to the checking out movement, but there are plenty of other occasions when knowing angles comes in handy, for example when approaching an opponent with the ball, the positioning of the goalkeeper, the passing of the ball in relation to defending angles, changing angles in attacking play, making runs, and so on. The triangular training routine described below helps you to work on movements involving your feet and body co-ordination. The results of this practice are fundamental to many of the skills in this book.

In the triangle routine (Fig 25), the player starts his work from one corner of the triangle, (cone position 1) with his body positioned sideways on, that is, his shoulders parallel to the line between cones 1 and 2; he is thus facing cone 3. This body position is important, as it helps him to turn correctly. The turns can be practised at each point of the triangle. The player moves from one end to the other by skipping along sideways. When he comes to cone 2 and has to change direction, he twists his upper

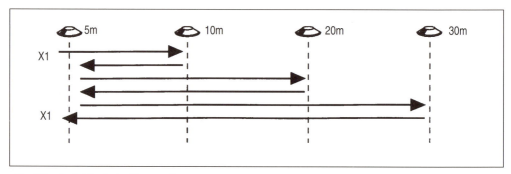

Fig 26   Individual shuttle running.

body to where he now wants to go, while at the same time moving across from one (imaginary) line to the other.

These techniques are used for example when changing directions during jockeying (*see* Defensive Working Formats).

Sharpening Up

The sharp turning angles required in defensive play (practised above) are soon put to good use because the turn in speed training work are based on this technique. The ultimate speed training routines are soccer-related in many ways, but do not in themselves simulate the whole range of soccer movements; it is the cone exercises that do that. The speed training routines and the long distance running examples are used mainly for fitness preparation. All the training formats can in fact be used in a complementary way, to supplement either fitness or running/turning techniques as and when required by the player throughout the season.

Shuttle Running
(Fig 26)

The two days spent on endurance running in week 6 will be of great value to the speed training sections of this programme. Both physical and mental strength are necessary to undertake speed work. In your interval routines you will have simulated all the elements of the soccer game. To make ultimate progress in your physical preparation, simply exclude all the slow work, and concentrate mainly on sprint work. This training is known as shuttle running, and it is the training routine which most closely resembles the fitness needs of the game itself.

Before launching into shuttle training, test the players' running fitness. Each player has to run three consecutive lengths of a 25m track, after which he rests for 45 seconds. He then repeats the same run sequence, and at the end is given him a further 45-second rest. The player repeats this run sequence for a third time, making a total of three sets of 3 × 25m runs. Each individual's overall time is recorded and compared to his next test times, which should give an indication of his fitness progress.

Shuttle running involves running short distances of up to 50m split up into sections of 10m, for example, 5 × 10m. The coach will usually determine how the player runs the set distances:

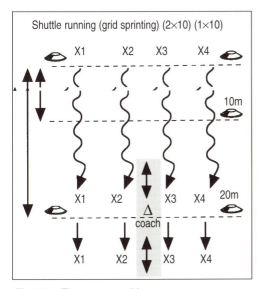

Fig 27   Team competition.

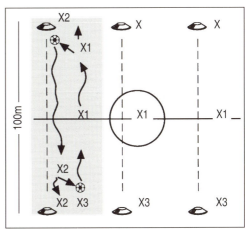

Fig 28   Long distance running: play the ball ahead of the runner.

thus he may want him to sprint all the way up to the 50m mark and back to the starting position, or he may want him to break up the distance into three sections. It is up to the coach to vary the exercise. Examples of shuttle running are illustrated in Fig 26. The main points to remember are:

1. The player must cover the allocated distances at the highest possible effort.
2. In between repetitions of 50m runs, the resting period is minimal – not more than 45 seconds.
3. Runs can be done in repeats of up to 5 x 10m split.
4. The player should run in shorts for maximum freedom of movement.
5. The player must ensure that his speed is maintained throughout the running exercise; slowing down to approach the starting/finishing line is not permitted.
6. The player must turn at a sharp angle at each turning point, as described above.

Exercises (Figs 27 & 28)

Fig 27 shows a group of four players performing a typical speed training routine. The coach here acts as a moving marker. The four players sprint towards him and back to their starting points. Meanwhile the coach moves towards the players up to the 10m marker, and the players turn and run to him and back to their starting points again. The coach returns to the start marker, or moves further back, and the players run to him and back again. The coach can position himself as far away as he wishes – it is the players' job to run to him. It is also the coach who decides how many shuttle runs the players do and the resting times between runs.

The exercise shown in Fig 28 simulates whole areas opening up in front of the player in possession of the ball. The running practice area is 100m long.

Player X1 starts with the ball at mid-point (50m out) and begins by running the short distance to player X2. He passes the ball to player X2 and takes his place. Player X2 controls the ball so that it travels well in front of him, and starts to run as fast as he can across to the other side towards player X3. He does not worry too much about his technique at this stage, the only thing he has to worry about is playing the ball in such a way that it keeps well in front of him. When he is near to the other side of the field, he passes the ball to player X3, who runs back to the other end of the field and passes the ball back to player X1, and so on. The coach sets the number of repetitions, for example five sets of 100m runs by each player.

SUMMARY OF SOCCER FITNESS CONSIDERATIONS

This training programme considers the well-being of all soccer players, consisting of exercises that promote the correct development of physical attributes. It is important to realize that specific training exercises (environments) do produce specific body shapes which can be the making or breaking of any potential talent, and that incorrect environments will destroy the player's ability to play the ball skilfully.

It is possible to create specific fitness training environments for specific positions on the field of play, but these must be carefully thought out, and the playing requirements of each position considered. For example, if an out-and-out defender has little to offer in terms of attacking skills, he could be helped by exercises that focus on developing his strength of running and stamina, such as working with heavier sets of weights and in a shorter-distance sprinting environment.

The solutions to this player's shortcomings cannot be used for other players. If you do not distinguish between the needs of different players and their positions on the field of play, you will in fact create an environment that will lower the overall playing standard of your team.

Remember this simple rule: the heavier the weight, the shorter the length of movement, and the lesser the skill. The same adage is true when developing the player's ball-play abilities. Thus if he moves the ball in a close-to-feet practice environment he is working to a short length movement, which again destroys skills. Rather, he should work the ball to the correct touch distance – meaning that the working environment must provide him with a format that allows him to play the ball to specific lengths on each touch. The cone formats afford the player the correct length of movement on the ball, which is essential if he wishes to achieve higher levels of skills. The cone positions are set up in such a way that the player acquires different ball-play skills, which is a key objective of this working programme.

REACTION TRAINING 4

Physical fitness training is largely concerned with two important body functions, which in effect are stimulated by appropriate training exercises. The first set of these routines conditions the muscles and cords of tissue to strengthen the skeletal structure. The second is concerned with the central nervous system, the means by which the brain tells the muscles to react to external stimuli. The brain is linked by the cranial nerves to the spine and there are reputed to be thirty-one pairs of spinal nerves that link the brain to the whole of the body: messages pass from the brain through these to the limbs.

There are many instances in play when players fail to react quickly and either lose or fail to win possession of the ball as a result. The worst time for indecision is of course in front of their own goal. Here, indecision and poor reactions to play situations cost goals. The following training routines help to develop the speed of thinking, which in turn quickens decisions, which in turn send the appropriate nerve pulse signals to trigger off appropriate muscle reactions and response to the decision process. They are designed specifically to improve reaction times (although an element of response time training is present in most of the exercises in this book).

THE CIRCLE EXERCISE
(Fig 29)

This exercise takes place in a circle 8m across, with eight cones regularly spaced round the circumference and one in the centre. Two players stand at a cone facing each other across the circle. The coach shouts out the following instructions in random order, and the players respond by moving in the required direction/s as quickly as possible. Sample instructions could be as follows:

Two or three right Both players move two or three cones to the right.
Two or three left Both players move two or three cones to the left.
Eight Both players run clockwise right around the circle back to their starting positions.
Z Both players run to the centre cone and back again.
Two right, one left Both players run two cones to the right followed by one cone back to the left.
One right, one left, Z Both players run one cone to the right, one cone back to the left, then to the middle cone, and then back to their starting position.

When either of the players makes a mistake it will be quite obvious because the players will not end up facing each other across the circle.

As you can see, these are simple

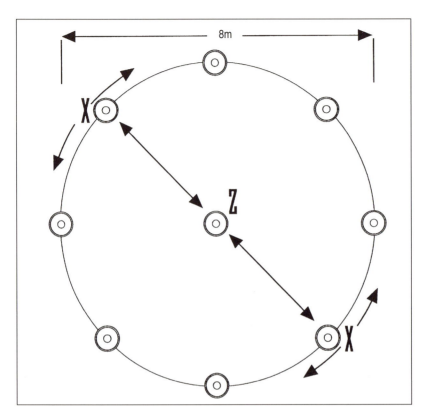

Fig 29
Change of
direction
format.

instructions which can be varied as necessary, but they begin to make the players think, and players need to think fast in competition with one another. The competition could be based on how many mistakes each player makes during a practice sequence; for example, make five and you are out of the competition. The working circle can be expanded and the number of players proportionately increased to match the number of cones. Alternatively leave one or two cones free.

THE CONE FORMAT
(Fig 30)
This working exercise is so simple and yet it does result in players reacting much more quickly to given tasks; only by interpretating quickly what is required will they be first to touch the right cone.

The right decision produces the correct course of action, and the more correct decisions made by the players, the better the chances of winning games. Making quick decisions is part of playing soccer. There are hundreds of times when decisions have to be made quickly during play, for example, the decision to challenge for the ball, to give cover, to attack space, to shoot, to dribble, to pass, to keep possession, to play the ball long, to play the ball short, to pass to

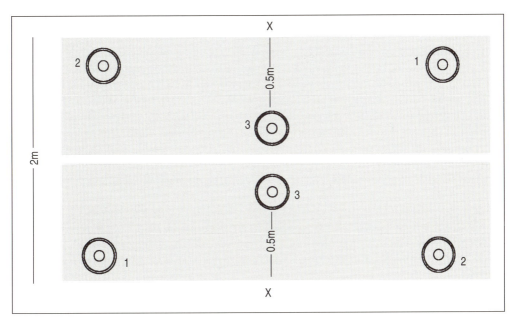

Fig 30   The cone format.

feet, to pass to space, and so on.

This is just a sample of the type of thoughts and decisions that are commonplace in play situations. Whether the problem is complex or simple is irrelevant: what does matter is that the decision to act is made quickly and that it is the *correct* decision. Whether you have time on the ball or not, deciding what to do has to be done early and acted upon quickly even though at times the resulting action need not be quick or furious.

The types of exercise described above are an important part of training as they help to develop the players' powers of concentration and speed of decision making.

How It Works

Three cones numbered 1, 2 and 3 are placed to the left, right and in front of two players, X, who face each other across the centre cones. The players work in competition with each other in trying to be the first to carry out the following instructions.

Touch right Players touch cone 2
Touch left Players touch cone 1
Touch 3 Players touch cone 3

You can also make the instructions mean the opposite of what they say:

Touch left Touch cone 2
Touch right Touch cone 1
Touch 3 Touch cones 2 and 1

You can make the exercise more difficult by introducing different message signals, by making the player remem-

41

ber a whole sequence of moves, or by adding moves such as turning, heading (an imaginary ball on the spot) and running on the spot.

You can also change the language as you wish – for example, 'touch west cone', 'touch south cone', 'touch blue cone', 'touch red cone' – because the whole point of this exercise is to make the players think and interpret the call into an appropriate action, that is, touching the correct cone. The easy option is to put the instructions into one word calls, such as 'north!', 'red!' and so on. If the coach shouts '1', both players touch cone 1 appropriate to their own position. If the coach shouts 'North', one player would touch cone 2 and the other would in that case touch cone 1, so in this example both players would be going the same way.

We could number the cones the same on both sides of the working area but this would be too easy, as the players could simply copy each other's moves. The cones numbered as they are forces each player to think for himself. When you think about this aspect of training you will realize that you are teaching the players to take responsibility for their own actions; they should not be given the opportunity to duck decision-making during play.

THE FENCE FORMAT
(Fig 31)

This routine is extremely effective in creating the sort of reactions required during a soccer match. The actual construction of the working format is simple: position four fences so that one is in the middle of each side of an imaginary square. Each fence is made of steel rods 18mm in diameter, the whole fence

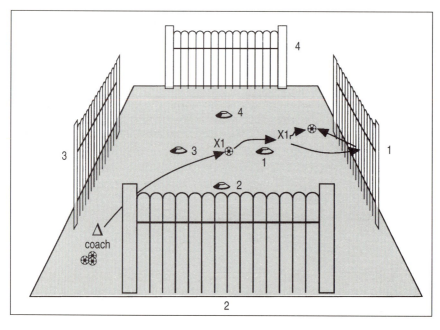

Fig 31
The fence
format.

being 4m across and 1.5m high. The base of the fence needs to be strong enough to withstand the strike and rebound of a ball without falling over. The gaps in between the rods of fencing need to be wide, but not wide enough to allow the ball to go through. Place a cone halfway along each fence but closer towards the middle of the square. Number both cones and fences 1 to 4, so that fence 1 and cone 1 are on the same side, and so on.

The exercise simulates the moments in play when the ball bounces off someone's foot and goes in an unpredictable direction, or when the player in possession of the ball suddenly changes direction. It aims to help players improve their reaction time to such changes of direction. The fencing is very effective in creating unpredictable ball movements to react to.

How It Works

To start the exercise, a player stands in the centre of the cone formation and the coach plays the ball to him. The player controls the ball, and plays it to the side of cone 1. He then picks up the ball with the instep part of his foot, and takes it with his next stride towards fence 1.

The reaction part of the exercise now comes into play: when the player is about 5m from the fence, he kicks the ball at the fence. The positioning of the fence rods is such that it is impossible to know in which direction the ball will rebound: it could be sent almost anywhere, hence the reaction training content of the exercise.

The player hits three strikes against the fence, reacting to the rebound as quickly as he can and con-

trolling the ball after each strike attempt. He then works the ball back to the centre of the cones where he might practise moving the ball with the inside of his instep, before repeating the exercise with fences 2, 3 and 4 in turn.

At this point this player can rest while another player runs through the skill sequence.

REDUCE THINKING TIME

Try relating reaction training exercises to a competitive environment. Here are some simple examples.

The Coach's 'To Me!'
(Fig 32)

1. The coach tells four or five players to walk away from him in any direction. Suddenly he shouts 'To me!', when the players must turn and sprint to him as fast as they can.

2. The coach asks his players to jog for a few yards and then drop to a sitting position. Timing his moment, he shouts the instruction 'Sprint!' and the players jump up and sprint to him.

How do the above examples relate to the game itself? Take, for example, the situation where you have to jockey up to your opponent to mark him tight. You attempt to do this, but he sprints past you and trips you up accidentally. You suddenly find yourself on the ground and now have to rise quickly and chase after your opponent to recover your position. The second exercise tries to simulate this typical situation. In soccer it is not enough to be physically fast, you must also be able to react quickly if you want to get to the ball first.

Further Examples

Do the Opposite (Fig 33)

Players stand in single file with the coach facing them. The coach shouts out a number of commands, and each time it is the player's job to translate the command into its opposite meaning and act upon it. For example, if the coach shouts 'Jump!', the players squat; if he shouts 'Left!', the players sprint to the right; if he shouts 'Face left!', they face right and so on. The players should try to carry out the opposite commands quickly, without hesitation.

The Numbers Game

The players are numbered and stand in a row facing the coach, who is some distance from them. When the coach shouts a number or numbers, those players have to sprint to the coach and back to their starting position again. The coach can choose from a number of

Fig 32　Speed reaction training.

Fig 33　Do the opposite.

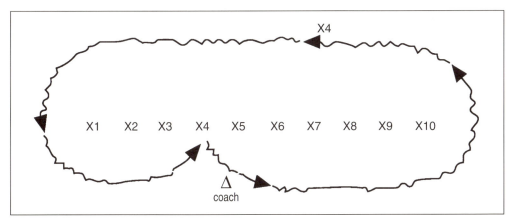

Fig 34   The Numbers Game.

command options: that is, he can say a few numbers at a time, just one number at a time, all even numbers, odd numbers, everyone, and so on.

Variation (Fig 34)

The players are again numbered but this time they sit in a row as shown. The coach shouts out a minimum of two numbers and the players involved get up and run as fast as they can completely around the row of players back to their places. The last man to sit down in his place does push-ups.

5 THE FIRST TOUCH

Up to now we have dealt with speed work and developing the correct turning technique, reaction training and speed of thought in decision making. The next step is learning good ball control. The different forms of running and fitness routine are fine as fitness goes, but it is introducing the ball to the training programme that actually begins to demand more effort from your players. This is inevitable because the ball weighs approximately 400g (16oz). The players will have to become much fitter because their muscles will need to be stronger in order to control the ball.

Players have to be able to control the ball in different game situations. There is nothing more frustrating than to see the ball arrive at the player's feet, only to watch him fumble and give the ball away. It is the coach's responsibility to make sure that the player is familiar with the skills required in dealing with the ball in a way appropriate to the game situation.

All training formats must include a gradual escalation of difficulty, both in technical and physical endeavour; thus as the player's mental and physical skills improve, the training exercises must get harder. When the ball is first introduced the soccer training routines must reflect the need to ease the player into the higher standard of work required. Not surprisingly, some of these formats can also be used to wind down the season's training programme, letting the players down gently after a hectic season. The idea behind this way of starting the season is similar, the gradual approach allowing the players to get into ball-work without any traumatic consequences. The golf touch format for example (Fig 36) is more about getting to know each other than about physical training, but at the same time the players are beginning to work on serious soccer issues. These formats do require some effort, as the players begin to get the feel for the ball, but this is what should happen at this stage of training.

There are major differences between ball possession skills and running with the ball. The first essential, however, is to get away from your opponent, and how to do so falls into two parts: choosing which skill to use, and the speed of actually getting away from the apponent. The following skills exercises relate to the moment when the practising player has managed, by using his skills, to leave his opponent stranded (flat-footed); the safe zones then have to be reached quickly, and doing so is crucial to getting free of opponent.

The work is mainly concerned with the individual making sure that he practises first-touch skills on the ball. This type of activity also makes sure that the player gradually improves his muscle/nerve and eye co-ordination reactions to the ball. When an opponent is first introduced to the working format any physical contact is in fact avoided; the exercise concentrates on the first touch of getting away from the challenger. Only after introducing these first-touch skills practice formats does the coach introduce a working format which is confrontational, where the player needs actually to deal with an opponent.

As far as I am concerned there are serious consequences to the way you practise skill work. There are a lot of misguided but well intentioned coaches who still insist on working to the two-touch formats. I will explain why we need to get away from this way of thinking. The next few introduction exercises are about one-touch play, but it should be appreciated that there are many touch play options in soccer.

ONE-TOUCH PLAY

When you look at the details of one-touch play, you will soon realize just how useful this can be in today's game. For example: the centre-half, in possession of the ball, is not allowed to pass it back to the keeper with any part of his leg, but he can head the ball back if he wants to. The practice exercises below give him the opportunity to perfect this type of skill. Not only that, but there are other skills that are in use during play that we can practise, for example controlling the ball with the thigh or chest, or playing the ball with the laces or instep of your foot.

However, there is an even more important point to this working format: it is based purely on skills. If the player

is inadequate in touch play, he will make many mistakes and lose possession of the ball. If he does so in a game situation, it can be costly. Here he has the opportunity to improve this side of his game without any drawbacks.

Introducing the player to first-touch play is very important to touch-play skills. This might be self-evident, but what might not be so obvious is the fact that the first-touch formats cannot be followed by restricting the player to the two-touch format when developing his skill repertoire.

Soccer Tennis
(Fig 35)

Set the exercise area up like a tennis court, except make it 20m long by 10m wide. In the middle, mark out a 2m buffer zone, which serves the purpose of a net. Two players face each other on either side of the buffer zone. Player A 'serves' the ball by kicking it from his hands across to player B, who attempts to return it back to player A's side of the court, and so on. You can only score a point when it is your turn to serve. If you serve the ball and it goes out of play, you lose a point. The winner is the first to reach twenty points. Each player serves the ball five times, then a change of serve takes place. Change ends after ten points.

The exercise can be modified to include the practice of certain other skills, for example the number of touches can be raised to three or even four before the ball is played back across to the other zone. The coach might also introduce working partners. The area of play can be extended to accommodate more players, and the rules of play can

47

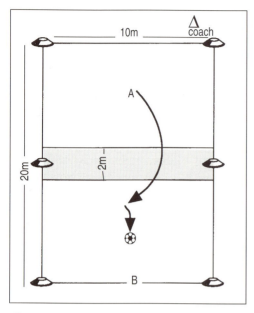

Fig 35   The tennis format.

be changed to suit a given theme, for example points can be given for completing a working skills sequence.

Such a sequence can be based on the following working example: the player receives the ball in his zone; if it comes on his head, he can attempt to cushion it and take the pace out of it, then bring it onto his thigh, then onto his kicking foot, before playing it with the instep to a partner or across the 'court'. The partner in turn can play the ball back (one touch) to the player, setting the ball up in such a way as to allow him to volley it (using the laces part of the boot) back across to the other side. The scoring system can be based on rewarding such completed sequences of work – for example, three successful touches of the ball, followed by a set-up pass – and a successfully played ball across to the other court could earn a bonus point.

Otherwise the game can be played according to normal tennis rules, adapted for soccer. The net was left out in this exercise, allowing the ball to travel at lower heights although it still had to clear the two metre buffer zone. A net might be put up as an alternative to the buffer zone, in which case the flight of the ball and the techniques in use would be altered to simulate skills such as the 'chip pass'. The touch techniques have to be more deft, as the ball has to fly over the net, and this alters the theme of the practice because the emphasis is more on ball control, which becomes more crucial because the first touch has to be perfect, giving the correct weight of pass.

SKILL NOT STRENGTH

It is not unusual to find that the player's initial instinct when kicking a ball is to strike it hard. Nearly all players at the beginning of their career equate the speed of the ball's flight with strength. However, strength destroys touch, and the player has to learn to control the ball skilfully with deft, precise foot movements; he will not be able to do this if he is concentrating on striking the ball as hard as he can. The training routines should teach the player to use different skills and to vary the strength as required. Being able to hit passes to different lengths comes from working to different play lengths on the practice ground. Likewise, the ability to strike the ball high or low only comes from practice. The different practice routines are designed to develop a wide variety of touch and body movement skills: this is the only way to build up a playing skills repertoire.

The best way to get a feeling of 'shaping' the ball is to take the strength out of the work at hand. You may be surprised how simple this is and how competitive the following exercises can be. Skills practice sessions can be boring, but it is possible to set objectives that do not seem directly skills related as the players enjoy the work while unobtrusively improving their skills.

There are players who would love to be more skilful but are afraid to be shown up in public, and this anxiety restricts their development. The nature of the following exercises disguises any individual skills failings or lack of technique. The key to setting up any working routine is to eliminate the psychological problems associated with skills training work.

Super Soccer Golf
(Fig 36)

This is fun to practise and removes any need to 'blast' the ball. The player is encouraged to develop a fine touch in pace and strength of striking the ball without focusing specifically on these skills: all he has to do is concentrate on getting the ball as close as possible to the cone flag. This type of training routine is best used in conjunction with complementary training exercises working on pace and strength of touch. All such training routines contribute immensely to the overall development of the player's touch, technique and skill repertoire.

How It Works

Nine cones ('flags') are placed at random

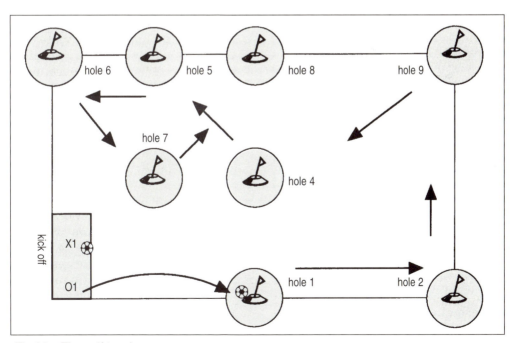

Fig 36   The golf touch game.

up to 40m apart, and numbered 1 to 9. The kick-off point is at an appropriate distance from flag 1. The players are paired off and compete against each other. At the kick-off point each player has a ball which he kicks towards the first flag, trying to get the ball as close to it as possible. The player who has his ball nearest to the flag wins one point.

A 'gimmie' (slang for 'point') can only be given if any ball played finishes 5m or less from the flag. If neither ball is this close, the players take one more shot each to see who can get closer to the flag. The closest ball then wins the point.

Thereafter the starting position for the next flag has to be in the vicinity of the one before, but must not interfere with the next two players coming up from behind. The competition is continued in this way until both players reach the last flag, and is judged on points.

SHAPING THE BALL

The first-touch formats must include practice in striking the ball to a more significant distance. The distances of the target objectives are extended, but not to such a length that maximum strength is required to propel the ball. The player needs to learn the different results of his kicking the ball in different ways. He also has to be able to play the ball without imparting any spin. Only a clean, dead-centre contact with the ball will keep it travelling in a straight line. The ability to shape the flight of the ball is another skill altogether which needs to be practised separately.

Accuracy
(Figs 37 & 38)

There is no such thing as a simple training routine. Every training routine has something to offer in terms of difficulty, and even the simplest of formats depends on the quality of work input. In other words, it is not just the training routine itself that makes a training session worth while, it is the player working hard on the quality of his touch that makes the exercises special. When confronted by the word 'accuracy', the player thinks in terms of targets. This is fine up to a point, but in soccer the target can mean different things; for instance, the target of a pass can be the feet or it could be a space. The different exercises will show that you can be accurate in many ways. In the following examples the players work on touch and shaping the ball to its intended destination. In exercise A they concentrate on being precise and direct, whereas in exercise B they work on shaping the flight of the ball.

The point at which the foot makes contact with the ball will determine the direction in which it goes. If you want the ball to go high in the air, aim at a spot low down on the ball (Fig 37). If you want to make the ball swerve, simply apply the inner toe/instep to the ball on the side opposite to the intended swerve direction. For example, if you want the ball to spin from right to left, strike the ball on the right-hand side. The amount of spin and flight deviation depends on how far over to the side you make contact with the ball; if you want to spin the ball a lot, strike/flick the ball on the extreme outer edge. Most of the forward strikes of the ball are done with

Fig 37   Strike points and lift of the ball.

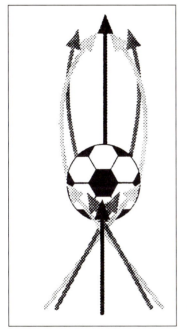

Fig 38 Striking the ball and the effects on its flight path.

the laces part of the boot.

Exercise A (Fig 39)

Two players, A and B, stand 40m apart. Midway between them two footballs are placed on 'tees' (cut down cones), 4m apart, positioned in such a way as to make a diamond shape with player A, player B, ball 1 and ball 2 at the corners. The players kick the ball to each other as straight as they can through and in between the two tees. The first player to hit one of the side balls is out and another player takes his place.

Exercise B (Fig 40)

Place two footballs (1 and 2) 1m apart on cone 'tees'. Players A and B stand 35m away from the two balls, one either side. Player A tries to kick a football to hit one of the two balls. If he fails to hit it (as shown in Fig 38), he lets another player take his place and player B has a shot. The competition now depends on who strikes either of the two balls first. The players enjoy putting the right shape on the flight of the ball, and there

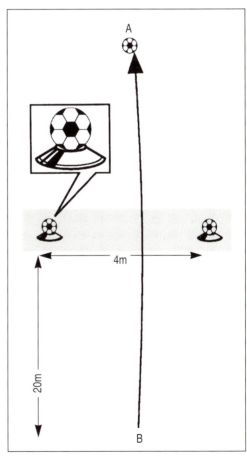

Fig 39   Shaping the ball.

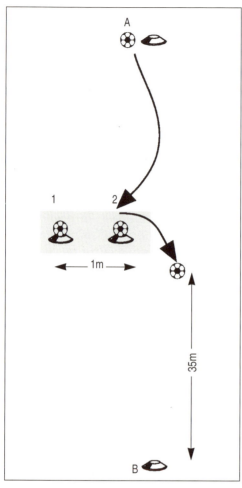

Fig 40   Hit the target.

is visible pleasure when someone actually does hit the target.

As you can see, simple practice objectives bring about the required skills without worrying too much about the details involved. This is acceptable to start with, but once the practice is under way the coach needs to work with the players on their technique of striking the ball.

EYE CO-ORDINATION

One of the most important aspects of ball control has little to do with technique. Keeping your eyes on the ball is but a flash of the eyelids: taking your eyes off the ball can be the difference between losing and retaining possession. The following training routine helps to deal with this problem; the practice involves receiving the ball with little or no time to spare in avoiding the oncoming opponent.

The Exercise
(Fig 41)

The practice area is 10 × 15m; these dimensions ensure the correct timing of the challenge. One end of the practice area, marked by cones, is the scoring zone. Player A, the attacking player, stands at the opposite end of the practice area from the scoring zone, player B (the defender) stands facing him just in front of the scoring zone; his approach to challenge for the ball will be in direct view of player A. The coach throws the ball up into the air. Player A has to keep his eyes on the ball in order to get it under control quickly, and to avoid the oncoming challenger. The timing of the challenge for the ball by player B is important to the practice theme: player B is permitted to run out to challenge for the ball on a given signal from the coach – just as the ball is about to be controlled by player A. The signal shout by the coach to player B helps to make the practice realistic, as it puts pressure on player A to keep his eyes on the ball, and to control the ball away from the oncoming opponent. If player A is successful in controlling the ball he can dribble past his opponent and get it into the shaded scoring zone. Points won could mean prizes.

Players can swap practice roles so that each player receives ten ball-control practice attempts as player A. Point scoring can be arranged as follows: getting past player B scores half a point, and getting the ball into the point zone a further half point – making a possible total of one point on each service attempt.

KEEPING POSSESSION UNDER PRESSURE
(Fig 42)

When the area of play becomes congested, keeping possession of the ball is a matter of controlling it away from opponents. The following exercise deals with the direction in which you choose to send the ball at your first touch in a crowded playing area.

How It Works

The cones are numbered 1 to 4 and placed in a 2m square configuration. The coach plays the pass to player A, shouting out a number from 1 to 4. When player A receives the ball, he knows that his first touch on the ball should send it to the cone number shouted out by the coach.

Try to get the player to use the strength and pace of the pass from the coach to really 'ping' the ball off the ground in that direction; keeping the ball flat on the ground may assist opponents in winning possession, so the skill of 'dinking' the ball over someone's foot is well worth mastering for tight situations. Make sure that the first touch is always under control; do not allow the player to get the touch wrong in terms of strength. If the touch is too strong then obviously the player has lost

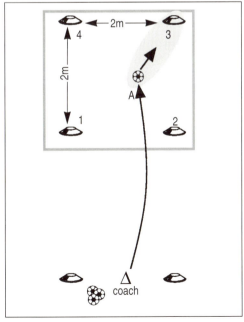

Fig 42   Directional touch, the four cone format.

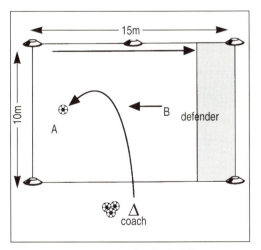

Fig 41   Eye co-ordination/ball skills.

possession of the ball. Standing still after the first touch can also be considered as giving the ball away to opponents and should always be avoided.

On receiving the pass from the coach, player A's body position is square on. The player should wait until the very last moment before moving to go in the direction indicated by the coach (cone 3 in Fig 42). In this example the practising player will use his right foot to touch/dink the ball to cone 3. The player uses his right foot to strike the ball (with the instep) and to stride off in direction of cone 3 all in one movement. If the player had wanted to go to his right (towards cones 1 or 4), he would have used his left foot to start off the stride/touch movement in that direction. This practice format thus allows the player to practise sending the ball in any direction with his first/touch stride.

This work can also be used to practise changing pace on contact with the ball. The player should change his pace so that he sprints past the cone placements for at least a few metres. When outside the cone placements he turns, using turning skills (where appropriate), then passes the ball back to the target set for this practice (the two cones placed to either side of the coach). The pass back to the coach must be correct in terms of pace, accuracy and height off the ground. The player should strive to pass back to the feet of his coach. The distance to the coach/cones is set to about 10m, but in practical terms the pass back to the coach varies between 10 and 15m.

WRONG-FOOTING THE OPPONENT
(Fig 43)

This training routine teaches how to deal with the ever present defender who is marking tight goal side of play. Losing such a marker is an essential skill, and this training routine works on the following: disguise of movement, checking out, changing direction, losing your opponent. The safe zones of this practice are there for very important reasons. It is important to realize that when you have managed to send the opponent the wrong way, the battle has actually been won.

Among other problems, getting away is a battle against the pull of the earth's gravity. The presence of the safe zones helps the player develop the muscles and reactions necessary for coping with this because they provide a target him to reach, thus not allowing him to stop once he has performed his skill (of temporarily wrong footing his opponent); this natural pause in the player's movement must be reduced so that the

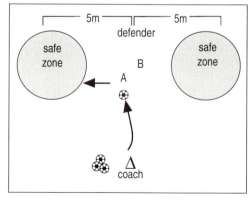

Fig 43   Man-to-man marking – getting away from the opponent.

play action is continuous. The body movements and the speed of reaction needed to get to the zones, ensure the correct training in this ball-control exercise.

How It Works

Player A (attacker) stands facing the coach, with a safe zone marked out 5m away on either side of him. Player B (defender) stands behind him. The coach plays the ball to player A, and player A works on dipping his shoulder to send player B the wrong way. In Fig 43, player A has got his first touch away from player B and is now on his way to his right-hand safe zone. Remember player A has his back to player B in this first ball-control working format. Player B can stop player A from reaching the safe zones, but is not permitted to challenge for the ball once player A has entered a safe zone.

Each successful attempt (entering a safe zone) can be rewarded by one point. The practising attacking player has ten attempts to get away from his opponent, giving him a possible top score of ten points. The ball must be under full control when the player enters the safe zone. Once this objective has been achieved, re-position the players as they were to start with.

USING THE OUTSIDE OF THE FOOT
(Fig 44)

The play area for this exercise is a square, 10 × 10m. The attacking player, player A, starts in the bottom right-hand corner; the defending player, player B, in the corner opposite. In the other two corners stand the coach, and a second player who stands in as coach 2.

The exercise starts with coach 1 passing the ball to player A. Player B must wait until player A has control of the ball before coming in to challenge. Once player A has made his first touch on the ball he moves the ball forwards immediately to confront player B. This time, instead of taking the ball to the side of the defender, player A plays it to service player coach 2. To do this, he uses the outside of the boot/foot, leaning the top half of the body towards the ball. Coach 2 returns the ball with his first touch back to player A, who has now passed player B and receives the ball behind player B. When this move takes place and player A has control of the ball again, the main theme of the practice has been completed.

The play can be continued with both players competing for possession of the ball and trying to reach either of the safe zones. Point scoring can add

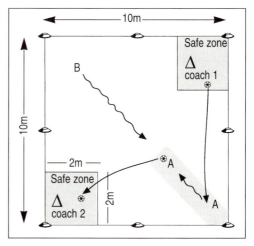

Fig 44   *The outside of the foot touch play format.*

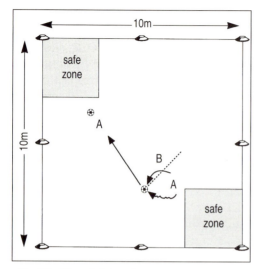

Fig 45   The dink touch move.

an extra incentive to this practice of dribbling skills, with one point being awarded to the first player to work the ball to a safe zone.

THE DINK TOUCH
(FIG 45)

The previous working formats concentrated on developing the player's ability to send the ball in a chosen direction away from opponents. This next exercise is similar in concept, only this time the opponent gets his foot to the ball.

How It Works

As before, the exercise takes place in a 10 x 10m square. This time there are two 2 x 2m safe zones marked in opposite corners. Player A starts at the corner of one of the safe zones with the ball at his feet, facing player B. The right foot is placed slightly under the ball, and will lift the ball over the foot of the defender/opponent. The technique is called the dink touch; the ball is played

sideways/forwards, away from your opponent.

The coach will signal to player B to go for the ball, and this is the start of the practice. When player B bites – 'bite' is defined as the moment a player makes a commitment to go for the ball – player A dinks the ball over his foot, which is possible to achieve because of the starting positions of both players.

Once player A has dinked the ball over player B's foot, he must perform a second skill – picking the ball up in his stride with the inside part of his other foot and knocking it forwards towards the opposite safe zone. The ball thus changes direction from the initial sideways movement of the dink to the forward movement of the second touch towards the safe zone. Player A then has to dribble the ball into the safe zone without losing possession to player B.

It is important to have the safe zone there for player A to aim at because it forces him first to change direction, and second to keep up his speed till safety is reached. It is all too easy to think the exercise is over and relax for a moment after performing the dink and stride; as with the previous exercise, it is vital to eradicate this tendency, as pausing simply allows the defender an opportunity to regain the ball.

Each player can try the exercise ten times. On each completed attempt, the practice can be started again by positioning players as described above.

THE SECOND AND SUBSEQUENT TOUCHES

The first touch skills are very special because they decide what happens next in play situations. Perhaps it is this fact that has led many coaches and players to pay less attention to the other skills in play. The first touch is important, but there are other important touches of the ball which have been neglected in recent times by many in the game.

For example, the second touch of the ball has several skill implications, the most significant being that it can send the ball in any direction. Another is passing the ball to a designated target.

Yet the skills factor does not end with the second touch of the ball: there is a third touch, which in certain game scenarios takes the ball forwards, making it a more 'forward directional touch'.

So thus far we have three separate skill touches: the first touch of the ball which controls it, and the second touch which could change the direction of play, setting the ball up for a third touch which moves the ball forwards. If you think that is about it, then think again, for there is a fourth skill touch on the ball, which stops the ball (with the foot on the ball).

In other words, there are different touch skills which should be recognized as such. All the exercises in this book look at ways of practising specific skill requirements. The eye co-ordination exercise (Fig 41) is a case in point, where the player works on his directional touch in a play scenario in which his first touch must be of the best quality if he is to get away from his opponent successfully.

THE TEST AND SKILLS MONITOR

The exercise below is designed to improve the player's close ball control skills and uses the techniques practised in this chapter. This makes it a suitable routine to use to assess a player's abilities and progress. Record the results in a chart as shown in Fig 47.

The Test
(Fig 46)

It is important for the coach to be able to distinguish between players who keep possession of the ball selfishly, and those who keep the ball for the benefit of the team. A player who takes on opponents and always ends up giving the ball away is in fact being selfish; he keeps possession for possession's sake, without an end object in mind. Possession should end in a pass to a teammate, or a shot at goal.

While you are in possession of the ball you can do what you will providing that the end result justifies the means. The team-player relationship should be based on ability, and if the player in question has the skills to go past opponents without losing possession of the ball, then this must be recognized as being good for team results. Players need to be aware of all possibilities and options open to them, and they need to know the effects of choosing a particular skill option. The team should be able to accommodate different skills, because there will always be times during the game when there is a need for an individual to do something special. Players should know their limitations, strive to improve on them, and play to their strengths.

The following exercise encourages players in possession of the ball to use a wide variety of skills to dribble past opponents. The coach encourages each player to develop and put together a

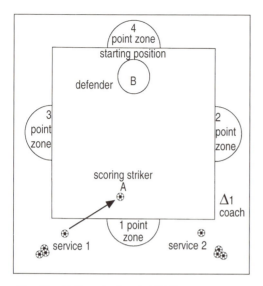

Fig 46   Ball control and dribbling.

sequence of ball skills, tailored to his particular abilities. A sample sequence (with reference to Fig 46) could be: play the ball with the outside of your right foot, when the opponent shifts in that direction, put your foot on top of the ball, drag the ball back, take the ball onto your left foot, change the direction point of your attack, play the double outside-of-foot touch, do a dummy, send the opponent the wrong way, change your pace of attack, pretend to go towards point scoring zone 2, change direction, go to scoring zone 4.

How It Works

The play area is a 10 x 10m square, with a semi-circular scoring zone attached to the middle of each side. These are marked out with cones and are 0.5m in depth. They are numbered 1 to 4, with zone 1 (the easiest to score in) being worth one point, zone 2, two, and so on.

The striker, player A, stands in front of scoring zone 1, facing the defender, player B, who stands in front of the scoring zone 4, which is thus the hardest to score in. Behind player A stand two service players with the footballs.

To begin, player A receives the ball from one of the service players; (these take it in turns to serve a ball to player A). He is then in a position to take on player B. The task set for player A is to use a ball skill sequence such as the one explained above to get past player B and get the ball to any of the scoring zones, thus scoring the number of points indicated by the zone number; for example, if he gets the ball into zone 2, he scores two points.

Player B times his coming forwards to challenge for the ball to the moment when player A has just controlled it. He is not permitted to tackle once player A has managed to get inside any point-scoring zone; a foot on the ball by player A inside any zone is enough to credit him with the points of that zone. The practice is restarted after each scoring attempt. The defender has the right to kick the ball out of the playing area, and when this happens that service-scoring attempt by player A becomes void. Player A has ten attempts to score points.

The objective of this practice format is for player A to accumulate as many points as possible out of ten service attempts. If he sticks to point zone 1, he will finish last in the points league table and the coach will have to take a look at the causes behind this apparent lack of ambition. Getting the ball to the other zones requires good all-round skills and it may be that the player has problems in this direction. A good coach will be able to sort out what is wrong. If the problem is a lack of skills, the solution is to take the player back to the appropriate skill practice exercise. This is the whole point of this skill progress assessment exercise.

The Monitor
(Fig 47)
Every training routine has something to offer the player in improving his skills, and generally concentrates on

what he requires. No one can improve his skills by just playing soccer. The game itself must be dismantled into small parts, analysed, the parts practised separately in the shape of the training exercises and then put back together for the player's benefit.

The coach needs to be able to monitor the progress made by his players. To do this effectively and to motivate his players, he can use a chart like the one depicted, recording the results of the exercise described above. This keeps a

---

Monitor Progress

The points league system

A working example: week 7. Training session – Monday morning 15/8

		points/			
Player 1–Edward					
10 Attempts		score comment	**Initial trial results–standards of play**		
Ball played to Edward					
Service	1	4	Excellent	points 29–40
Service	2	3	Above average	points 19–29
Service	3	4	Average	points 9–19
Service	4	3	Less than average	points 8–12
Service	5	4	Low rating	points 0–8
Service	6	0	Defender – kicked/out of play	
Service	7	3	Good work by both players	
Service	8	4		
Service	9	3	Edward has achieved fine standards of skills	
Service	10	4		
Session total		32	= excellent work	

League table points					
	week 7	week 8	week 9	week 10	total
Player 1, Edward	32	33	36	37	138
Player 2, Adam	31	31	34	35	131
Player 3, Andrew	29	30	35	36	130

Fig 47   The skills monitor. The league points are booked down over a set period of time, and are used as a guideline for checking skills progress. Set the standards according to initial trial results.

record of each player's results over a period of time, and adds a competitive element to training by showing a league table of points.

Many normal working practices in soccer today started off as simple misconceptions; the skills assessment exercise above is a case in point. A similar format is used by many coaches for developing skills with the ball, even though it represents an end product rather than the means to achieve it. Dribbling skills and ball-control skills should be practised in special separate training routines. All skills are different and cannot be acquired by using incorrect practice environments. The test and skills monitor are used to assess the ability of each player because they show what he can do with the ball. The actual development of ball control happens elsewhere, by using such training routines as the one-touch working routines and other cone formats to work on the players' wider range of skills.

PASSING AND BALL CONTROL 6

The pass itself is in fact a one-touch play skill, and as such belongs to the one-touch practice formats. However, the passing skills are special; they come first in the order of technical merit and should initially be worked on in isolation. The variation of working skills used in passing is amazing, and when analysed it can be seen that the players are in fact working on a number of skills such as touch, pace, direction of the pass, even the occasional knee pass technique. Therefore this initial introduction is very important, particularly as these working formats explain the function of the players within the team shape as far as the art of passing the ball is concerned.

The exercises below form the basis of all passing combinations, the simplest being the first short pass play option within the team play structure. Fig 48 shows the two-man working format, while Fig 49 shows the three-man version. The latter is the more important of the two because it explains the relative positions of selected team players within the system of play. This positioning of players allows you to work on both short and long passing techniques.

PASSING TECHNIQUES

The shape of the foot limits the techniques available to the player, but even so, the more skilful can pass the ball in a variety of ways, improvising with the lean of the body, spin of the ball, pace and strength of touch and so on. Even without improvisation, however, you can pass the ball in different ways by simply using different parts of the foot – the inside, the back, the laces, and so on.

What makes any player special is the all-important ability to pass the ball accurately over any distance. The shortest pass possible can be played with almost any part of your body. Some say that using the instep of your foot gives the largest contact area with the ball, but the majority of skilful players use the laces part of the boot to play a wide variety of passing variants.

The height of the ball can be varied by using the upper part of the body, almost like a rudder on a ship. If you lean back with the top half of your body this helps the foot to get under the ball, which will make the ball fly high. Leaning forward with the top half of your body will help your head to stay above the ball. To keep the ball low you need to concentrate on getting the laces part of your boot to strike the ball mid-on, with a good follow-through. As with all working skills, however, it is not that simple: even if your body is leaning towards the ball, your foot could still make contact with the underpart of the ball, making it rise up into the air.

Passing is therefore a question of mastering your body and foot co-ordination, and the following practice formats are ideal for learning to pass the ball over any distance. Remember that every practice you do has to be taken seriously because even a simple task has direct implications for other soccer issues.

SHORT AND LONG PASSING COMBINATIONS

The Team Shape

By adding a third player to the practice (Fig 49) you are in fact creating a basic team structure: player 2 can be in defence, while player 3 can be part of the midfield and player 11 the striker. The shape of the team can be set up to adhere to a pre-determined passing sequence. Fig 49 shows the short and long passing combination set-up, in a straight line for practical practice reasons. In fact the shape of this formation can alter during play while still adhering to the correct passing working sequence.

The shape of the team is vital when working on ball possession skills, because if the players are positioned too far from each other, they will rely on the long ball to retain possession. This obviously has a longer flight time, which allows the opponents time to reposition and gives them a greater chance of gaining possession of the ball. With the short passing game, if the passing is short within a restricted area, the ball falls into the hands of defenders.

It is very important to understand that adhering to either the short or long passing game as the only playing option damages the skills development of players. It is essential to use different passing length and movement combinations

as this teaches players to look up and helps them to develop a wider range of skills.

The Two-Man Working Format
(Fig 48)

Ten players stand in two lines of five, facing each other: thus player 2 faces player 11, player 3 faces player 10, player 4 faces player 9, and so on. Behind players 11 to 7 four lines are marked out, parallel to the line of players, at distances of 10m, 20m, 30m and 40m from the row of players 2 to 6. Initially players 11 to 7 stand on the 10m line, so the players are 10m apart. Players 2 to 6 are each in possession of a ball. The coach starts the practice by giving specific instructions.

The Coaching Exercises

1. The players with the balls start by throwing them by hand to their opposite numbers. Then both players try to keep the ball in the air for as many headers as they can. Players can receive a points reward if they can manage a certain number of passes in a row, say ten.

2. The players with the balls start by throwing them to their opposite numbers. Then both players try to keep the ball off the ground for as many passes as possible, using any touch sequence and any part of the body except the hands. Rewards can be given as in Exercise 1.

3. Short passing, one touch only. The distance between the players is 20m. The players with the balls start the practice, by knocking the first pass.

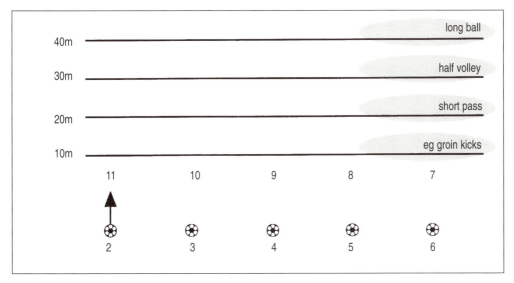

Fig 48   The two-man (ball control) working format.

4. Players 11 to 7 move back to the 20m line to practise half volleys. The players in possession kick the ball in such a way that it bounces in front of their opposite numbers, who allow it to bounce once before kicking it back as it rises from the ground. As in Exercise 1, players can be rewarded if they can pass the ball in this way ten times in a row, in full control of the ball.

5. The players with the balls start the practice by playing the ball in such a way as to make it fly through the air with enough height so that their opposite numbers can chest the ball down to their feet before playing the ball back in the same manner. Repeat a set number of times.

6. Players 11 to 7 move back to the 40m mark to practise the long ball pass. The players in possession kick the long ball pass to their opposite numbers, who

control it before kicking the ball back. Vary the height of the service.

The Three-Man Working Format

These practice routines are about player positioning. Obviously, the players will move around during the passing practice, but this does not matter because the passing sequence will still incorporate both short and long passes between players.

Exercises (Figs 49a & b)

1. The players split up into groups of three, with a striker, midfielder and defender in each group. The three players, numbered 2, 3 and 11 in Fig 49a, stand in a line so that player 3, the midfielder, stands between the striker (11) and the defender (2). Player 2 starts with a short pass to player 3, who passes it back. Player 2 now strikes the ball long to player 11. Player 11 plays the short

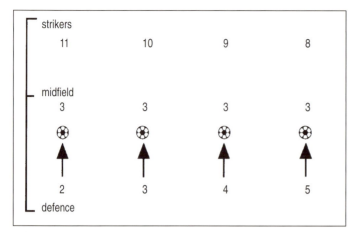

Fig 49a   The three-man (ball control) working format.

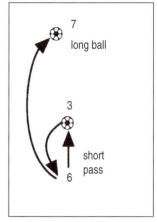

Fig 49b   Team shape.

ball to player 3, who plays it back. Player 11 now strikes the ball long back to player 2, and the sequence can begin again.

2. As before, the players split up into groups of three, with a striker, midfielder and defender in each group, and take up the same positions as in Exercise 1 with the midfielder in the middle. Player 2 starts the practice by playing the ball to player 3. Player 3 then runs with the ball towards player 11 and plays a one-two with him; receiving the ball back from player 11, player 3 runs with the ball back across to the other side to do the same with player 2. Player 3 repeats this run as many times as the coach wishes – say five runs – before changing places with either of the outside players.

SOCCER PLANNER 1 – BALL CONTROL

This working planner shows a typical training session with a random selection of loosely related ball control topics.

Note that stages 2 and 3 are only an introduction to the skills formats. It is important to distinguish between ball control, dribbling and running skills, which are different skills that need to be practised in appropriate training formats. The straight line cone formations that were widely used for training in the past can be used for fitness training (stage 2). The art of dribbling in the modern game is completely different, the difference lying in the need to possess other skill dribbling variations.

Stage 1
(Figs 50–53)
A warm-up of 20 minutes. The tempo of the running must be varied and must not include sprinting in the first phases of the warm-up. The first phase (approximately 15 minutes) should be well broken up; use your favourite stretching exercises to intersperse aerobic warm-up exercises – sample stretches are shown in Figs 50 to 53. Start with lateral exercises such as press-ups and arm circling, followed by dorsal exercises

Fig 50–52   The kick out and stretch sequence.

Fig 53   The warm-up continued: working on abdominal muscles through the use of natural body tension.

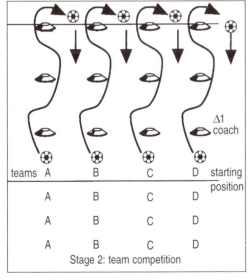

Fig 54   This working format is not strictly a ball control skills exercise; the emphasis is on achieving fitness.

such as trunk bending to the front or sideways, or the kick out and stretch sequence; finally do abdominal exercises such as sit-ups.

Keep to a standard routine set by you or your coach or to the training sequence given in this book. The routines are selected on the basis of your physical needs.

Stage 2
(Figs 54 & 55)

This should last 20 minutes. Practise different individual dribbling skills, encouraging the player to create his own moves. He could try to emulate the dribbling skills of top players.

You could hold a team dribbling competition. Mark out four identical obstacle courses of three cones spaced out at 10m intervals, as shown in Fig 54.

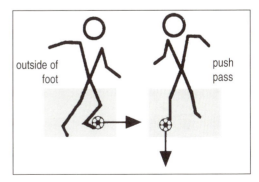

Fig 55   Practise passing.

Divide the players into four teams, which will compete against each other to see which team can finish the course first. Each player has to dribble the ball round the course using the techniques shown in Fig 55, to a course decided by the coach. This exercise is purely for fitness training, it is not a ball control skill format in the full sense of the word.

Stage 3
(Figs 56 & 57)

Continuing the dribbling theme, the players are positioned in a circle and are paired off, as shown in Fig 56. The coach nominates one pair to start off in the middle, one of whom will be the defending player. The players on the outside pass the ball to the dribbling player on the inside, who tries to beat the defender by dribbling past him. The outside players help the dribbling player to keep possession of the ball, but if one of the outer players makes a bad pass he and his partner automatically

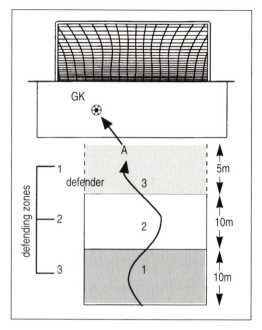

Fig 57   Taking on defenders.

become the inside pair. Continue the practice for 20 minutes.

Another exercise uses a more direct approach. Line up three defenders, 1, 2 and 3, in a row in front of the goal, so that player 3 is nearest to the goal and player 1 is furthest away, as shown in Fig 57. A goalkeeper waits in goal. The striker, player A, has to get past all three defenders (starting with player 1) in turn. If he beats all three he can finish with a shot on goal. Continue the practice for 25 minutes.

Stage 4
(Fig 58)

Fig 58 shows a team exercise that encourages players to take on opponents in the correct zones. The players are divided into an attacking and a defending team. The attacking team –

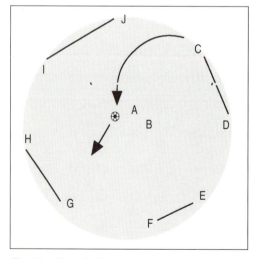

Fig 56   The circle format.

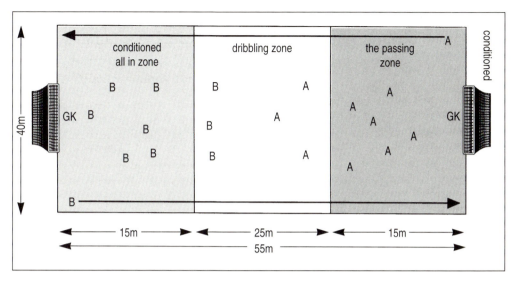

Fig 58   Team work format: stage 4: take on defenders.

team A – must adhere to the following rules. In and around their own penalty area (on the right in this example) the players must pass the ball. They are encouraged to dribble past their opponents *only* once they reach the midfield area of play and beyond. It is simply bad form to encourage players to take people on in front of their own goal; however, they should take on defenders inside the opponents' penalty area. Continue the practice for two sets of 15 minutes.

7 INTRODUCING THE TEAM

Based on what he has observed thus far and before events can unfold any further, the coach must give a lot of thought to the overall assessment of his playing staff. It might be said that at a professional club success is measured by the club's standing in the league, but getting promotion is a very difficult issue and cannot be achieved as easily as you might imagine. Thankfully, the players and the club can find success at most levels.

There are many reasons for a club's existence. In today's world, money controls a large part of our life, and money can have an enormous effect on the club's success. Translated into a soccer point of view, players have to earn a living playing soccer because in practical terms you can't reach high standards of play on a part-time basis. The morale of the club is always a factor, and poor morale among the players can wreck the best of plans. It is not my intention in this book to highlight problems in this direction, suffice it to say that the coach should have the full support of his players.

CREATING A TEAM

Eighteen first team players is the minimum number required to sustain a strong team. Throughout the playing season injuries can decimate your playing staff. It only takes one or two key players to be injured and unable to play

for the team to lose its chances. Injuries apart, the balance of the team needs to be maintained in specific areas of play; for example, in defence the coach may choose a player for his outstanding tackling, ball distribution and heading abilities, whilst his choice for attacking play may require a player who has a wider range of abilities such as ball skills, pace of movement with the ball and strength in attacking heading.

The pool of players available can become a vital source of tactical options, such as could be observed in the 1994 World Cup competition. The secret of success comes from the ability of the coach to place players in their respective roles according to their skills. Each player complements another to create either an attacking or a defensive type team. The most successful team in the USA 1994 was based on an all-round capability.

THE ATTACKING SYSTEM
(Fig 59)

The 1, 1, 4, 4, 1 system is the ideal base for modern attacking play, where players should be able to attack creatively from almost any position in the team structure. The Brazilians demonstrated this ability in the World Cup in 1994. This is the style of play which has an exciting future, and the clearly outdated flat back four and the channel positions in attacking play will hopefully come to

Fig 59   The 1, 1, 4, 4, 1 system.

an end. Tackling from behind was outlawed because it was negative and ugly and detrimental to the quality of the game.

THE TEAM
The balance of the team depends on many factors. Success comes from the correct assessment of the players' abilities and skills for the purpose of team effects in play. The best teams in the world have outstanding individuals in key role positions, that is in central defensive positions, midfield and up front, though of course this does not mean that the rest of the team can be discarded and the positions filled with mediocre players. The outstanding individuals are usually especially effective in certain skills, which contribute immensely to the team success. Different players have different characters and abilities. Here are just some of the finer points to look out for.

The Goalkeeper
A typical goalkeeper is tall and agile, aggressive but controlled, and always shouting at his co-defenders, which is a positive attribute. The two things I

watch for when choosing a goalkeeper are the techniques he uses for handling the ball (safe hands) and co-ordination. He should also have fast legs! Honesty and integrity are vital for obvious reasons; as coach I need to be able to trust him completely.

The Left Back
This player must have masses of talent. He does not need to be aggressive as long as he has plenty of skill. Often a cheeky character with plenty of pace, he is able to skin anyone coming out of defence and is practically impossible to pass. He also has to possess the ability to move into forward attacking positions in support of the attacking players.

The Central Defender (1)
In this position I would place a ruthless man who takes no prisoners and who has no fear of any opponent. His feet would be as tough as they come with bruises to show that he has been in many a battle and come out on top.

The Sweeper
This name is used only because in his defensive role the sweeper covers for his back two, three or four defenders. He can also be regarded as the play maker. This player is a moderate person. The game of football to this character is an exercise he goes through without any undue emotion – he is calculating, brilliant, unnerving to watch, and possesses a great range of skills and concentration.

The Central Defender (2)
This player has to have the ability to keep on his feet, to control opponents

without fouling them. This type of man will think before he leaps, which in this position is a desirable attribute most of the time. He complements the other central defender with his ability to give cover, but once in possession of the ball he must have remarkable ability in using it well.

The Right Back

It is very difficult to find an exceptionally good right back player because not many players like to play in this position. Sometimes a great personality can be found, but he must have vision and be able to pass the ball accurately over long distances. When defending, the full back can control the flanks effectively and cancel out the early/late cross of the ball into the box. Players at the back must be able to create counterattacking movements when in possession of the ball, not only by moving it through passing, but also by pushing into forward positions themselves.

The Outside Right Midfielder

This must be an extrovert who has fun on every turn. On the field his pace should be second to none with skills that are electrifying and determination that is ferocious. He must be able to nutmeg the best and still come away with his shirt in tact.

The Inside Right Midfielder

Ideally this player has a terrific shot on goal, but very rarely does. One cannot plan for this type of player as he must have everything – skill, determination and the right amount of aggression. When a goal attempt comes off, it comes

off spectacularly, and you can hear the crowds cooing with admiration. He is an unpredictable player, which adds to his undoubted skills.

The Inside Left Midfielder

This is a truly gifted player. He is strong in the tackle, and a huge force in the team, and has the ability to split any defence with his wonderful vision. His passing is second to none. He is often a little bit of an introvert, and does his talking on the soccer field.

The Outside Left Midfielder

This player has abundant skills and plenty of pace and power. He has the ability to get past defenders as if they are standing still. Often a very sensitive type, you cannot push him too much as his response might be negative; gentle persuasion usually works. Many opponents will underestimate this player – at their peril!

The Spearheading Striker

The job of this player in my system is to co-operate with everyone in attacking play. It is particularly interesting when he combines his playing talents in partnership with player 2, the play maker. This position demands a player who can perform to high standards in many playing skills: he must be able to hold up the ball in order to bring players into the game; he must be brave, physically strong, have pace, plenty of stamina and good concentration; he must be able to turn defenders; he must be good at passing the ball and at finishing.

THE BOSS

The coach/manager has the necessary

experience to place a player in the position best suited to him and the team. Sometimes this is unpopular with players but in my opinion players are not able to perform this task correctly, mainly because they are pre-occupied with the work created for them during play, and are therefore not in a position to assess their own performance and the team play accurately.

A good coach will always spot bad playing habits (team or individual) developing and immediately take steps to return things to proper working order in training.

The coach – and the players – should also keep an eye open for problems associated with drug abuse or alcoholism. Players should be encouraged to spend more time coaching youngsters in the community, building on a natural interest that would take them away from environments that are destructive to the mind and body. Many are not even aware of the dangers involved in what seems at first to be an innocent pastime, having fun with friends.

There may also be psychological problems arising from the pressures associated with sustaining quality performances week in, week out. Such expectations can lead to considerable anxiety, especially if the player is in competition for a first team place. The coach will have to be sensitive in his handling of stressed players.

It is only through this unique ability to achieve the right balance of all the various factors that a good coach can put together a winning unit called the team. It is not widely appreciated, however, that the success of any club depends on *everyone's* attitude to working and training. The job of coach can be very difficult because ultimately the actual end product – 'the game of soccer' – is in the hands of his players.

8 DEFENDING

The most important single team issue in soccer has to be the ability of the team to play to a given shape and as far as skills are concerned there should be no difference in that sense between all the players. What should be recognized, however, is that each position on the field of play has specific requirements.

The first team topic deals with defensive plays, because no team can be successful without a well-organized defence. Every player should be confident in his role in the team, which gives him the base to use his skills. The following topics are the building blocks of a player's whole game. I will describe in detail how any playing system works, how to use the system in attack and how to construct a defence. Technical and tactical knowledge is provided, including many examples of using relevant skills.

A GAME OF NUMBERS

I cannot conceive of losing a game because my players were unable to adapt to situation, whatever it may have been. It is equally inconceivable to defend a goal with four players while five opponents are attacking it. It is a basic rule that in the vicinity of the ball you must give cover to the challenging player, especially in your own defensive third of the field; wherever possible you must try to outnumber the opponents by at least one. However, while I believe in

total attacking soccer, this certainly does not imply that you do not keep a shape in defence. It means simply that every player has the duty to go forwards *and* to defend. The responsibility here has to be collective: it is the working basis for keeping the shape in play.

The 1, 1, 4, 4, 1 system has five players in forward positions and five in defending positions. The opposing team thus has to use six strikers to have any chance of scoring a goal. They also have to defend in the correct numbers. It is impossible for the opposing team to do both things at once, but with this system our team can. Fig 61 shows the basic defending principles which are the building blocks of this system of play, the beginning of keeping the shape, that is, maintaining the correct positioning and distance between the players, usually about 10m in general play.

THE DEFENDING WORKING BASE
(Figs 60 & 61)

Teamwork starts with defending principles: without the knowledge of how to defend properly, it will be impossible for you to construct your system in defence. In practical terms, this system will allow your team to win possession of the ball, and give it the capability to counter-attack quickly in numbers. The team shape of 1, 1, 4, 4, 1 is shown in Fig 60. The arrow from the sweeper to a

Fig 60   In the modern 1, 1, 4, 4, 1 system, the sweeper should move to the position indicated by the arrow.

line with the back four indicates a need to move forward. The position as shown to the rear of the back four could otherwise be counter-productive in a defensive situation.

Getting to know the correct body positions in defence will help your team to take care of several problems at once, the first being to eliminate the threat of the first attacking player, who by definition will always be trying to create an opportunity to strike on goal. If he fails to create such an opportunity, he may be able to pass the ball to someone else who could.

Study the first challenger's body position (in Fig 62 player 1), and the timing of his challenge to the man in possession of the ball, as this determines the eventual directional attack or outcome of play. The defender has positioned himself incorrectly, allowing his opponent a free hand. His body position is square on to the opponent, so he will not be able to stop the opponent's progress into wide areas. If player 1 was on his own, without cover, the man

in possession of the ball could attack his goal to either side of this challenger.

The picture shows clearly how the system of play works in defence. The defender's body position can control the direction of the opponent's attack. In Fig 61 it might have been better if the first challenger was further to the left of his opponent, from which position he may have been able to force the opponent to come inside and onto the covering player (player 2). Instead, the team could now be exposed to a crossing of the ball situation. This is not always something to be avoided, and the option of sending opponents inside or outside will depend on your strength in defence. Always try to achieve the shape at the back of your defence as shown in Fig 66.

THE THREE DEFENCE POSITIONS
(Fig 62)

When establishing your defence, the first defender in place is known as the 'first challenger' (jockey) once he is in position. Your team also needs to position (wherever possible) a second defender, known as the 'covering player'. The third player in this defending base is known as the 'zone defender'; this position is the 'anchor' for the system of play. Fig 62 shows how the defenders position themselves in the vicinity of the ball. They will have other key duties, such as picking up runners from the back, protecting the back unit, positioning to cover key areas in front of the box and, if play continues, inside the box. If the opposition have attacked in numbers, all hands are on deck to protect vital spaces in the vicinity of

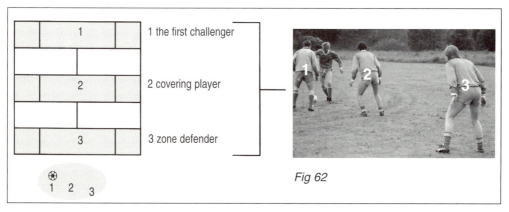

1	1 the first challenger
2	2 covering player
3	3 zone defender

⊛ 1 2 3

Fig 62

Fig 61   A constructive defence.

this initial defensive unit.

The First Challenger
(Fig 63)

The whole process of defending starts with the first challenger, who is always going to be the man nearest to the opponent who is in possession of the ball. The way the first challenger behaves is vital to the success of defensive play; he should try to make the attack move in the desired direction by the way he

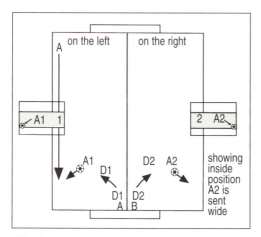

Fig 63   Jockeying.

positions himself. The position taken up by the first challenger (with regard to the ball) can also be used in other areas of play, though not as effectively.

In Fig 63, the first challenger stands sideways on to attacker A1, sending him to the left or right of the goal area, depending on which side of the field the attacker is. In this case, player D1's position is similar to player 2's in Fig 61, the covering player. These positions are known as being goal side of the player and ball – forcing opponent A1 into wide positions (away from the goal). This is the first principle of defence, commonly known as 'jockeying' your opponent.

The Covering Player
(Fig 64)

In Fig 64a the covering player (D2) has positioned himself to the side of player D1, and is helping him to force the attacker (A1) wide to the left. In some situations it is the covering player who decides how D1 (the first challenger) should act. He can instruct him either to send player A to the left or to hold

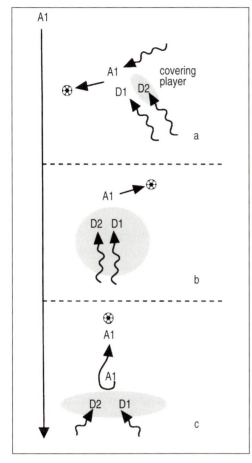

Fig 64   The very best in defending.

him where he is, or to tackle him while he gives cover. We know that the challenger's body position dictates to his opponent the direction in which he has to go, but once there is a covering player helping out, it is the covering player's job to dictate play, and it is his position alongside the first challenger which will decide the opponent's direction.

In Fig 64b the opponent is being forced to go right (infield). This time the covering player's position is such that the attacker is unable to go into a wide position.

In Fig 64c the first challenger (D1) and his covering player (D2) have succeeded in forcing the opponent (A1) to turn round and move away from the goal. This is the best outcome in defending. Forcing the opponent away from the goal buys valuable time for your team players to return goal side of the ball and to re-establish the defending shape.

Communication

In order to help each other, the defending players must communicate with each other in a clear and instructional manner. Being precise is vital to success, and all players should learn to communicate. Soccer language cannot be too complicated or colourful, however, because of the laws on ungentlemanly conduct.

Remember that when the first challenger is in position, he is unable to see what is happening behind him; it is therefore the responsibility of the covering player to give the first challenger as much information as possible. In every situation helping each other in this way will build confidence. Possible instructions to the first challenger are as follows:

Instruction	*Meaning*
Send him left	The challenger should position himself on the incoming attacker's left-hand side.
Send him right	The challenger should position himself on the incoming attacker's

Stand up	right-hand side. The challenger must not challenge hastily, as there is no cover available and there is a need to buy time.
Cover's on	The challenger can try to win possession of the ball.
Stay tight	The challenger must not allow the opponent to turn with the ball.
Push up	The challenger should get close to the opponent, ready to defend.
Pick up	The challenger positions himself to defend tight, close to the appropriate opponent.
Away	Do not take your time, get rid of the ball quickly, play the ball out, safety first.
Man on	If the challenger wins the ball, this warns him of someone coming to challenge for the ball.

The Anchor Man
(Figs 65–67)

The zone defender establishes the link between the players challenging for the ball and the rest of the team. His position acts as an anchor for repositioning the other defending players; the whole team takes its lead from him.

The anchor man always positions himself in line with the action to defend the area to the side of the challenging and covering defenders. The first challenger is always the man nearest to the player in possession of the ball; it will not always be player D1 as in Fig 66, because the attack will come from different directions. The defensive positions aimed at, however, will always be those shown, regardless of which players actually end up in them.

Fig 65 shows the full range of defending positions combined against a

Fig 65 The back unit.

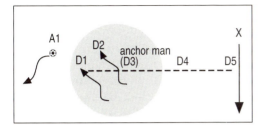

Fig 66   The back unit in position.

central threat on goal in the 1, 1, 4, 4, 1 system. The picture shows the need for quick defensive changes in response to attacking play. The two full backs are in fact out of position, and need to come a lot closer to the wide attackers. The attacking player in possession of the ball could take full advantage of the incorrect positioning of the two full backs by playing the ball wide to his right or left.

Fig 66 shows how the defending players adapt to new situations in play. The anchor player (D3), seen second from the left in Fig 65, turns to support the full back, and is now the covering player (D2). His new position (in field/cover) sends the opponent (A1) into a wide attacking position. The original challenging player now repositions in an anchor role (D3). The original covering player takes up a zone-defensive position (D4), and the full back stays more or less in the same position (D5), appropriately positioned to the back of this defence. This shows a flexible response system, based on the three body positions in the vicinity of the ball.

The distances between the positions in defence of your goal vary depending on the danger to it: the greater the threat, the tighter the shape, in principle. Remember that in very wide touch line situations, the first challenger sometimes has to cope on his own.

The Pace Of Approach

The speed at which you approach your

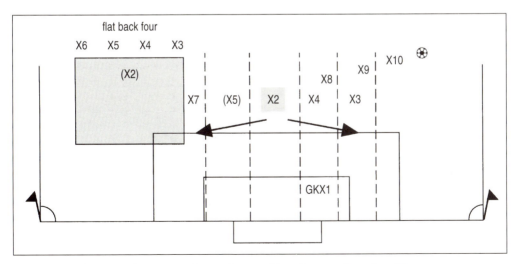

Fig 67   The flat back four can no longer be considered as a safe option. The sweeper X2 has been positioned to show my alternative to this flat back defensive shape.

opponent is important: do not commit yourself too soon. When you watch a sheepdog at work, you can see him forcing the sheep to do his bidding without actually approaching them too closely, and the first challenger's job is similar. He must force the opponent to go in the direction of his choice. When defending on your own, the choice of sending your opponent wide, away from goal, is the only option you have. The defender's strongest body position is always the tie/chest side to opponent. The opponent will always try to go onto the weakest side of the defender, which is the defender's arm nearest to him.

The challenger's sideways-on position is deliberate, not only because it helps him to control his opponent's body movement but because it helps the other defenders to know what the first challenger is doing and so react appropriately.

When giving cover to the first challenger, the second defender must be the correct distance away from him (*see* Fig 61). Be very careful not to get too close to the action, because if you do, the opponent may be able to get past both of you in one movement.

DEFENSIVE PRIORITIES
(Figs 68 & 69)

There are exceptions to the three-man-plus zone-defending system because at times play stretches the shape causing problems with numbers at the back. In such situations there are defensive

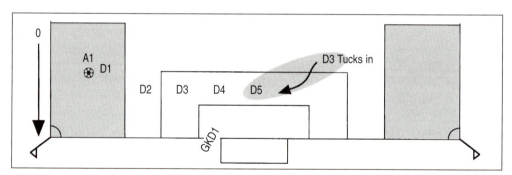

Fig 68   D2 anchor position.

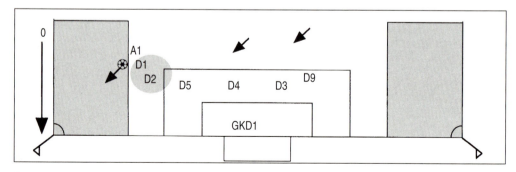

Fig 69   The system with cover from D2.

priorities, although the fact is that in very wide positions the danger to goal is minimal. The danger is always in and around the penalty area.

Sometimes the defending situation is that shown in Fig 68, where the opponent A1 has to be taken care of by just one player (D1) without cover. When players filter back goal side of the ball, and the opponent ventures further in, the immediate defending priorities will require sufficient numbers to employ the full working defending system as shown in Fig 69.

SOCCER PLANNER 2 – JOCKEYING

This planner practises the correct approach and timing for making the first challenge. The initial approach to the opponent was described as 'jockeying' – standing up and controlling the opponent's movement away from dangerous positions close to goal – it is important to realize that it is quite possible to win possession of the ball without tackling. The following training

routines should practise most of the technical skill requirements of challenging for the ball.

Stage 1
(Figs 70–72)

All warm-up sessions should include stretching exercises, and these should be performed prior to any vigorous activity. The skittle format below can become part of the warm-up session, but this form of exercise must come later in the programme. The stretching exercises can be very simple, using your own strength to pull gently on you own muscles, extending their length to cope with further activities.

The Skittle Format (Fig 73)

This exercise can be done with any number of players. You do not need a ball, just an open practice area. Fig 73 assumes there are ten players participating. They stand in rows in an inverted skittle formation, with four players in the front row, three in the second and so on. They must stand far

Fig 70   Groin stretch.

Fig 71   Hamstrings.

Fig 72   Thigh stretch.

enough apart so that there is space to run around them. The players are numbered 1 to 10.

The coach starts the exercise by shouting out two numbers. While the rest stand still, the first number heard becomes the runner and the second number becomes the catcher, and the catcher then chases the runner through the formation. The practice stops when

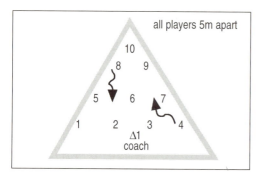

Fig 73   The skittle format.

the catcher touches the runner or when the coach says 'Stop'. It should last 20 minutes.

Stage 2

Back to Back (Fig 74)

In this fun training routine, two players stand back to back with a row of three cones facing player A and three facing player B. The cones are numbered 1, 3, 2 in each row, with cone 3 in the middle, cone 1 to the right of each player and cone 2 to the left. When the coach calls a number (1 to 3), each player has to try to turn round and reach the numbered cone called *behind* him. The players are allowed to use the upper part of the hand to try to turn around each other's position, but they are not permitted to

grab or use the hand in any other way. The practice should last 3 minutes per pair.

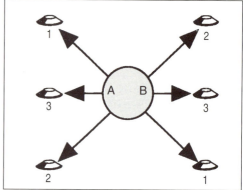

Fig 74   Back to back.

One on One (Fig 75)

Split a 20 x 20m practice area into three separate sections, a central zone and two point-scoring zones on each side of it, one worth one point and the other five. Two teams (A and B) of players are each numbered from 1 to 11 (or however many players are participating).

The coach shouts out a number and the two nominated players from teams A and B compete for the ball in the middle zone. Once a player wins possession and is in control of the ball, his opponent cannot tackle him, he can only jockey him away from the point areas. The aim is to score points by touching the ball inside either scoring zone. Only one touch place is counted. In order to score again, the player must re-enter the middle zone, and start again from there.

The jockeying player can prevent him from coming out, but he is not permitted to enter either point-scoring zone. The players have 3 minutes to accumulate points.

Alternatively, once a player has won possession of the ball and has made it to a scoring zone, he can be given 10 seconds to get out and back to the middle zone; the other player will try to prevent him leaving the scoring zone by jockeying. If he does not make it in the time, or if the jockeying player wins possession of the ball, the practice is restarted by the coach in the middle zone. The exercise can be timed to last 3 minutes per pair, or played in sets of five attempts.

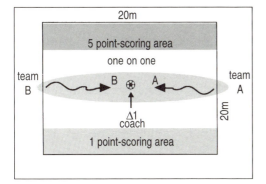

Fig 75   One on one.

Stage 3
(Fig 76)

Small-Sided Game

Use a scaled-down playing area of 60 × 40m, with a scoring zone marked out in two opposite corners. Two teams of six players line up on each side of the centre line as shown. The players initially compete for the ball in the middle of the field, and the player who wins possession of the ball becomes the attacking player; he then has to try to reach one of the point zones to score. He is obliged by the rules to take on the nearest defender, who has to try to position himself in such a way as to send the attacking player away from the point scoring zones.

The challenging team must provide a covering player to help the challenging player win possession of the ball. Possession has to be obtained cleanly – tackles are not permitted in this practice. One player from the defending team must always be scoring-area-side in a zone-defensive position. Offsides are not in play.

The practice should last 30 minutes.

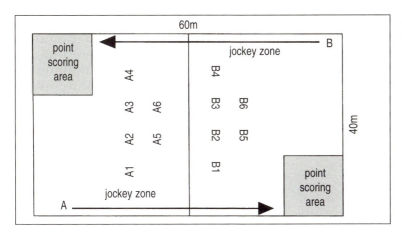

Fig 76   Small-sided game.

Practise timing your approach to the man in possession and positioning yourself sideways on to send your opponent in the direction *you* choose.

Stage 4

The Full Game Format
This exercise takes place on a full-sized pitch with two full teams, A and B. Initially a normal soccer game is played to give players time to adjust. Then the coaching conditions (given below) are introduced. During the first 30 minutes of practice the game will be stopped several times, as and when the coach feels the need to point out references to the coaching theme (jockeying), or change elements of the theme to help bring about the desired effects of the practice. This form of practice concentrates on improving the players' overall team abilities in all aspects of defending play. Remember that restrictions are not without risk, and there is always the knock-on effect of conditioned practice play, namely a temporary loss of form. This can be prevented by making sure that players train to the correct balanced four-stage working plan.

Rules and Objectives
1. Neither team is permitted to tackle opponents. Winning possession of the ball must be performed from a jockeying position.
2. When the first challenger is in position, give cover wherever possible.
3. Both teams must endeavour to work the team shape around the anchor position.
4. Endeavour to position a double anchor in the direction of play (with the zone defender at the furthest point).
5. Players work on presenting the three defence positions as shown in Fig 62.
6. The team shape at the back should be constructed according to the principles of presenting a first challenger, covering player and zone anchor (*see also* Figs 209–214).
7. There are no offsides.

Note The total time of the practice depends on the amount of time spent stopping the game in the first 30 minutes. With 20 minutes or so spent on the warm-up and a further 30 minutes playing conditioned or full games of soccer, the total time spent on most practice sessions can be as much as 1 hour 45 minutes, which is the average for this sort of working session.

SOCCER PLANNER 3 – AN INTRODUCTION TO TACKLING
The skill of getting the ball, rather than the man, needs to be practised to perfection. In today's game the referee has instructions to punish severely any bad intentions. It is not that difficult to receive a yellow card, and two cards in one game and you are off the field of play.

This soccer planner concentrates on acquiring the right attitude to tackling. The player making the correct challenge for the ball can be the difference between winning possession of the ball and giving away a penalty. A badly timed tackle could also mean the player responsible being sent off, which could cause further defensive problems, especially if the player is a key member of the team. However, the new laws demand this strict referee action in certain potential goal-scoring situations.

The jockeying format preceded the tackling one because the first skill is the basis for the second. This order is also a working approach to the problem of winning possession of the ball. With tackling, it is a matter of getting your timing right, picking the right moment to go for the ball. In most game situations, the first approach to the player with the ball is that of jockeying the player.

There are exceptions to this rule. When defending the front part of your goal, you may have no options other than to block tackle for the ball. In this case, the first challenger's efforts go to timing the tackle correctly, attacking the ball, not the man. The co-operation of the other players is crucial, as the opponents will do everything in their power to try to get the ball into the back of the net. Cover must be provided tight to both sides of the challenging player.

For some players, tackling can be very difficult because of fear of injury. However, this skill topic should be treated like the other topics, and practised systematically as shown below. If you do not practise tackling in the right way, you will not understand what is involved, and are therefore more than likely to respond incorrectly to a tackling situation. Tackling is a dangerous business and should be approached with utmost respect. The players should be well prepared in terms of equipment as well as attitude, so that no one comes away from this working session with any injuries.

Stage 1

The warm-up session can contain many elements from this book. Consider this option: in some parks there are natural features such as rocks, large boulders, trees, paths, hills, climbing equipment – a whole range of natural or man-made features. This type of equipment can be utilized for parts of your warm-up session.

For example, start the warm-up by jogging towards some trees; when you get there, stop, do stretching exercises, followed by ten press-ups; get up and jog on, this time jogging in and out and through the trees. Jog on towards some boulders; once there, stop and do stretching exercises, for example a groin stretch. Go past the boulders jumping on and off as you go along, follow this up with a three-quarter paced 100m run. Walk for 100m; stop, do stretching exercises, walk up a steep hill, come on down to a level area, walk for 100m, run at three-quarter pace for 100m and walk for 100m. Do stretching exercises, then walk up to the finishing line/park gate. Without doubt the warm-up can be fun, and natural equipment can provide you with a good warm-up session. Take care and plan the route, and ensure that the features used are left undamaged. The warm-up should take 30 minutes.

Stage 2

The Block Tackle – One on One (Fig 77)

This working format considers the first moments of the challenge, and familiarizes the players with this type of situation. The objectives are:

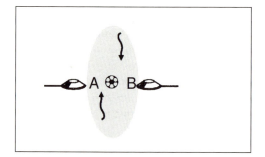

Fig 77 Block tackling one to one.

1. To learn the tackling technique.
2. To overcome the fear of tackling.
3. To time the tackle correctly.

Players must take all precautions to protect themselves from injuries by wearing the proper kit for this practice session, and by conducting themselves appropriately.

Position two cones in line (the tackling line). Two players, A and B, stand on either side of the line between the cones. Player B stands on the line with the ball, with his foot firmly in position behind it and facing his partner square on. He must try to place the ball over the line on player A's side, while player A tries to get the ball off him.

Player A is not permitted to lunge at the ball, and the over-the-top/ball tackle will be punished with a fine; the block tackle is the only technique allowed in this practice. He must attack the ball in a controlled way and get his foot to the ball, and must stop the ball from coming over to his side. If player B gets the ball over the line, or as soon as player A gains possession of the ball, the practice stops and the players swap roles.

The technique of winning a point is to roll/push the ball over the leg/line. The first player to reach ten points wins; only the player in possession can score a point. The defender is not permitted to kick the ball through the legs of the man in possession. Once the ball is rolled/pushed over the line by either player the point is credited or not as the case may, be and the ball is given over to the opponent.

Group Practice – Winning the Ball (Fig 78)

On a 20 × 30m play area there is room for seven pairs of players to do this exercise. Mark out a broad 10 × 30m centre line (the tackling zone), then divide to create two zones. Divide each of these in half again, thus creating four 5 × 30m zones. The two outermost zones are scoring zones.

The players all start in the middle, positioned as for the one-on-one exercise (Fig 77). The objective of the player in possession is to attempt to get the ball over the line and get past his opponent. If he is successful in this, he is allowed to run on free to the point scoring zone. If the tackling player wins the ball, however, he can also score points

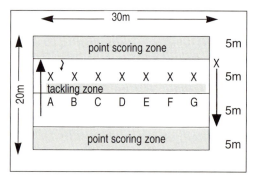

Fig 78 Group practice – winning the ball.

by running on to the opposite scoring zone. Once either player has got past his opponent the other is not entitled to recover in order to prevent a point being scored. Once a point has been scored, the practice is restarted from the middle by the losing player. The first player to make ten successful tackles is the winner – not the player who first scores ten points.

Stage 3

Conditioned Small-Sided Game (Fig 79)

Mark out a play area of 60 × 40m, divided up into three 20 × 40m sections. The middle section is the tackling zone. Three teams of up to eight players can take part. Initially team A starts the practice in the left-hand zone with three soccer balls. They must get through the tackling zone, where team B will try to stop them. Any player in possession of the ball must take someone on in the tackling zone. Once any A

player is through the tackling zone he is free to score a goal individually and is not impeded by anyone, as the right-hand zone is not in use. If a B player wins possession he can try to score in the A zone. When a goal is scored as a result of a good, clean tackle it is worth two goals in value.

The C team at this stage is resting in the right-hand corner of the play area. The coach swaps the teams around so that each team gets the chance to practise tackling.

The first team to twenty goals wins the game, or the practice can simply be timed to last 20 or 30 minutes.

Stage 4
(Fig 80)

This exercise is played on an ordinary full-sized pitch with two full teams. However, each half of the pitch is divided into two and the area in front of each goal is designated the tackling zone. There are no offsides, but otherwise normal soccer rules apply in the middle

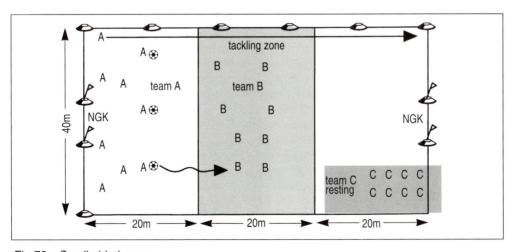

Fig 79   Small-sided game.

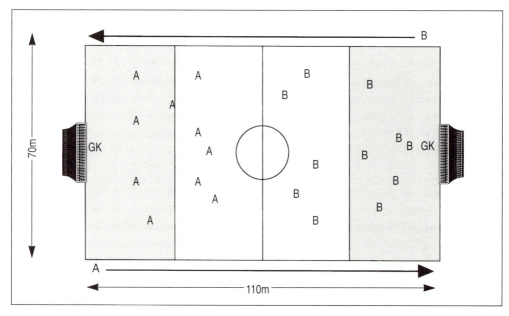

Fig 80   Full game format (conditioned).

area of the pitch, although special conditions apply in the tackling zones:

1. When the player in possession is attacking inside the tackling zone, he must take on at least one opponent before passing the ball to someone else.
2. When a defender wins possession inside the tackling zone, he is restricted to two touches of the ball. This is to encourage loss of possession and bring about further tackling confrontations. If the defender takes more than two touches of the ball inside the tackling zone, the ball is returned to his opponent on the edge of the zone to continue attacking play.
3. If a player wins possession of the ball through tackling in the opponents' half of the field, a goal scored as a result is worth double goal value.
4. Defenders may not give cover in this working session.

This practice should last 30 minutes. After that, the special tackling zones can be removed and another 30 minutes played with normal soccer rules.

PLAYING SYSTEMS 9

Soccer is a team game, and this was proved without doubt when the Brazilians won the World Cup in 1994, they won it by consistently keeping to high standards of play throughout the competition. Some of the World Cup matches represented what is best about this wonderful game: the one-touch play by the Argentinians and others was breathtaking, the speed of approach play was awesome, the skills on show should have been admired, and what is more important, the lessons learned should be put into practice.

The 1994 World Cup was the best for some time. It showed that soccer is a growing game, that countries in Africa are beginning to match the established nations, and that even if you are brand new to the world's biggest team competition, with the right attitude and aspiration any nation can win. The best free kick of the tournament in 1994 was scored by an American called Bruce Winalda. The evidence of progress made by many countries was not hard to find – think of the game Nigeria versus Italy. The lack of experience by the Nigerian players to play out the game with just seconds to spare, was the main reason they did not make further progress than they did.

Sadly, the media tends to focus on one or two star players and sometimes for the wrong reasons, while many wonderful, talented individuals are neither recognized nor mentioned because they are not newsworthy. Instead of recognizing that in soccer there are many different types of skill, the media only concentrates on the finishing product, the goal itself, as if the rest of the game was incidental.

From a playing/coaching point of view, if the end product is a goal, two very important questions need to be asked: how and why was the goal scored? That is, both individual skill and overall team strategy play a part in bringing about a goal. In coaching terms these aspects complement each other because training work involves practising both. Most winners of any competition show that a successful team is made up of many different skills and individuals. The sight of the Brazilian team holding hands is a case in point.

The work in this book clearly reflects the evidence shown in the 1994 World Cup that attacking and defending play must be well balanced for any team to be successful.

TEAM PRIORITIES AS DEFINED BY AREAS OF PLAY

There are practical reasons for defining areas of play. For example, knowing how to defend as an individual in and around your penalty area will always be the first defence training priority. The eventual shape of the team is determined by the positioning of all the players, the average distance between them being approximately 10m.

The player positions create the playing system: in place it is an organized working platform from where to perform the many skills required by the game. Its shape in attacking play will change constantly around the vicinity of the ball, especially if the players are allowed to leave their allocated positions. When a player is in possession of the ball, the attacking movements must be creative. When the attack has failed, for whatever reason, the first team priority must be to return to the correct working shape.

Fig 81 shows the full team recovery shape goal side of the ball in front of the penalty area. The team is now ready to implement the defending principles as discussed in previous chapters. The diagram gives no idea of the field dimensions because the shape can in fact be kept fairly intact anywhere on the field of play. The length and breadth of the shape may change dramatically, but in general terms the positioning of players within the team structure will ensure (barring injuries) that, when closing ranks against the opposing team, they can return to these positions quickly.

There are times during play when the speed of your own attacking players

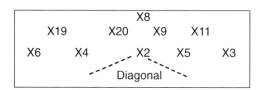

Fig 81 Double bank defensive shape.

has left the shape stretched to breaking point. When this happens, the number of players left in position will not be sufficient to sustain the shape. This is important, because if the ball is lost at such a time, the team shape is short in numbers in midfield and so vulnerable to counter-attacking moves. To help the players deal with these situations, the field of play is split up into three sections for training purposes: the attacking third, the midfield third and the defending third. These three separate zones are used in many of the coaching exercises, which reflect the need for all players to conduct themselves differently in the different areas of play.

When the ball is lost, the players need to know how to behave in that phase of play. In any game play situation they need to assess what is happening quickly and take the correct action. As you read the following game scenarios you will realize that at times the first team priority may not be to regain possession of the ball.

The play scenarios describe in general terms what happens, and the action carried out by the team in particular play situations. Maintaining the shape is a direct result of correct playing decisions.

In the Opponent's Third of the Field

Play scenario: our players have failed to score a goal and have lost possession of the ball to the opposing goalkeeper. The opponents are moving out very quickly, so we are forced to move out with them to comply with the offside law. The only course open to us at this stage is to get goal side of the opponents and to harass them as much as we can in order to slow them down. As yet we are unable to establish any serious challenge for the ball.

As you can see, there is little chance of establishing a real defence in the opponents' third of the field. Our immediate thought should be to protect our own goal. In this situation the coach always allocates the initial defensive responsibility to the strikers or midfield players. There is little we can do except to go along with the opponents and prevent them from attacking freely into forward positions; we can do this by getting in their way and forcing them to play the ball away from their intended directions. Because they are in possession of the ball in their own defensive third of the field there is space in front of them. This fact also forces us to withdraw towards our half of the field.

The Midfield

Scenario: we have managed to slow down the opponents' progress with the ball to just inside their own half of the field of play. We are increasing in numbers, but still cannot present more than a one-to-one competitive challenge; we occasionally manage a two-to-one situation, but this is an exception. There are many individual battles in this area of the field, but the opponents still have sufficient room to pass and move forwards. We can only hope to put pressure on them to make them make mistakes and give the ball away. The pace of the game is too quick to establish any shape in the vicinity of the ball.

As you can see, the midfield area is a battleground where action is constant and explosive. It would not be wise to

hold our line of defence on the halfway line because of the vast spaces still behind us and in front of our own goal. The good thing about the midfield area is that it can become restrictive with regard to time on the ball. The key to defending in this area is to control the forward and directional movement of our opponents, and where possible to intercept, tackle or force them to play the ball back.

Our Own Defending Third

Scenario: the opponents are still in command of the ball, but we have now slowed them down effectively, reducing the area of play to just in front of the penalty zone. We have recovered in sufficient numbers, and are now in position to hold the line of defence. The very nature of falling back to defend our own goal, while holding our line of defence, will momentarily check our opponents' movement.

In truth there should be little difficulty in positioning the back four unit, which should be more or less already in place. When this defensive line-up is in position the remaining team members slot in and defend as shown in Fig 81 and previous diagrams. The resulting shape should be the double-bank defensive unit. The sweeper's role (2) in this play scenario is to give diagonal cover to anyone in need of help.

OLD AND NEW SYSTEMS
(Figs 82–85)

The 4, 3, 3 system would not stand up in the modern game, the numbers in the different departments of the 1, 1, 4, 4, 1 system would see to that – compare Fig 84 to Fig 82. The same applies to

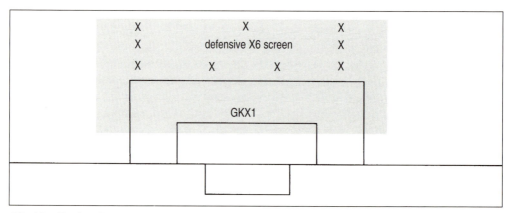

Fig 82   England's shape in 1966, winning the World Cup.

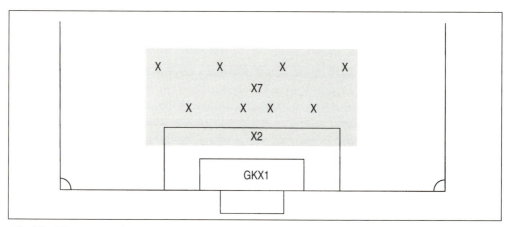

Fig 83   The catenacio.

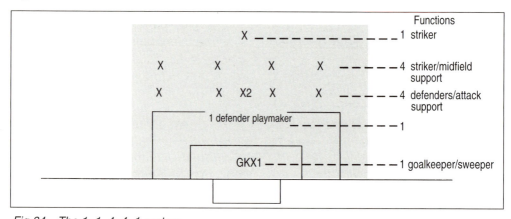

Fig 84   The 1, 1, 4, 4, 1 system.

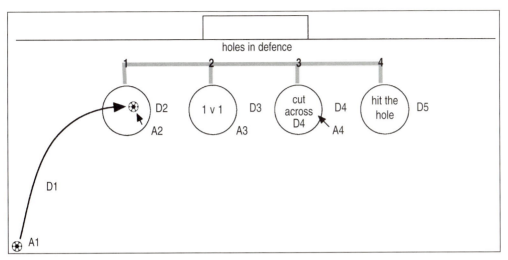

Fig 85   The 4, 4, 2 system is full of holes, which are weak points without cover.

the old-style catenacio. It looks good on paper – *see* Fig 83 – but when put to the test, this system would also find itself in trouble against the modern formation. The old-style sweeper could not cope with the modern game because of the changes in the laws on offsides. His position behind the defence exposes them to all sorts of problems. Today's opponents are much fitter and could beat him for pace. Also, the overlapping full backs could attack from wide positions or play a diagonal ball against the sweeper, in which case there would be little he could do to protect his goal.

Even the 4, 4, 2 system is being tested to the full now, although out of all the old systems in play, this one comes close to coping with the modern game. However, in my opinion the long-term prospects do not look good for a rigidly played channel position 4, 4, 2, and the athleticism of today's players and the development in skills will see the end of this system as it stands. The speed and skills of players is devastating to the flat back four. The shape itself is not that far out in terms of numbers, but when confronted with the attacking style of the 1, 1, 4, 4, 1 system it is vulnerable to counter-attacking play. However, the adaptation of the 4, 4, 2 to the future game is not that difficult; my transformation as described in this book took just a couple of moves (*see* Fig 88).

You should adapt the way you use the 4, 4, 2 system and the type of players you use, as well as the shape. The players' ability to change the shape in attack is just one of the skills that is required to make progress into the future.

The secret to success in soccer lies in being able to win possession of the ball (a successful defence). An effective team defence will adhere to the three positions described in Chapter 8. When your team is unable to defend in this manner and keeps to a rigid zone defensive formation, the back four unit will be in trouble for various reasons. The way player 2 works in the 1, 1, 4, 4, 1 system comes from an understanding of the weak points in the flat back four positions.

Fig 85 highlights the problems faced by such a line-up by showing typical actions taken by attacking players when confronted with such a defence. Each circle represents a weak point of the flat back four unit. This hole is representative of the holes right across the team formation. Circle 4 is representative of all the holes across this line-up. In passing terms, the ball can be played into holes or to feet. The fact that there are only three strikers up front in this example is not an issue because this diagram illustrates different attacking ideas against the flat-back line-up.

CHOOSING YOUR OWN SYSTEM OF PLAY
(Figs 86 & 87)
There are many reasons for choosing a system of play. In some countries there is pride in keeping to a particular playing system, and changes are very slow in coming. Yet to be successful, the team system has to adhere to certain realities. With the advent of modern technology in television reporting, the game has fast become a media/spectator event. However, in order to appeal to the audience, the players have to be extremely fit and skilful, and in today's soccer game the playing system has to work equally well in attack and defence.

I have used several systems of play in the past, for different reasons. Some systems of play were devised for a one-off match situation, others became part of an experiment to find the right player combination/team balance. Different systems of play can alter the numbers in different parts of the field, especially when your players are capable and have the courage and willingness to try something new; the key is to work for each other. The examples of playing systems

Fig 86 The old system: vulnerable team position on the field of play. Note the position of the back four, especially the central defensive position of X2 and X3.

given in this chapter come from my own personal experience, and from playing scenarios from around the world.

On one memorable occasion, the creation of a playing system happened because I was given the opportunity to save a club in a crisis situation. When I took over, this team's playing system was the 4, 4, 2 one as shown in Fig 86. Look at the way the back four were positioned. When England played against this system they won hands down, as they found plenty of holes to play the ball into and create attacking play options.

This club had no money to spend on transfers and was left with young, inexperienced players to get it out of trouble. I realized that to play the same system as everyone else could only spell defeat. I had to come up with something different, fast. In what seemed like a desperate move at the time, I changed the playing system and gambled on the opposition's set way of playing. I reversed the 4, 4, 2 system and played a one-off which in fact brought about a sensational result. I played two defenders behind the midfield four players, taking up an in between position as shown in Fig 87.

We won the game 3–0 with just two at the back, yes two! All three goals came from counter-attacks. This opponent had evidently planned to play attacking soccer (being the home team) and came a cropper. It was certainly a shock to them, as they had expected something else and were unable to adjust their strategy to cope with the numbers now facing them up front. The one-off had worked, and I started my work with a positive result which no

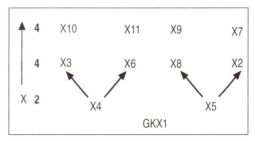

Fig 87   While the 2, 4, 4 system assured victory away from home, it could not be used on a regular basis.

one had thought possible.

In the following games, I made several important changes. The first change was to introduce the team to the conventional back four unit, which eventually had to be bolstered by an additional player. In order to achieve this I withdrew one of the strikers, who was very experienced, and put him in charge at the back in a special role, leaving just one striker up front.

The opponents were absolutely baffled by our system and even experienced players found it difficult to adapt to our way of playing. With the right attitude we gained enough points that season to finish in second position in the league. I will not forget occasions during the season when travelling to an away game where the odds of winning were heavily stacked against us; everyone thought we had no right to win, but win we did.

When things are difficult you must not be afraid to try something different. No one, not even the best teams in the world, have a monopoly on winning every game. In fact many teams at the top do not adapt to new situations readily. The evidence for this lies in many shock results around the world of soccer.

TEAM TACTICS

There are three separate skills involved when using any system during play, all of which are equally important to the success of the team. They are: (a) the initial system of play; (b) the positional changes within the system; (c) the individual abilities of the players within the system. The first two of these, the team skills, can be described as the working team tactics. The individual skills that influence play will be discussed later.

It should be appreciated that even simple tactical ploys can make a difference. For example, one-touch play can influence the style of passing and team movement. It can also be useful to change the passing format to short and long combinations, not only to change the direction of the attacking play, but also to vary the speed of passing and movement. Another way of varying the speed is by keeping possession of the ball more – this tactic has an immediate effect on the speed of play.

Defensively, the movement of the whole team shape can best be described using the analogy of a shoal of fish. The movement in unison of the fish des-cribes exactly what should happen: the reaction of every player in the team should be identical, the distance between them altering depending on the danger to own goal – the closer the opponents get to goal, the tighter the shape becomes. Effectively it ranges from being 40m plus in length, to the size of the defensive formation shown previously. The positioning of the first challenger and giving him assistance/cover wherever possible are always the most important considerations.

The positioning of each player in the system of play and the ability of players to change positions during play (changing the shape) are modern concepts. The following examples of positional change may astonish you in their simplicity. In the case of England v. Sweden, the failure of England to adapt could have cost them their place in the 1994 World Cup.

Changing the Team Shape
(Fig 88)

In simplistic terms, the team consists of the back unit (defending third), the midfield unit (midfield third) and the

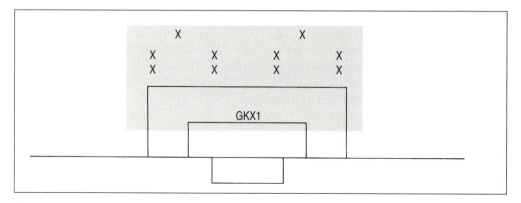

Fig 88   The 1, 4, 4, 2 system.

striking unit (attacking third). In many respects, what distinguishes a playing system is how it divides its players up between these key areas. However, the shape of the team can be altered during play. You can start off with the 4, 4, 2 shape, for example, and end up with the 1, 1, 4, 4, 1 and such a positional change can be devastating if your opponents are unable to adapt and alter their numbers in key areas of play.

The choice of system is up to you, but remember that if your team shape is badly constructed, you will not be successful. Look at the system played by my old team (*see* above) shown in Fig 86; on paper this system was very close to the English style of play, the 1, 4, 4, 2 system shown in Fig 88. The positioning of the first defender in front of the second central defender in Fig 86 created too many holes in defence. When I had the opportunity to play my team against a team using the old system, I took the chance to position my players in a 2, 4, 4 counter configuration, as described above. The opponents fell back into the penalty box because of the mess they were in, in terms of numbers at the back. None of the opposing players ventured past the halfway line.

Of course I could not keep using this system throughout the season because not everyone is so naive. The point is that if your team is capable of positional changes, these are tactical options that can win you games. There is no such thing as an infallible system. If you set out a shape and it compares badly with your opponents' and you do not change it, you can expect a negative result.

Sweden Vs England

The tactical game played by Sweden here was astonishingly simple. Sweden lulled England into a false sense of security by playing in channels within the 4, 4, 2 line-up, none of the players venturing out of their allocated positions and the shape never altering during the first half.

The first 45 minutes of this game were uncompromisingly hard, both teams using strong tackling methods within the 4, 4, 2 working shape. England came out on top in the first half, coping well with numbers in midfield, and creating a fine goal-scoring opportunity. On the balance of play, England deserved to go in at half time one goal up.

The Second Half (Fig 89)

The winning formula was difficult to find because Sweden and England played to similar styles. All credit must eventually go to Sweden for finding the winning solution; the Swedish manager probably thought something like this; 'England are matching us in numbers

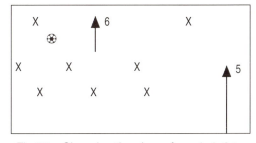

Fig 89   Changing the shape from 4, 4, 2 to 3, 4, 3 in attacking play. Sweden's shape is altered in the second half, to that shown in this diagram. Player 6 attacks from midfield, which in turn is bolstered by player 5.

because they are also playing the 4, 4, 2 system [*see* Fig 88]. However, they are flat at the back, and do not seem to be too concerned with protecting this defensive unit from the front. We will also continue to play in channels, but our system will alter the shape in attack to take full advantage of this lack of cover. Our midfield player (6) will move into a forward attacking position [*see* Fig 89]. The move from midfield to attack by player 6 will be supported by player 5, the right back. This player will move out of defence and into midfield, but only when we have possession of the ball.

'The three-up-front shape resulting from these changes should create some chances for our team. England are lacking in depth, especially in central defensive positions, so this could be our chance to finish off some of the moves with a direct shot on goal. With the warm weather helping the flight of the ball, who knows what can happen. All you need is that one chance in front of goal, and we're in. When we lose possession of the ball, we will simply revert back to the 4, 4, 2 system, and defend accordingly.'

The Winning Shape in Play

The above positional changes worked. England stayed in channels as before and did not adapt or respond to the positional play changes made by Sweden. This meant in effect that Sweden had the advantage of increased numbers in attack. The extra midfielder/striker up front did eventually breakdown England's defence and created goal-scoring opportunities for Sweden.

Moving the Ball from the Back

The shape can affect play the minute your team wins possession of the ball. Your team can impose the numbers game from the word go, co-ordinating the movement of players and the ball from the back into forward attacking positions.

Below is a frame-by-frame breakdown of positional changes during play. The game scenario is that the opponents have just failed to score a goal and the keeper is in possession of the ball. The whole point of this example is to show how positional changes can be used to play the ball forwards, rebuilding the shape of the team while retaining

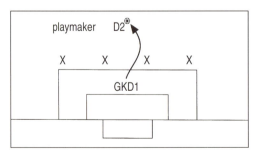

Fig 90 First move: the keeper throws the ball to defensive screen/playmaker.

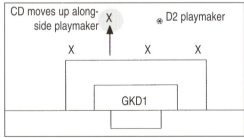

Fig 91 Second move: one of the central defenders pushes up alongside the playmaker.

possession. This type of team movement forces opponents to go back towards their own goal because they have to maintain the numbers required to defend vital areas of play.

Possible variations are also shown. For example, in Fig 92 the 4? shows a possible formation position ahead of the defending shape. Equally the number of players up front at this stage (1?) can be other than that stated. Thus the lone striker up front here can in fact already be supported by other players. Anything is possible when you have possession of the ball; when you have lost possession, the sweeper can become a defensive screen, his position as shown in Fig 90. In this situation the back four unit would drop off, and the sweeper would keep his forward position, adjusting only to the position of the ball on the field of play. Acting as a defensive screen, this could delay opponents long enough to allow other players to come back to protect the back unit accordingly.

Changing the Shape in Four Moves (Figs 90–93)

Move 1: The ball is thrown out by the keeper to playmaker D2, who keeps possession long enough to allow other players to get into forward positions (Fig 90).

Move 2: One of the central defenders has moved alongside him into a supporting position (Fig 91).

Move 3: The two full backs have moved forward and are now spread wide across the field. At this point player D6 (one of the central defenders) has been left behind – he could in fact take up the sweeper's role. The ball is now played by the playmaker (D2) into a wide (left full back) position (Fig 92).

Move 4: The full back is now in possession of the ball, with player D6 protecting this unit at the back in a deep covering role. His position gives cover in case the attacking moves break down and the opponents play the ball over the top of this defence.

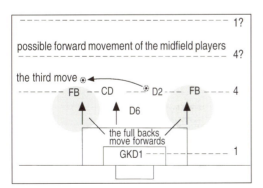

Fig 92   Third move: the two full backs move forwards; one of them receives the ball from the defensive screen/playmaker D2.

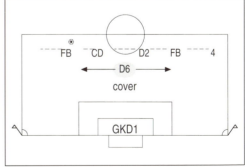

Fig 93   Fourth move: the whole playing unit has moved forwards without risk and still has the shape in a forward position.

As you can see these four moves allow the team to implement attacking play moves that put players into forward positions. The way the players move creates different shapes in play and alters the numbers in key areas. Good organization requires that certain players take up each other's roles to protect key defensive positions; in this example the movement of the back four unit has left the central defender 6 in a covering/sweeper's role. This is acceptable in this example because the attacking players are in possession of the ball.

If they were to lose possession of the ball, the back players would drop off into defensive positions as before; player 2 in that case would be left where he is in order to protect the front part of the back unit in a defensive screen role. If the danger to goal became even more threatening, he would drop further into the back defensive unit. In extreme dangers revert to the key defensive positions of first challenger, covering player, anchor man, and try to get the shape to its full 1, 1, 4, 4, 1 format (*see* Fig 81).

Moving the Line of Defence

The following examples illustrate organizational aspects of your defence. The team unit has to respond to a given formula, you cannot leave things to chance. It is true that in the event good players will respond instantly to given play situations, working out problems and solutions. The whole point of coaching is to give the players the best possible chance to make the correct decisions in these instants. The following chapters will show how the team should adapt the shape in different play situations.

Holding a set line of defence is not an accident, nor is this task performed with everyone doing what they want. Make sure that only one player is responsible for giving orders at the back. In the following working examples the zone defender (D3) controls the position of the defending line. The communication signals, simple one word messages, are worked out on the practice ground, and are shouted out by controlling player D3. On hearing the messages all the players respond accordingly. The most common signal/word used in response to the ball being played out of defence is the message 'Out!'. Every defender, without fail, moves forward in response to this message.

The Goalkeeper's Kick (Fig 94)
The opponents have failed to score a goal, and the keeper has possession of the ball, which he then kicks out of his hand. Player D3 shouts out the command 'Out!', and very player in defence responds to his call.

The goalkeeper is in a difficult situation because he must not take too much time in kicking the ball out of his area. Nonetheless, he takes a little time on setting himself up for the kick so that player D3 can start the process of moving his defence into forward-of-goal positions. Only then will he proceed to kick the ball out of his hands.

D3 assesses the flight of the ball, and decides that the flight is sufficient to move his line of defence 20m up field (shaded line in the diagram). He knows that when the ball is in the air he can move forward safely. The minute it comes down to earth, he must be ready

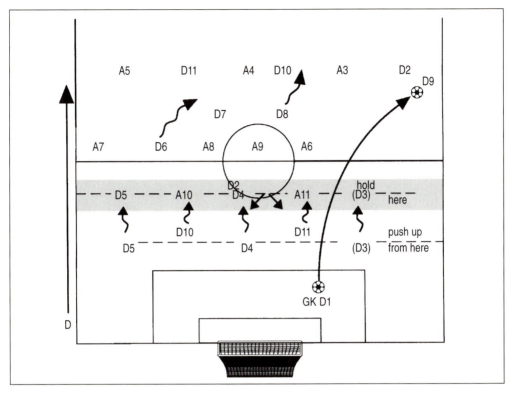

Fig 94   Push up and support play.

to hold his line of defence. All players hold the shape in the new position. Player D2 is poised ready to give cover defensively.

The pushing up of this defensive shape is not haphazard, but is calculated to press the shape closer together, which closes down space for the opposition. In this situation, if the opponents happen to win possession of the ball, the shape will make the area congested (tight) and they will find it difficult to play the ball forwards.

In today's game the possible alongside position of players in defence, afforded by the new offside law, can cause problems by exposing defenders

to any number of attacking possibilities. It is therefore very important to work with an organized defence in order to protect your goal.

Using the Long and Short Passing Combination (Fig 95)

In some game situations the response of the back four unit is co-ordinated to the short and long passing format. In Fig 95 the defensive player D4 plays the short pass to player D8 and has the option of moving to position X. The short pass forward to D8 combined with this slight push forward of the back unit is designed to draw opponents towards the ball. The return pass back from D8

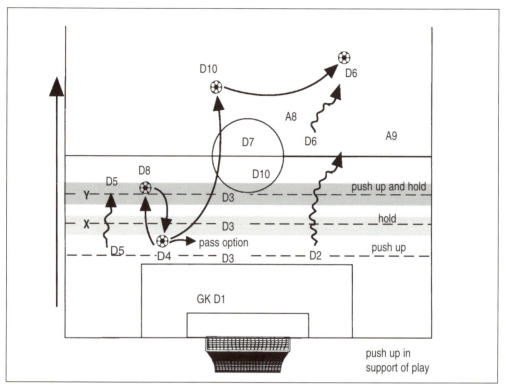

Fig 95   Using the long and short passing combination.

to D4 is deliberate – it buys time for the other defending players to move forward to hold position X.

Keeping possession of the ball in this situation is very important. There are various ways of doing this. For example, the pass by player D4 can be played to player D3, which would have the effect of keeping possession of the ball, but would defeat the objectives of the previous pass by allowing the opponents time to push up. D4 will instead play the long ball to player D10, leaving many opponents on the wrong side of the ball. This long pass puts pressure on opponents to fall back goal side of the ball. Once D4 has made this forward pass, he will join the line of defence held by D3 in position Y in support of play. The whole back unit will again adjust according to the flight and position of the ball.

Watching the Kicker (Figs 96 & 97)

Player D3, standing in position X, controls the line in a very special way, observing the play in front of him and continually assessing the situation. When he sees the ball played from opponent A2 to A4 he holds his nerve and line of defence, watching carefully what A4 will do next. D3 waits for the moment when opponent A4 is about to

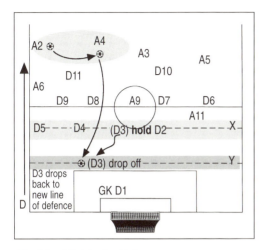

Fig 96   Watch the kicker.

Fig 97   The offside signal.

kick the ball and it will become clear where he is aiming. In this instance, the ball is being played to the back of D3's defence.

The moment D3 knows where the ball is going, he can 'drop off' to gather it up, timing his moment to move to coincide with the kick. He should gain possession as a result. The rest of the players will move quickly to support D3's possession of the ball, re-adjusting to position Y.

Fig 97 shows the opposite situation. I wanted the players in the back four to respond to the kicker, using the moment when the ball is about to be played to move the whole unit forwards beyond the opponent on the left (wearing the dark strip). The position of the ball shows the perfect timing of the players' coming out, leaving the opponent in an offside position.

ATTACKING PLAY

We have looked at defensive organizational requirements, and as you can see

there are ways of making sure that the player has his say in what happens. No one can pretend that you can stop opponents from scoring goals, but an effective defence can make it very difficult.

Attacking play is a completely different proposition, but it should be remembered that it is a good defence that makes it possible to attack in the first place. The difference between good teams and bad teams is that the good teams know what they are doing, defensively and in attacking play. Yes, it is important to adapt to real game situations, but when it comes to attacking play, it is very much to do with team work and individual contributions. You do not actually need to practise attacking play with opposition in order to get good at soccer! I will stake anything on this statement.

Why am I so confident? Because soccer is a game of skills, and as such can be taught individually as well as collectively; the separate skills will eventually create one single effective team unit. Good organization and technical skills go a long way to making a successful team. Teaching the player his working position on the field of play

101

can be done without opposition, and example exercises are given below. They are designed to overload or attack certain areas of play. The following practice formats all take place in one half of the field.

Setting up the Cross
(Fig 98)

This exercise takes place in the attacking half of the field. Four attacking players start near the middle of the field, in a row as shown. Player A1 has the ball and starts the practice by playing the ball wide to player A4 on the right midfield. A4 takes the ball in his stride and goes on a run down the side of the pitch, at the end of which he crosses the ball into the box to one of the other attackers, who will have got themselves into the right position and

will attempt to score.

There are two important coaching issues here. The first of these concerns the timing of the runs. The far post runner (A1) has to be quicker than the rest, as he has the furthest distance to run and he should aim to arrive early at his post. The run to the near post (A2) is nearly as long, and like A1, the player must arrive early. The shortest run is the straight run down the middle (A3) and it is best to come late onto the ball from this position. Choose your players accordingly; for example, choose good runners for positions A1 and A2, and a good header for A3, as he will be closest to the goal.

The second issue is the quality of work. The crosses of the ball must come at the correct height and distance from the keeper. The timing of the run must

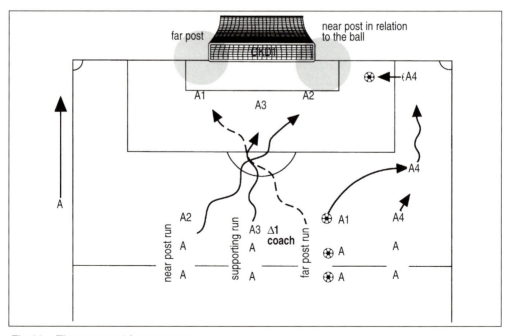

Fig 98   The near and far post runs.

put the attacking player into position just in time to attack the ball. Good timing means you can use the pace of the ball and the element of surprise to add power to the finish. Arriving early in the box removes any element of surprise, so the finishing power is reduced, although sometimes this does not matter.

Attacking Runs from Deep Positions
(Fig 99)
This working example shows the attacking run of the full back, supported by the rest of the players. Their job is to provide anchor support for the run, as well as take opponents away from the intended route. Clearing the route will not be that difficult, because opponents have to keep goal side of the ball.

The exercise can be carried out with or without opponents. In either case, all the players participating start off in the midfield. The coach passes the ball to the full back, A2, whose intended route to the box is down the right-hand side of the field. Players A3 and A11 act as anchor men for A2 as he works his way down the field. Players A6 and A7 run into the middle of the opponents' third to take defenders inside. A5, A8, A9 and A10 do the same on the far side of the field. In the diagram, A2 completes his run successfully, and it is A9 who finishes.

Blind Side Run
(Figs 100 & 101)
The slow motion account below is a detailed breakdown of the movements

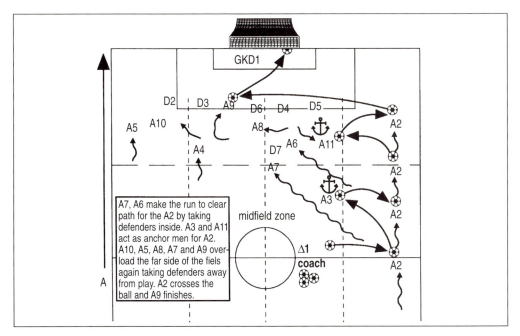

Fig 99   The overlapping full back.

and skills involved in changing the point of attack. The initial passing and movement disguises the real intentions of the attacking players, until the short pass from A8 to A6 carries the real signal of the team's intentions.

The coach starts the practice by passing the ball to A5, who passes it to A10. A10 then passes it to A3 *away* from the intended direction of play. This across-the-field pass is supported by appropriate running patterns by attackers A11, A7 and A9, who are careful to keep running in flat positions, keeping out of penetrating runs into the opponents' defence. The opponents are therefore happy to keep position in front of them and to build their defensive position on the right (from an attacking point of view) side of the field. Once this unbalanced defensive posi-

tion is in place, the ball is played back to attacking midfield player A8, and from him to A6.

A6 is excluded from play until the moment when the team is ready to play this tactical move – he is positioned centrally deliberately for the purpose of changing the direction of the attack, from the right to the left side of the playing field. On receiving the pass from A8, player A6 controls it, and pretends to measure up for a pass to his right before suddenly changing direction, and playing the long ball across to A5.

The pass from A8 to A6 was the signal for A5 to start his forward run. He now picks up the pass on the blind side of the opponents, taking it round to the back of their defensive shape, and finally sending the cross left to right away from the keeper.

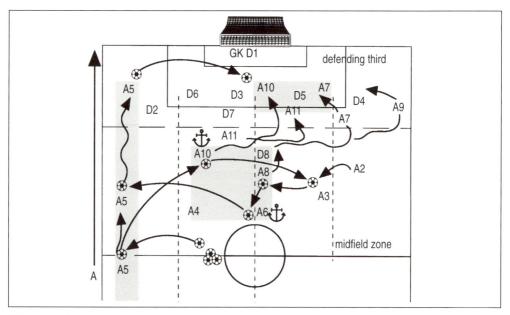

Fig 100   The central midfield players concentrate on short passing, leaving A5 to make the blind-side run.

Fig 101   Player A5 attacking the back of this defence.

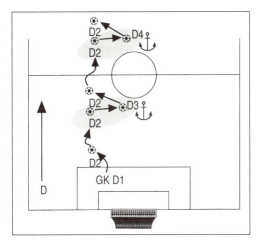

Fig 102   Anchor play.

Fig 101 shows the devastating effects of such a run. Most of the defenders (in the dark strip) are caught in no man's land. The shape at the back has disintegrated, with some of the defenders watching the ball, and it is rather obvious that the distance from the opponents invites danger. Opponent 2 holds back at this point, timing his attacking header run according to what the kicker does and the position of the ball.

Defining Anchor Play
(Fig 102)

Anchor players are positioned along a runner's route to help him retain possession of the ball. In this example, players D2 and D4 are in anchor positions ahead of the runner. If the runner comes under pressure he can pass the ball to the anchor, and continue his run up the field; the anchor will pass the ball back to him when he is free of opponents. The anchors help D2 to retain his momentum and continue his attacking run into the opponents' third of the field.

This type of run and anchor positioning can be used for long or short running distances, almost anywhere on the field of play.

10 DEFINING ROLES – THE SWEEPER

The defensive back positions in some systems of play have become very vulnerable since the introduction of the new laws on offsides. The flat back four line-up would not be my choice for a defensive strategy without the application of certain safeguards to back it up.

There are many ways of safeguarding the back defensive shape in play. The defending players must endeavour to have the first challenger, cover and zone defender provide a defensive shape in the vicinity of the ball. In addition, each midfield player has defensive responsibilities: this is a must. Remember the general defending principle of one man, one opponent – plus cover. There is no such thing as a three- or four-man defence, as some people suggest: everyone in the team has some sort of defending role to play. The modern sweeper's responsibilies are rather special since his positioning can see to it that the back unit is protected; his role is explained in the following working examples. The flat back four cannot in all seriousness be expected to cope with today's modern attacking play.

The purpose of having defined roles for each player is to give your team a solid base from which to work; understanding roles can help you to create different systems of play. Accepting the numbers argument, why should you play the same system as everyone else? Try to compare your working patterns to that of your counterpart in the examples given. Are your running patterns similar? Do you have to run longer distances? In changing your system of play you must consider the running distances for each player. The modern game demands different types of running, and again this is important from a fitness point of view. Different types of running require a different training format.

As you can imagine, knowing the function of each player will also help the coach in his selection of working exercises. Such considerations have been taken into account, and the results are put into practice within specially formulated working formats. All this information is required to formulate a team-play strategy. Each player can function within the team as an individual, or his role can be specifically designed to work closely with other players. Team tactics can be greatly simplified by giving a special role to one or more individuals – shadow training in the previous chapter was an example of this – so that each player knows exactly where to run when the ball is played in a particular way.

It is not that difficult to implement such tactical running patterns, as these can be pre-planned and set up to work within the team in a specified way. Obviously such work should be kept secret and only displayed during play, and it is also advisable to work out several play running patterns, so that the team can be unpredictable.

THE MODERN SWEEPER
(Fig 103)

The modern sweeper knows exactly what is expected of him in certain areas of play and has a clearly defined role to play. This does not mean that he functions like a robot – on the contrary, he is entitled to improvise in attacking situations.

Defensively, he is very special: first defender, covering payer, zone defender and attacking forward all rolled into one. The conventional positioning of the sweeper is not the way for my D2. The modern game does not allow him to stay at the back of the defence, as this would open up all sorts of possibilities to opponents. The modern position for the player decrees that he performs his duties from *within* the back four unit, giving cover on a diagonal run.

There are also all sorts of other playing possibilities and options open to him, as shown in the diagrams below.

Defensive Roles

Temporary Full Back (Fig 104)

D2 takes up a defensive role. D6 has switched to a midfield supporting position. D2's task is to fill the gap left by D6, that is, to become a temporary left back.

A Defensive Screen (Fig 105)

D2 has been deployed to challenge for the ball early. He takes up a position in front of the back four and acts as a defensive screen for his main unit.

Front of Goal Protection (Fig 106)

D2 protects the front of goal during

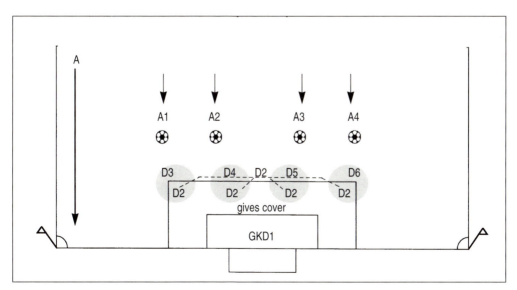

Fig 103   The tactical function of D2 in defence – he adjusts his position to give cover.

corner kicks against his team. He positions himself inside the near goal post.

Playing Opponents Offside (Fig 107)

D2 and his colleagues all move forward upon a signal given by D2, leaving opponent A1 in an offside position. D2 times his forward run to coincide with the moment that A2's foot connects with the ball. See Fig 96.

Attacking the Ball (Fig 108)

D2 attacks the ball during a free kick against own team. He positions himself in the centre of the wall formed by his colleagues to protect the goal. His aim is to be the blocking player, getting his body in the way of any shot on goal.

Protecting the Goalkeeper (Fig 109)

The goalkeeper moves into the ball's flight path and catches it. D2 immediately runs behind him towards the goal to give him cover and to protect the goal.

Attacking Roles

Turning Defence into Attack (Fig 110)

To attack D2 goes forward, intercepts the ball and quickly turns defence into attack by moving out and attacking the space ahead of him.

Competing with the Opposing Goalkeeper (Fig 111)

D2 competes with the opponents' goal-

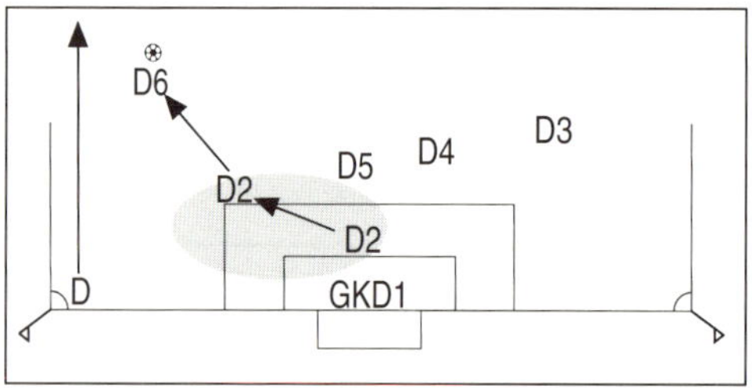

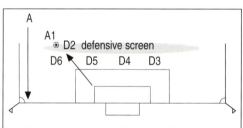

Fig 104   The sweeper as temporary full back.

Fig 105   Providing a defensive screen.

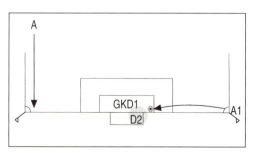

Fig 106   Protecting the front of the goal.

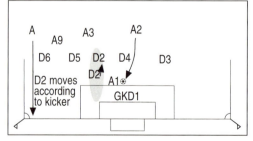

Fig 107   Playing opponents offside.

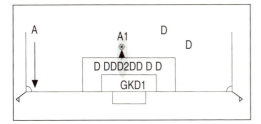

Fig 108   Attacking the ball.

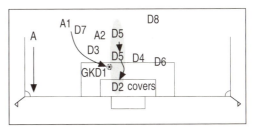

Fig 109   Protecting the goalkeeper.

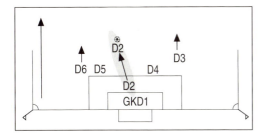

Fig 110   Turning defence into attack.

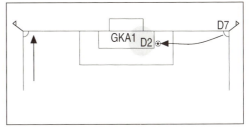

Fig 111   Competing with the opponents' goalkeeper.

keeper during corner kicks for his own team. He positions himself close to the keeper, where he will be able to attack the ball in competition with him.

Back-Up (Fig 112)

D2 acts as back-up to the player who executes the free kick (zone position). He takes up position between the halfway line and the opponents' goal so he can try to slow down any counter attack should his team lose the ball.

THE SWEEPER AS CAPTAIN

As the team's captain, D2 has the responsibility of adjusting the team's style of play according to the game situation. He may feel that the opponents are not good enough to warrant extra cover, or he may feel that by defending in front of the back four he can contribute to attacking play without risking his own goal. He continues to evaluate the state of play throughout the game, basing his decisions on a continuous assessment. If, for example, he notices during the game that one player on the opponents' side is very fast and skilful, he may make a decision to allocate one of his midfield players to mark this opponent while he himself concentrates on securing the midfield position.

I want my captain to contribute to the game during play. Team play is about partnerships; the final decisions are up to the manager/coach, but all eventualities must be taken into consideration. The style and the system of play have to be flexible. There is no point in setting out your stall and refusing to change it if things don't go to plan.

The captain can alter minor details during play: for example, he can support the back four unit in co-operation with

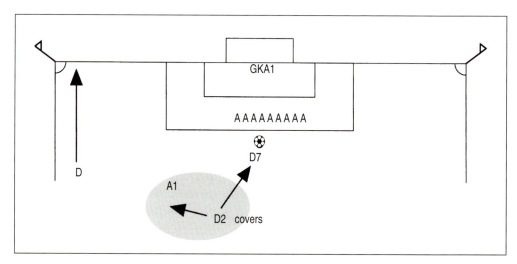

Fig 112   Providing back-up in a free kick situation.

other midfield players. Some of the functions described for him can be taken up by any midfield player, for example his role as in Fig 105 can be performed by a midfield player for a specific tactical reason. If he puts himself in between the full back and one of the central defenders, this screening position can sort out any wide threat on goal, sending opponents inside/outside. This is just one example of the sweeper/captain's midfield defending responsibilities.

There are three main categories of set piece:

1. Free kick directly/indirectly resulting from a foul
2. Corner kick
3. Throw-in

In today's game you are not permitted to bring down your opponent intentionally when they are through on goal: if you stop him by fouling him you will most certainly go for an early bath. And if you are fouled in this way, the law of the game not only sends off your opponent but gives you the opportunity to take a direct free kick on goal. For lesser infringements, the punishment is an indirect free kick. Often the law does not seem adequate, and the punishment does not justify the crime, especially when a promising move has been destroyed and the resulting free kick comes to nothing.

This state of affairs can be slightly improved by some very clever planning. If there is any compensation for a foul, it has to be gained by working out the moves that follow the awarding of a free shot or header on goal. Set pieces do result in goals, but only about one out of ten attempts will succeed. This does not mean they should be taken lightly if awarded against your side. Free kick

situations are a threat in front of goal. Imagine, for example, that you have five minutes of the match left and one of your team-mates gives away a free kick on the edge of the box: one or two clever moves by the opposition and your side is a goal down.

You cannot always help giving away corner kicks and throw-ins, especially in today's game, but there are no excuses for intentional fouling. Nevertheless it happens, as players are only human, and then you must be prepared to deal with the situation; by recognizing the possibilities open to your opponents, you stand a good chance of protecting your goal.

In the following examples we will discuss the functional responsibility of some of the key players involved in those situations, considering the problems of free kicks from both a defending and an attacking point of view. In most of the diagrams only the immediate working players are shown, because the most important issue here is to show the key team positional plays in action; showing the whole team would be a distraction.

CORNERS

Corner for Your Team
(Fig 113)
In a 'corner for' situation you must protect against a counter attack and

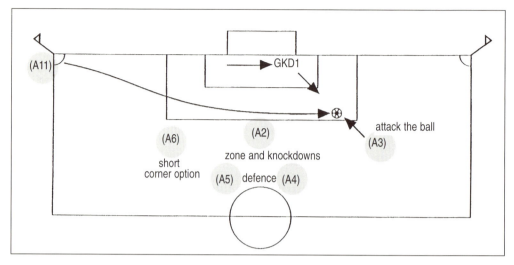

Fig 113   Defending positional responsibilities of the back unit on corners for your team.

position the players accordingly.

• A4 and A5 take up a central defensive position on the halfway line.
• A2 has an in-between position and guards against opponents counter attacking on either side of the central position.
• A6 is positioned for defence in case the ball is miskicked. He could also be used for a short corner, but his priority is to defend that section of the field if things go wrong .
• A3 is positioned to attack the ball, and A11, taking the corner, will pass to him.

Corner against Your Team
(Fig 114)

The safest defending option in any free kick situation is to use man-to-man marking tactics, and wherever possible secure the area beyond the man-to-man marking area by placing any free player in the so-called in-between positions.

These are positions which secure holes to the back and front of the man-to-man marking area.

• D8 stands nearest to the corner and will watch out for the near-post flick.
• D3 takes up position about 1m away from his nearest post to the corner.
• D2 positions himself on the inside of the near post.
• D6 positions himself on the inside of the far post.
• The goalkeeper (DGK) has a clear path to the ball and is positioned towards the further half of goal.
• D4, D5, D7 and D9 position themselves along the edge of the six-yard box.
• D11 and D10 take up in-between positions, guarding holes in the defensive line-up.

When all plans fail there is one very simple rule to make defensive life easy, and that is that opponents score goals

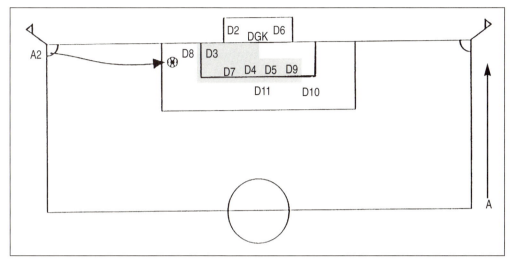

Fig 114   Defending responsibilities of the back unit on corners against: watch out for 'flick on' to the far post.

and not areas of play. What this means is that the defensive positions are not zone defensive positions but are allocated defensive positions, each player being responsible for picking up someone near his allocated zone. The area of this zone may change, in other words each player may need to move closer to close down the opponent nearest to him. The only time this system does not work is when a defender's allocated area is threatened by a taller attacking player. In that instance the players swap places accordingly.

What you need to keep in mind is that any corner situation poses a threat to key defensive areas of play, and these areas have to be secured – you cannot afford to allow opponents to roam free. Taking up the positions described above does help to protect your goal, but if the ball gets knocked out of the area, the defenders must *immediately* move to close players down.

DIRECT FREE KICKS

Free Kick for Your Team
(Fig 115)
• A8 plays the ball to A6.
• A6 plays it wide for A7.
• A5 is a decoy for A7, and times his run inside to mask A7's move into a wide position.
• A2 and A3 attack the final pass from A7. They must time their runs correctly to be in place to receive A7's pass. They should also be good at heading.
• A4 positions himself on the half-way line to counter the long ball sent out by the defence.

In all free kick situations players are free to improvise, and that is why I have not included all eleven players in any diagram. The goalkeeper's position is obvious but the number of defenders you leave up-field is usually determined by the number of opponents. Remember

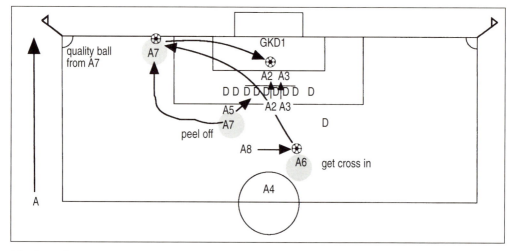

Fig 115   Back players involved in the free kick for: A2, A3 and A5 are used for their heading abilities.

to attack opponents at speed, because this will always give you the advantage of height to the ball. Success is determined by the timing of your attacking runs: if your run is too early you will miss the ball, and at best you will not attack the ball with any telling force; if your run is too late the defenders will be in a better position to defend against the cross. It is also possible that a mistimed attack could leave you stranded on the wrong side of the ball.

Free Kick against Your Team

In Front of Goal (Fig 116)
• D4, D8, D9, D10 and D11 form the defensive wall.
• D5 attacks the ball, hoping to block the shot on goal.
• D2 covers the back of the wall.
• D6 defends the left side of the wall.

The allocation of these positions is based on the individual players'

strengths in defence. The main danger will come from the shot on goal and not from the short game. If a pass is played, the closeness of the situation does not give the opponents many options. You can afford to stay tight because the flight of the ball will be of short duration; this will prevent the opponents from attacking the ball at speed, which could be your only compensation in this situation.

From the Corner of the Box (Fig 117)
From this angle the most dangerous free kick is the swerve shot, in this example, from right to left. The wall therefore has to cover the inner post and give a certain amount of protection to the rest of the goal.

• The goalkeeper positions himself 1m away from his goal line favouring his left post and 0.5m away from the centre of the goal.

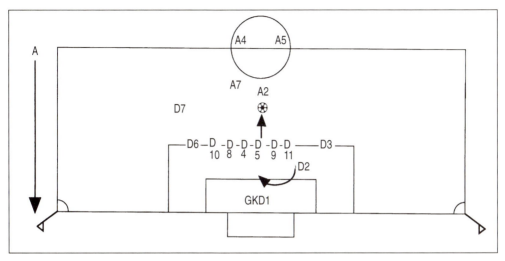

Fig 116   Team D positions for protection of goal – D5 is hoping to block the shot on goal.

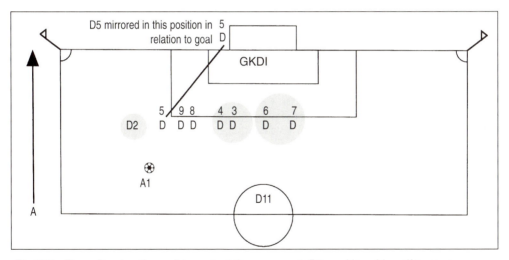

Fig 117   Team D using the wall to protect the near post. D5 positions himself to cover just outside the line of the near post. The keeper must be alert to all possibilities – striker A1 can swerve the ball right to left, around the wall.

- D5 is one end of the wall and positions himself to cover the line from him to just outside the near post. The other players in the wall line themselves up goal side of him.
- D2 protects the side of the defensive wall.
- D3 and D4 prevent opponents from attacking the space in front of goal and position themselves 0.5m behind and to the side of the wall.
- D6 and D7 take up a zone position on

115

the edge of the box, blocking any attacking run; be careful how you challenge in this situation.

It is up to the keeper to decide how many players he requires in the wall. He bases his decision on his assessment of the danger to his goal. The wall has to be made up of the most reliable players. The best place to sort out who takes part in the building of such a wall is on the practice ground. The last man in the wall (D5 in the diagram) lines the wall up to cover the near post. Once he is in place the keeper positions himself by taking into account the three key points of the far and near posts and the position of the ball.

From the Side of the Box (Fig 118)

This is a dangerous situation because the ball can be crossed into the box and from this angled situation it can be attacked at speed. The attacker may feel that in this situation the angles are inadequate for him to succeed with a direct shot on goal in which case his options then are obvious: he will most likely play the ball to the far or near post. You must prevent opponents from attacking this space.

•   D4 and D8 position themselves towards the far post to give you depth in defence, preventing the opponents from entering unchallenged.

• D2 and D7 are positioned towards the front part of the box and are prepared to stop the opponents getting a run at the ball. Being goal side should give them the advantage of being first to the ball.

•   D5 defends against any ball played behind the wall and guards against the chip pass into this hole.

• D11 attacks opponent A2, but only if the ball is played to A2.

•   D9 takes care of the ball played towards the touch-line.

• D10 aims to block the ball, if possible.

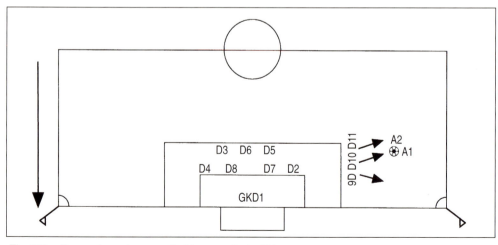

Fig 118   Every player knows what is expected of him.

THROW-INS

Down the Line
(Fig 119)
Throwing the ball down the line makes life difficult for opponents, because the player in possession (A3 in the diagram) can throw it in such a way that the ball is held between the touchline and another attacking player, A6. In most cases the opponents' only option is to try to kick the ball out, which again returns possession to the attackers.

The Long Throw-In
(Fig 120)
When the opponents are marking tight man to man in the vicinity of the throw-in, use the long throw to keep possession. This will take care of any tight marking problems. Remember that you cannot be in an offside position from a throw-in.

In this example the two attacking players A8 and A9 have taken full advantage of the long throw by player A3 and have attacked the ball with pace from well outside the area.

It is worth remembering that the throw-in can be just as difficult to deal with as any cross of the ball because it can be made more accurate, and the lesser pace on the ball can hinder a defensive clearance.

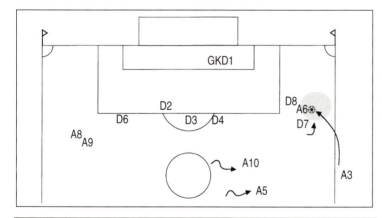

Fig 119   Throw-in down the line.

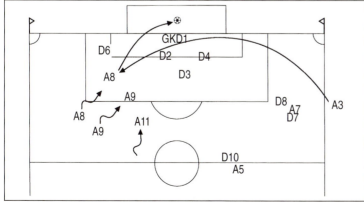

Fig 120   The long throw-in.

117

12 MODERN ATTACKING SKILLS

All touch play formats are essential skills exercises which focus on the different types of skill required during play. The first touch is very important (*see* Chapter 5), but there are other touch skills which are equally so, and they will be practised here. The greatest mistake made by many coaches was to introduce the two-touch working format and stick to it rigidly, come what may. Of course there are times during the game when the player needs to work to this touch play sequence. The mistake is to simulate this play requirement by practising it continuously for 20 to 30 minutes at a time.

Think about what is actually involved in taking players on in tight game situations. Think about what you need to practise when the ball is played to you from different angles. The skills of movement and bringing the ball under control are not reflected by the two-touch working formats, which concentrate on 'getting rid of the ball'. Always trying to get rid of the ball will not promote the development of skills in soccer.

The future of today's game depends on the media as well as domestic games, and the big clubs already make use of the media money-earning potential in the form of various competitions. However the media's main concern is whether games are interesting to watch, and this will only be so if skills rather than brute strength are on display. Therefore it is important to separate the working skills to understand what they are about. The training sessions need to vary, and somewhere along the line need to include all aspects of play. The exercises in this chapter adhere to this coaching requirement because they teach the player many different touch skill options on the ball.

The inexperienced player starts off working the ball with strength rather than technique, being unable to judge the strength needed to strike the ball to achieve the height and distance desired. This difficulty is caused mainly because he cannot distinguish between the different types of technique and their uses in play, and this leads to all sorts of play problems, limiting his pass options and causing him to make inappropriate choices during play. Correct training soon sorts these problems out.

However, there are far too many players whose only contact with the ball comes in match play situations, and the long-term problems experienced by players who are brought up on a diet of playing five-a-sides or proper games of soccer as the sole means of training are easy to see. These players lack many of the skills necessary to play the game properly, which is not surprising as they will be lucky to have five minutes on the ball in total in one match. Time spent on one training routine even for one half-hour would afford more touches of the ball than all the games in a season put together.

When a potential player works in a five-a-side environment, in tight, confined spaces, the first habit he develops is the head down syndrome. This head down position on the ball is forced on him by the closeness of opponents, and means he cannot see anything other than the ball. This naturally limits his playing options severely, and his passing becomes coincidental.

It is possible that many well intentioned people have not given this subject any consideration. The skills of dribbling and developing a range of playing options are built on a wide variety of practice formats. The length of touch and movements on and off the ball by players are vital parts of these skills, and they cannot be learnt in the tight working environments which are enforced by certain possession formats (such as five-a-sides) and which are practised without a specific end product. These formats adhere to the running and tackling game, but do not produce the type of skills demanded by the new soccer regulations.

There are even more important issues at stake. When using the practice formats not only has the player more touches of the ball, but the nature of the exercises does not cause as much wear and tear as playing too many games.

The following topics on attacking play include a wide range of skills exercises, all teaching how to keep possession of the ball. There are different ways of going into forward attacking positions, so running patterns combined with passing skills should be learned.

Attacking play is based on movement. The players have to be able to cope with all the different types of movement required, such as running off the ball, dribbling, close ball control and choosing where to pass it. To help with this, the first of the attacking skill exercises is concernned with foot co-ordination.

FOOT CO-ORDINATION

This training routine is designed to make both your feet move equally well. Some people have one foot which is less efficient than the other, so the less efficient foot has to be trained to a proficient standard – the good leg used at the wrong time can become the wrong leg in a specific game situation.

The cones are positioned on the ground shoulder-width apart for each player in all the following exercises. It is very important that when practising with the cones the feet move precisely this distance, as the mechanics of moving both feet the right distance makes the lazy leg move as it should. Training the leg to respond helps to rebuild the muscle nerve links to the brain, and developing muscle–brain co-ordination improves ball-control skills.

Close Ball Control
(Fig 121)
One line of ten cones shoulder-width apart are placed as shown. The player works to the following instructions.

Straddle Skips
The player straddle skips sideways to the end of the cone line. It is important to keep the body positioned sideways on, and the feet to cone width.

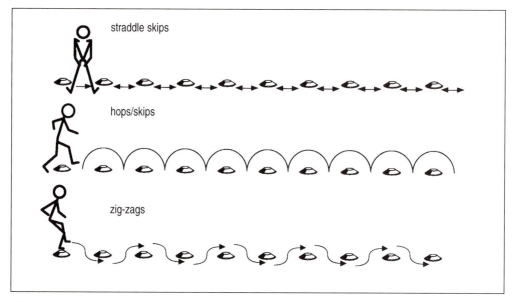

Fig 121   Improving foot co-ordination.

Hops / Skips

The player hops/skips over the cones to the end of the line, making sure that he does not touch any of the cones. The feet/knees have to be high, just like a sprinter, and the speed through the cones should be as fast as the player can manage.

Zig-zags

The player starts with both feet placed on the ground to the left of the first cone, facing up the cone line. The first move is with the left foot going across his body to jump to the right-hand side of the second cone. From then on, the right and left feet alternate cutting across the line to the end of the line of cones. This exercise is a good basis for developing close ball-control skills.

Adding the Ball
(Figs 122 & 123)

Set up two lines of ten cones side by side. The player starts the practice by standing sideways on between the two lines, in the square formed by the first two cones of each row. The ball is placed at his feet. The player starts to skip/straddle on the spot, playing the ball from foot to foot using the inside/instep part of the foot.

Once he has begun this movement, he concentrates on moving himself and the ball sideways along the row, working with the ball from one square to the next, and trying to get the distance touch right each time. The player in Fig 123 is concentrating on the right foot touch; to focus the work on the other foot, simply turn the player round to face the other way. The coach can decide the number of repetitions for each

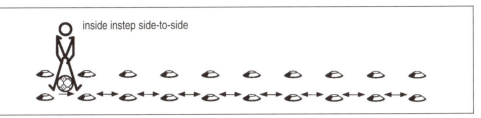

Fig 122   Two lines of ten cones, running parallel to each other, are placed on the ground shoulder width apart.

practising player. The practice session should last 25 minutes.

This practice has a number of significant benefits. Firstly, the staccato rhythm – the ball is given very short, quick touches – teaches the lazy leg to move in time with the good leg, so both feet benefit. Secondly, the exercise works on the all-important habit of never leaving the ball still for more than a fraction of a second. This develops the player's dribbling ability, teaching him to use this tiny pause to implement other skills, and helping him to repel opponents' challenges. Thirdly, moving the ball in this way allows the player to develop his touch with the instep part of either foot, which is the part of the body most used in soccer.

To develop this last skill further,

complement the skip straddling exercise with a knees-up, return-the-ball exercise. The ball is thrown to the player from a distance of 2m, and the player has to return it using his left or right instep. This helps to develop his passing technique by teaching him the correct foot position in relation to the ball.

Off the Ball Skills
(Fig 124)

The previous exercises are examples of close ball-control movements, whereas this one practises movement 'off the ball'. It is a figure-of-eight running training exercise which concentrates on developing both the right and left foot passing technique, by simulating a player passing and going for the return ball during play.

Set up two cones, A and B. The

Fig 123   Developing the use of both feet.

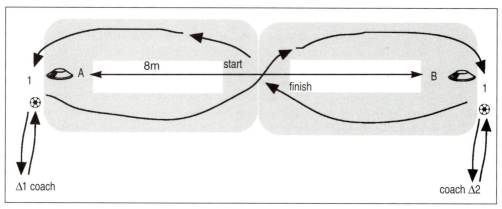

Fig 124   Movement off the ball.

coach stands near cone A, and a second 'coach' near cone B; both have footballs. Player 1 starts between cones A and B. He runs round the back of cone B and receives a ball from the coach, which he returns; he then runs diagonally across to cone A, passing round the back of it and receives a ball from the other coach. He then runs to cone B again, completing the figure-of-eight shape and starting the exercise again. The player should work to sets of ten repetitions; the total practice time should be 10 to 15 minutes.

RUNNING WITH THE BALL – AN INTRODUCTION

It is vital to distinguish between the different types of running with the ball. Close ball control and dribbling are two different skills, and ball control running can be divided further into three categories: attacking short space openings, taking on and going past an opponent, and attacking vacant space well ahead of the runner.

Dribbling with the ball is a quite different skill with different require- ments and is only loosely related to the running formats – the relationship ends where the skills of taking on opponents begin. When dribbling with the ball, the player should be allowed to stop the ball for a fraction of a second, as practised above (*see* Fig 122). With constant practice the momentary pause within the movement will become second nature. This pause allows the player mentally to introduce natural skill changes during play, which straight line cone formats do not.

Look back at Fig 54 (in Chapter 6). This format should only be used during fitness training, rather than to practise dribbling, because this training exercise focuses only on work with a constant speed and length of movement. This movement environment does not simulate real game situations. The coach who asks the players to run faster through this cone format causes even more damage to the development of dribbling skills, as attacking players who stick to a constant speed are easily dealt with. It is constant changes in pace, in coming to and going past opponents, that are a defender's nightmare. The following exercise will develop this type of attacking flexibility.

Attacking Short Space

Soccer running should be performed in a realistic game situation. The long distance running exercises have already been discussed. Short distance running is tackled here. In the example below, the players practise many important link elements to do with the runner. The middle zone of the practice area simulates attacking space conditions in play.

How It Works (Fig 125)

The play area is marked out with cones to be 70m long and 30m wide. This area is then split up into zones, a 10m running zone in the middle flanked by two 30m possession zones. The middle zone will be free of players, and used for the purpose of running with the ball from one zone to the other. The front part of each possession zone has a 3m deep skill entry zone, where the players will take on defenders as in a real game situation.

Two opposing teams of twelve players are each split up into two teams of six and positioned at either end of the working area, creating a competitive game in each end possession zone. Although the teams have been split up and are separated by the middle zone, they still belong to each other, so that team A players at one end are on the same side as team A players at the other.

The object of the exercise is for each team to try to link up with its other half by sending a runner across the running zone. To do this, the team has to keep

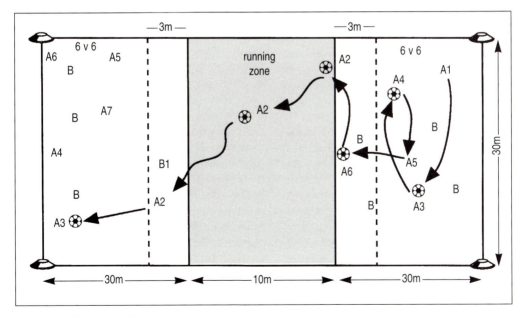

Fig 125   Attacking short space.

possession of the ball for at least four consecutive passes. This entitles the team in possession to release a runner to the other side. A successful link-up scores one point.

Each of the two opposing teams (the team not in possession) presents one challenger (in turn) to the oncoming player (the runner). A defender of the opposing team will position himself in the skill entry zone, from where he will defend the possession zone. If the defender wins possession of the ball, he simply plays the ball to one of his own players, and his team tries to make four consecutive passes, and so on. Otherwise the attacking player continues his run. If he makes it to the opposite half he has to stay there, as it has to be a different player from his side who will go back if his team wins the chance.

The first team to ten points – ten successful link-ups – wins. There can only be one runner at any one time. Sometimes, depending on the strength of one team, there may be an imbalance in team numbers. The difference in team numbers between the two sides in either half should not be more than two players at any one time; if the imbalance in numbers is greater than this, the teams are allowed to balance out.

ATTACKING RUNS

Any club that wishes to stay at the top of its profession can only do so nowadays if it plays soccer in an attractive attacking way. The following practices reflect the changes in the laws of the game, and promote skills which would never have seen the light of day if tackling from behind had been permitted to continue to dominate. This sort of tackling game was simply used as an excuse to propagate the type of player produced by outdated training methods, and was boring to watch.

Now for the first time in a decade of negative destructive play, it is possible to make attacking runs without being brought down; the following training diagrams show the skills required to make such runs. There are basically three types of running scenario: playing the ball into space, keeping the ball under close control, and cutting across the defender. The skills reference points are numbered 1 to 4 (7 in Fig 129) on each diagram, and are key skills application areas. The skills in use at these points are taught in working formats from appropriate chapters of this book.

The theme of each working run concentrates on what you need to do once you have used your dribbling skills to go past the first challenger. The direction and the way you run is crucial. Straight runs will always get you into trouble, so working out when to cut inside or go on the outside of your chasing opponent is worth practising.

The best way to describe each working format is to present step-by-step descriptions of the movements required to perform the various tasks involved when dribbling past defenders. However, before describing the three types of run, I shall briefly discuss the end product, which is of course the finishing or striking of the ball on target, in this case one of the two offset goals.

Setting Up the Practice
(Fig 126)
Set up the playing area as shown. There

should be two improvised 8m-wide goals positioned at one end of the practice area; goalkeepers are optional in this working practice. Players A2 and A3 can be positioned as shown to help with finishing. To start the practice for the next three topics, the defending player or coach plays the ball to practising player A1, who starts in between the two lines of cones at the far end of the playing area. After this initial pass, the coach/defender takes up a defending role. The main cone lines to the sides of the practice area represent the right and left touchlines on the field of play.

The End Product

As you can see, the practising player,

A1, starts at a position in between the two goals, so approaches neither of them head on. This is arranged deliberately, for several reasons.

The first reason focuses on the need to strike the ball on target to the far post. This angled approach to the goal fosters a clear appreciation of the far post finish. This is not a random objective: statistics prove that the far post finish has a greater chance of scoring a goal than almost any other type of finish. If the keeper fails to hold on to this ball the supporting strikers may have the opportunity to strike it into the back of the net.

Conversely, the finish to the near post helps the keeper rather than the

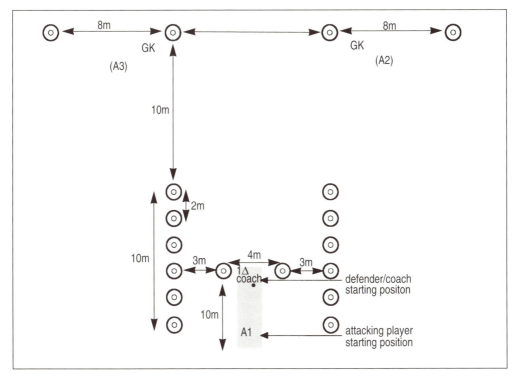

Fig 126   The set-up for practising attacking runs.

striker, because his position in relation to the ball and the attacking player covers most of the goal target, so he is naturally in a good position to protect his goal. The statistics also show that if the keeper fails to catch the ball at the near post, he will more often than not clear his lines by sending the ball out for a corner kick.

The goal positions also reflect the need for the attacking player to practise finishing with both the right and the left foot. I believe that if the ball comes onto the player's left side then he should finish with his left foot; transferring the ball to the other leg (good leg) may reduce his chances of scoring a goal. The position of the cones in relation to the two goals forces the player to work to a right or a left foot finish.

Finally, remember that although this routine includes finishing, this is not the focal point of the practice. This practice session and the exercises relate directly to the three major coaching tasks required to go past opponents.

Playing the Ball into Space

The first topic concerns itself with playing the ball into space behind the defender, rather than trying to run with it close to the feet.

How It Works (Fig 127)

The coach/defender starts by playing the pass to attacking player A1, and follows it to simulate the oncoming defender. A1 dinks the ball to his right side away from the coach/defender as and when the opponent bites (tackles for the ball).

A1 then plays the second touch to send the ball into free space behind the defender and ahead of the runner. The

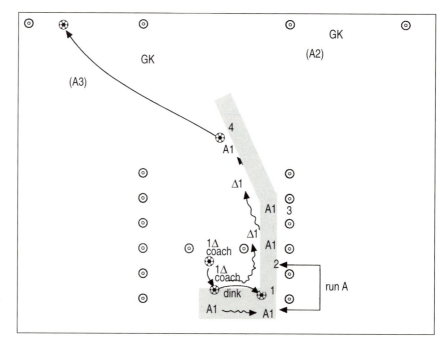

Fig 127
Playing the
ball into
space.

sole purpose of this second touch is to use this space in order to gain an advantage over the defender – the first skill practice objective (skill point 1 in Fig 127). It is important that the second touch does not play the ball out through the right-hand cone line as this would be considered loss of possession. More importantly, the second touch of the ball must reflect a good positive attitude and have sufficient strength to enable the ball to travel to at least the gap alongside the gate.

At the same time A1 changes his pace to reach skill point 2 where he then attacks the space and ball, kicking the ball well forward of his run, at which point the defending player is set to chase after him (skill point 3) to put pressure on him. On reaching at least the fifth cone from the start, A1 controls the ball and cuts across the channel and the defender to finish with a shot on his left-hand goal (skill point 4). The target is the far post.

Keeping Close Control of the Ball

There are times when you cannot allow the ball to travel forward of your run but must keep it close to your feet, times when your opponents are marking everybody else in the vicinity of play, and other than the man who is chasing you, there is no one to challenge you for the ball. The opponents are caught in a no-win situation. You are in control of the ball and they know that if any one of them leaves the player he is marking to try to challenge for the ball, the chances are that you will pass the ball to the now-free player, which could prove to be even more of a

threat to them. Rather than risk this happening they keep to their man-to-man marking duties.

It is therefore up to you to take full advantage of what is happening around you and to attack the opened-up spaces. When your team-mates are marked tight in this situation, they should help you to take further advantage of the unfolding play scenario by taking opponents away from your intended run direction.

It is important to keep close control of the ball because if you allow it to run free, the opponents may feel that they can leave their charge and nip in to win possession.

This practice format follows the work done on this issue previously, only this time the player needs to deal with a chasing defender. This exercise does not concentrate on other issues such as cutting across the defender at this point, because cutting across the defender with the ball requires different running patterns, which will be dealt with in practising skill 3 (Fig 129).

How It Works (Fig 128)

The coach/defender plays the ball to attacking player A1, then follows up the pass (directly) to simulate the oncoming defender. A1 dinks the ball to the left side of the coach/defender (skill position 1), then picks up the ball with his next stride, controls it, and changes direction to a forward running position (skill position 2). Going forward now with a change in pace, the ball is in close control at his feet. The defender gives chase (skill position 3), and catches up with A1 at skill position 4.

Now comes the clever bit. When the

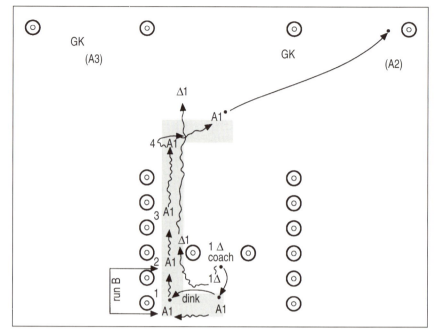

Fig 128 Practice requirement skill 2. Run B.

defender runs alongside A1, A1 will suddenly put his foot on the ball, perform an under-foot turn to turn inside the defender and then go on to finish in the right-hand goal, aiming at the far post.

Cutting Across the Defender

The last of the three exercises in this practice session concerns itself with the situation where the attacking player has gone past the defending player but has not been able to shake him off. This practice is about cutting across the line of run, the attacking player making sure that the defending player is held behind him.

In today's playing environment the attacking player is greatly helped by the fact that the defending player is not allowed to tackle from behind. The wrong approach by the defending play-

er to win possession of the ball can be a sending-off offence. Therefore this exercise is worth its weight in gold.

How It Works (Fig 129)

The start of the practice is the same as for the previous two previous exercises – that is, the coach/defender plays the ball to attacking player A1 and follows the ball up in a direct line (this is important to the practice as it is a way of simulating defending play conditions with an oncoming/chasing defender).

On receiving the ball, A1 dinks it to the right of the oncoming defender/coach (skill point 1). This initiates the first part of the movement required by the practice format. For the sake of acquiring the whole range of running skills it is important to practise the next move in the following way. On the second touch A1 redirects the ball to go

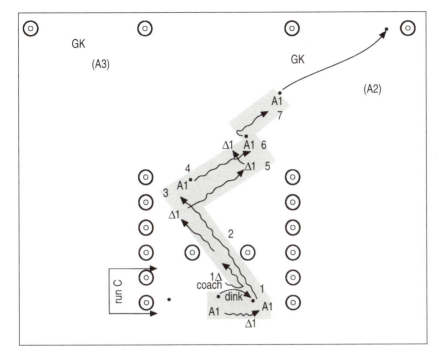

*Fig 129
Cutting
across the
defender.*

inside and through the small gate behind the coach (skill point 2). This approach forces the attacking player to come inside and to the back of the defender. It also puts him in the correct run position for this exercise.

The attacking player is closely followed by the defending player/coach to skill position 3. A1 keeps the defending player to the back of him by making sure that the run pattern is angled. At this stage A1 runs towards the left cone line before suddenly turning inside with the ball just ahead of the defender (skill position 4). A1 now takes further advantage of his forward position by changing the angle of his run a third time (skill position 5) and then chooses his direction of attack (skill position 6). The position of the two goals gives the attacking player the option of going to

his right or left, allowing him to practise changing the direction of his attacking run at will and sending the opponent the wrong way. Once this has been achieved successfully A1 finishes with a strike on target, again aiming at the far post (skill position 7).

The best solution to staying ahead of any defender in these circumstances is to learn to run with the ball in such a way that the attacking run does not afford the defending player the opportunity to run to the front or side of you. It is important that once this attacking run position has been achieved, the follow-up angle of the run keeps cutting across the run of the defending player. The angle of the run is right to left, then left to right. Do not spend too long running in one direction, or running at the same pace.

129

THE SKILLS OF DRIBBLING

Changing the Pace

Sending the opponent the wrong way, changing your direction of approach, encouraging the opponents to come to the ball, are all part of the soccer skills of dribbling. This practice format concentrates on changing pace.

Preparation (Fig 130)

Set up the practice area as shown in Fig 130. The practising player (A1) starts off alongside cone A. He walks with the ball at his feet from cone A towards cones 1 or 2, which mark out the directional change zone where he will change direction. He must use only one foot to touch/push the ball forwards to ensure the correct speed of approach to the working area/opponent. His next task concentrates on keeping close control of the ball, in preparation to change his pace and running direction. At any moment the coach will give a (pre-arranged) signal telling the player to suddenly change speed and direction.

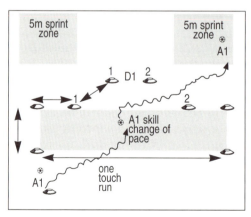

Fig 130 Changing the angle of run.

Once the player is accustomed to walking with the ball and reacting to the signal by changing pace and direction, he can go on to complete the full exercise. Player D1 can be released to put pressure on A1. D1 comes into play when A1 reaches cones 1 or 2.

The Full Practice (Figs 131–134)

There are three separate sections in this working format. The first concentrates on the skills of ball control running, and changes in the pace of work. The second phase works with the actual skills required to send the opponent the wrong way. The final phase of the practice works on skills co-ordination, changing the pace and direction to get away from the opponent.

The player runs with the ball from cone A to the directional change zone marked out by cones 1 and 2. When inside this zone the player is required to perform one of the following skills on a given signal from the coach: change direction with the outside of the foot, change direction using the inside of the foot, or work out a double bluff move – foot over the top of the ball dummy, drop the shoulders, send the body in a different direction. The player should improvise and create new skills, turning with the ball, to practise sending the defender the wrong way.

Once the player has performed one skill from this playing repertoire his next touch of the ball will send the ball out of the directional change zone. The first touch of the ball, sending it between either the cones marked 1 or those numbered 2, changes the pace of this part of the exercise. Moving through cones 1 represents moving to

Fig 131   The forward touch...

Fig 132   ...followed by a change angle to the left using the outside of the foot.

Fig 133   Follow through the path of the ball.

Fig 134   Finish with a strike option.

the left side of the oncoming defender, and moving through cones 2 represents moving to his right.

Once the player has passed the cone markers he sprints with the ball to the 5m sprint zone; he is now allowed to use both feet. From the sprint zone he walks back down the side of the practice area to the starting position at cone A to begin again. The practice should last 30 minutes.

The Oncoming Opponent

When you are confronted by an oncoming opponent or one who simply bars your way into forward positions, the first thing you should do is position yourself at an angle to him regardless of how far away he is (in practical terms up to 10m away). The first rule is never to permit the opponent to come close to you, especially head on. The angle of the first touch on the ball is vital – it must be played to a sharp sideways-on position. Playing the ball forwards in tight game conditions is a bad habit which you must avoid. The only time you would play the ball forwards is when there is no opponent in your way and there is plenty of free space ahead

131

of you. The cone set-up in this next exercise is such that it makes sure of the correct angle of the first touch.

The pace of touch is just as important as the first touch direction. The first touch of the ball sideways and away from the opponent enables A1 to control play because it allows him to change direction quickly in relation to the position of the oncoming opponent. In applying such an angle, he is in fact removing himself from the opponent's dimension in play, and the opponent can never get back into his line of work unless he allows him to challenge for the ball from a head-on position. In all other circumstances the opponent can only cut across this dimension, and as long as you keep your body position at an angle in relation to the opponent, and use the bite moments (when the opponent challenges for the ball) to shift the ball away from the challenger, you will always be in control of play.

Changing the angle of approach is very useful, especially if the defender is holding his ground, as it will force him to adjust his position. To do this, the defender needs to come across and towards the ball, which opens up attacking areas of play. The defender's sideways-on position allows the attacking player at least one option of going past him. See D1's angled approach to A1 in Fig 135.

How It Works (Figs 135 & 136)

To set the cones up for this exercise, all you need to do is to stand up straight and put your hands out to the side of your body, then position one cone on the ground to either side of your extended arm length.

Player A1 is positioned slightly behind and centrally between the two angled cone positions. Defender D1 faces him with the ball 8m away, and starts the practice by playing the ball in to A1. D1 then moves forwards to try to win possession of the ball, but he must move in a direct line towards player A1. It is important that he moves at the correct speed (see Fig 136). Player A1 makes sure of the quality of his first touch away from this oncoming defender. The ball must be played at a sideways angle to the back of the two cone positions (alternately). The actual challenge for the ball can be left out at this first stage of the practice.

After the initial direct approach practice, where the sole concentration is on the first touch direction, the next stage concentrates on the sideways-on approach by the attacking player, who is still in possession of the ball. D1 plays in the ball to A1, and A1 completes his first touch, which puts him at an angle to the challenger – see the

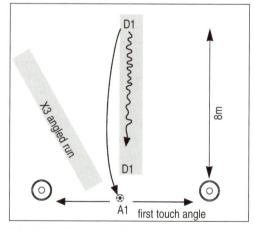

Fig 135   D1 moves forward to try to win possession.

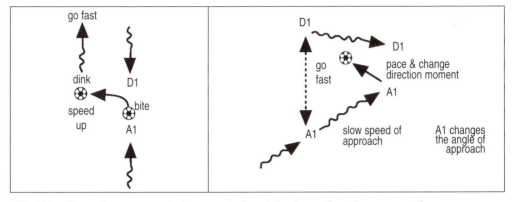

Fig 136   On a direct approach the speed of work is slower than the opponent's.

shaded area on the diagram (ignore the cone placements for this angled scenario).

The practice ends when the attacking player has turned the defender and retained possession of the ball. Both players then return to their starting positions and begin again. The players can swap roles after each completed sequence. Alternatively work to repetitions of ten angle practice attempts per working player.

The Attacking Player A1

Make sure that the first touch directs the ball to your side of the cones. Shift yourself away in one movement, using the inside/instep of your foot to go to the right or left. When the opponent comes at you from the side, make sure that you are patient and wait for the bite moment before making your next forward touch. All your efforts go into turning the opponent, so you should always make sure you are positioned at an angle to him. Do not allow the opponent to face you.

The Alongside Opponent

In some respects oncoming opponents are easier to deal with than those approaching at an angle, especially if they come towards the player in possession without trying to control their pace, because the momentum of their run can be used against them when the right moment is chosen to change direction with the ball.

The same cannot be said of an opponent who has managed to come alongside and has matched the working pace of the player in possession. This can happen, for example, when the player in possession is going down the line. If his run is in a straight line, the opponent will not only match him for pace but, because he is not burdened by the ball, will gain the upper hand, forcing the ball away from the attacker's possession or out of play.

To deal with the alongside opponent, the first skill is to keep the ball on the foot furthest away from your opponent when running. Try to keep the ball close to the left or right side of your running line, use the hand nearest to your opponent to protect your own working

133

space, and make sure that your opponent does not cut across you. It is also important not to lean into or against the body of your opponent, as this will only slow you down further and put you in the wrong body position for getting out of the situation.

The next skill is to change the pace of your work, for example to speed up or slow down, and to keep on changing your rhythm. A change of pace will create a moment of indecision for your opponent, giving you the opportunity to take control. All you need is a moment to give you a half-metre lead on him, then you can use this opening to come inside him (or outside, depending on where you are on the field of play).

This change of angle away from the straight line run will help you regain control of the situation, because when you come inside or outside your opponent, he will have to turn his body momentarily in order to match your new run direction. When this happens, turn and go the other way, only this time put more distance into your touch on the ball so that the ball is played further away than on the first bluff touch. Make sure that the touch on the ball takes it away at a sharp left or right angle. Once this is achieved you are well on your way to keeping possession. These skills are practised effectively using the following three-line cone format.

The Three-Line Cone Format (Fig 137)

Set up the practice area as shown in Fig 137, arranging the cones in three lines of seven facing player A1; he has to work his way through the lines of cones, which simulates evading a defender.

The exercise is described below from the point of view of player A1 who starts on the left of the cones, but it can be performed from the other side too, with player A2 starting from position B and working his way through the cones from right to left.

The coach plays the ball to player A1, who takes it up with the inside/instep of his left foot. He then brings his

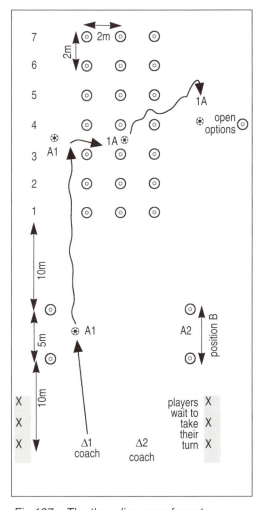

Fig 137   The three line cone format.

right foot into play, again picking the ball up with the inside/instep of his foot; the right foot doubles up as the stride-off foot, taking the ball up as the player strides forwards towards the cones.

In this example the player makes his run with the ball to the left of the three lines. He runs alongside the outside of the first line of cones. At cones 1 and 2 he effects the change of pace, and just past cone 3 he turns with the ball using his left foot, changing the direction of his run from left to right. On turning into the cones he immediately puts into effect other close ball control skills – touching any of the cones is equivalent to giving the ball away. Once through the cones the practice of changing angles in relation to the opponent has been completed.

Alternatively it is easy to set up a finishing opportunity on the field of play as an end product to this practice. Thus instead of the single cone to the right of the lines of cones, a suitable portable goal can be set up. The practice should last 40 minutes.

The Direct Challenge

The Gate Format (Fig 138)

This exercise simulates a direct challenge for the ball. It is designed to teach the player in possession to deal with several challenge attempts in a short period of time.

Set up two squares with cones, 10 × 10m in size, so that they share one corner, resembling two diamonds side by side (like a squared figure-of-eight). Set an escape gate 1m in width in the centre of each side of each square and number them 1 to 4.

Two working players take part in

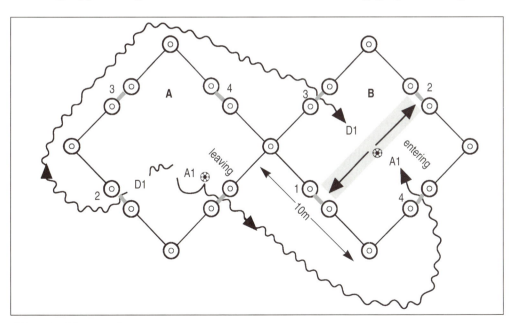

Fig 138   The gate format.

this practice format. They each start in the same square and the attacking player (A1) has the ball; he will try to keep possession and get out of the square while the other player (D1) defends every gate within each shape and tries to win possession. If D1 wins possession of the ball the players swap roles.

Thus A1 must take on the oncoming opponent in order to make his escape; he then enters the next square through any gate. D1 is not allowed to go after A1 through the same gate, but must leave the shape through the next gate (if A1 leaves through gate 1, D1 has to use gate 2 and so on); he can enter the next square through any gate except the one used by A1.

Entering and leaving the shapes in this way ensures that the player in possession of the ball has the opponent coming at him from different angles, which gives him many opportunities to practise playing the ball away at an angle. Also, he will always be first in the next square because the defender is not allowed to follow him through the same gate.

The player in possession is allowed to have ten change angle attempts. Alternatively, the coach can decide how to work the exercise based on how he sees events unfolding.

VISION

You cannot play soccer seriously if you cannot read the game or play with your head up. To acquire this ability means that the player also has to acquire the skills that go with it. For obvious reasons 'vision' is useless without the ability to pass the ball. The first exercise below is designed to give the player

practice at both these vital soccer skills.

Vision and Passing
(Fig 139)

Position five players as shown in Fig 139. The distance between the four outside players, A1 to A4 (two at either end of the practice area), is set at 30m. A special 10 × 10m short-pass zone is marked out in the middle of this configuration, with the fifth player (D1) standing in the centre. This set-up is designed deliberately to simulate the shape in play. Two of the outside players start with footballs (A1 and A2 in the diagram).

The players practise playing short and long passes continuously. The player in the middle has a special function in this exercise, controlling the exercise by deciding who to play the ball to. His job is to use his vision and body language to receive the ball. He does this by lifting his head up and looking up at the player on the outside who has possession of the ball. When the player in possession looks up at this 'head up' signal from D1, and the players lock eyes, the player in possession must play the short pass to D1.

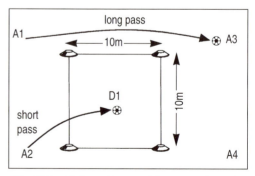

Fig 139 Vision: short and long passing. To start the practice place one soccer ball at the feet of player A1 and A2.

Meanwhile, the player who has the second ball and is not involved with this exchange of passes (A1 in the diagram) plays the long ball to the other end of the shape (to A3). As he does this, D1, who has received the ball in the middle zone, turns with it to select another player to look up at and play the ball to (A4 in the diagram).

This short and long passing sequence is maintained in a constant flow throughout the practice, and the players must be constantly looking up and assessing the situation in order to select the right choice of action.

Seeing Options Early

The following exercise is to teach the player to assess his passing options and make early decisions about what type of technique to use and where to pass the ball; it is astonishingly simple.

How It Works (Fig 140)

The practising player A1 begins the exercise in a specially marked out starting area. The target players receiving the ball (numbered 1 to 3) stand facing player A1 but different distances away from him so he has the option of making either a long or a short pass. The coach with the ball positions himself an appropriate distance away from the starting position.

Player A1 turns his back on the coach and target players and jogs slowly away from the starting position. When the coach thinks that he is far enough away he passes the ball to him, at the same time shouting a number between one and three. The pass has to be timed correctly so that A1 has enough time to turn, control the ball,

look up and play the ball as per instructions; when A1 hears the shout he knows he has to turn quickly to face the oncoming pass from the coach, and then pass the ball to the designated target player, using an appropriately chosen technique with great precision, hopefully!

This exercise can be made more difficult in various ways. The simplest method is to place players ('defenders') between A1 and the target players. Alternatively, the target players can move from place to place when A1 has turned his back to jog away from the coach. This makes sure that gauging the correct length of pass is left rather late.

Quick-Fire Passing

Do not be misled by the simplicity of this exercise. It is the best way to assess the quality of passing work by any player of any standard, as it has been designed to show up any faults in passing techniques. The pressure on the

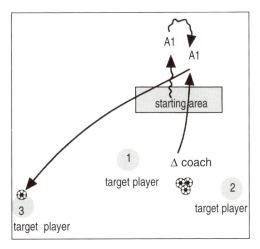

Fig 140   Vision: seeing early options.

137

working player comes from having to make the right choice of technique and having to time the pass accurately, while at the same time trying to decide which player (if any) is suitably positioned to receive a pass. This is an important practice consideration because moments of indecision do arise during play.

Players need to be able to make quick decisions, as opponents' actions mean that any decision may have to be altered as quickly as it was made. The player may be about to make a pass when, at the very last moment, an opponent runs across the line of his intended pass, cutting off this opportunity. A quick decision not to pass to the intended player and some skilful adjustments help him to retain possession of the ball and pass it to someone else.

How It Works (Fig 141)

The practising players stand about 5m apart in two rows facing each other; the distance between the rows is about 10–15m, and they are slightly offset so that no player is directly opposite another. This arrangement creates the right angle for the passes, allowing the ball to travel without hindrance provided the passing player makes the right decisions. The players work to a short and long passing sequence, where the long passes cover about 20m and the short passes 10m.

The practice begins with A1 playing a short ball to A6, while A2 plays a long ball to A7. This short and long passing sequence is then maintained to achieve the desired coaching objectives. The exercise is called 'quick-fire passing' beacuse two balls are being passed the whole time; you could practise with more balls but this increases the risk of ball collision and the practice could lose its momentum.

To make sure that the quality of technique and accuracy of passing is maintained in a realistic enviroment, the exercise is carried out according to certain rules. The players must control the ball, set it up and pass accurately. A mistake by any player is considered as giving the ball away. All the players have five lives, which means that they can make up to five mistakes during the practice. If any player reaches this

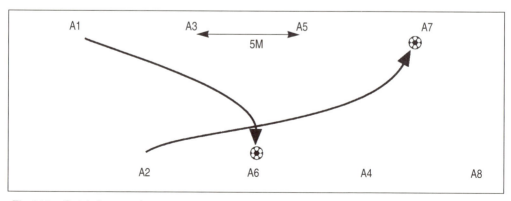

Fig 141   Quick-fire passing.

number of faults they could do a forfeit, such as press-ups. Alternatively, leave in the player(s) who have made the least mistakes when swapping players in and out of the exercise. The player(s) with the least errors wins the competition/session.

The quick-fire format can be made to work to any skill standard by simply adapting the rules. Begin the practice by allowing the players to use four touches of the ball, thus catering to the lowest of standards. The difficulty of the exercise can be increased by reducing the number of touches on the ball. You can appreciate that the ultimate test of skill must be to play the ball on the first touch.

Even this can be made more difficult by asking the players to construct shapes out of the base shape during passing – the easiest shape to achieve is the circle. The change in the working shape is possible because of the combination of short and long passing options and because there are two soccer balls in play all the time. The base shape can represent two tiers in any system in play – whether this is the midfield section or defence is left up to you.

Passing the ball involves two important skills. The first is of course the technical ability to kick the ball; this has already been practised in previous exercises. The second is perhaps even more important – it is the skill of 'vision' we have been practising here. In soccer terms, having vision means that the player possesses the ability to look up when in possession of the ball. This definition includes the ability to play the right pass at the right time.

PASSING PATTERNS

If you were to position yourself in a central position on the field of play as shown by player A4 in Fig 142, then the easiest way of interacting with other players would be to pass the ball in a readily recognized pattern. Technically speaking the man in possession of the ball can do this while hardly moving from this central play position – the players running off the ball in fact do all the hard work by creating passing options for the player in possession.

The running patterns can be organized beforehand and can include such tactical variations as anchor play options. Study the full range of running and passing options given here. Read about the relationship of the short pass to the feet and other passing possibilities described in later chapters. Remember that coming short to the player in possession is a fundamental skill on which other passing and movement combinations are built. Never underestimate the simplicity of this first move.

There is no limit to the passing possibilities once the players are aware of the different running and passing options open to them. Fig 142 looks at attacking play passing options.

Typical Passing Options
(Fig 142)

The Long Ball (Option 1)
There are two main reasons for choosing to play the long ball. Sometimes being closed down on the ball gives the player in possession no alternative but to make sure that the ball is played far enough up-field for the opponents not to pose an

immediate threat to his goal. This long pass may give his team the chance to reposition goal side of the ball. The second reason is more positive. This is when the long ball is used to penetrate into the opponents' defensive positions. A direct approach on the opponents' goal can be very effective.

The Wide Ball (Option 2)

This is very useful because play can at times be restrictive going down the middle. Switching play will release pressure on the team in possession of the ball by making it possible to free areas of play while retaining possession. Playing the ball in this way creates more room to play and more time on the ball.

The Holding Pass (Option 5)

This pass to anchor man A7 is a holding pass, which allows players to regroup in support of play. The ball does not penetrate the opponents' defensive positions and is not an immediate threat to goal, but it does provide time to move other players into forward attacking positions.

The Overlapping Pass (Option 6)

The ball is played into a wide position by A4 to allow his team to attack from full back positions.

The Support Pass (Option 7)

This is an anchor tactic in play for both forward and defending play scenarios. It is important that the player in possession of the ball is supported from behind in case he mistimes his play and has to pass the ball backwards (remember that the law allows the pass back to the keeper, although the keeper must not pick the ball up with his hands). It is also important from a defending point of view, since losing possession of the ball in front of your own goal without cover could be disastrous. (Anchor skills are practised in the attacking practice section of the Half Field Format, in Chapter 17).

Support

(Fig 143)

Players must work together to support each other in attacking and defensive situations. It is the player in possession

Fig 142 Support play options. (1) The long ball; (2) the wide ball; (3) the short ball option (in-field changing angle); (4) the short pass, direct to feet; (5) medium pass; (6) the overlapping pass; (7) the support position, pass to anchor player.

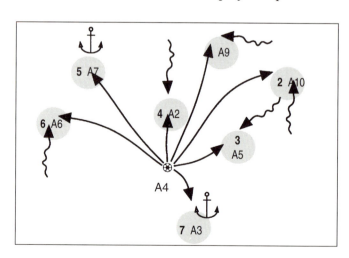

of the ball who dictates what happens next, but in order for him to control play effectively he must receive the right support from his own players. This support is known as your playing options.

In the following example, player A4 is in the process of attacking the right full back (on the left side of the field). The flat back four positioning of the defence (team D) works in favour of the attacking players, who now have several options. For example, player A4 could take on the opposing defender (D2) on the outside, going down the line; or he could play a passing move known as 'pass and go' with player A6 on his right (inside). Other passing possibilities in this situation include playing the diagonal ball inside along the ground, or playing the ball over the top of the defence. This is known as 'playing the ball into holes', for example, into the space beyond the second central defender (D4). The in-between position of attacking player A7 makes him the

favourite to get to this type of ball.

The Right Playing Option

The most common fault in play occurs when the player in possession of the ball does not select the appropriate type of pass for a particular play situation. Depth in defence means that opponents are well positioned, and barring your way forward. When this is the case the correct choice of pass can make all the difference between retaining or losing possession of the ball.

Practising different passing techniques such as chipping the ball (getting the laces under the ball) is simple enough but in itself is not the complete answer to the player's problems. We need to look further, because giving the ball away can happen in different play situations.

For example, the player in possession could find himself isolated through no fault of his own with no one left close enough to pass the ball to. This is quite

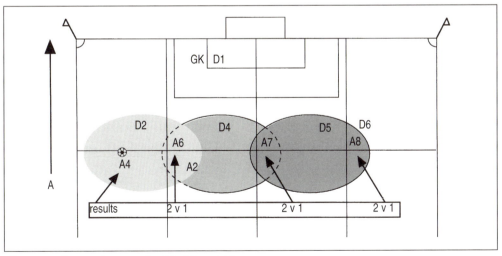

Fig 143   Supporting runs by A2, A7 and A8.

common, and occurs for two main reasons. The first is that the need to score goals sometimes overrides all other considerations and inexperienced players do tend to go forward of the player in possession. Oddly enough the second reason springs from good, solid, positive thinking, which alas sometimes goes against team defending requirements. This is the case when players 'think positively' and take it for granted that the player with the ball will not lose possession.

This natural instinct should be encouraged and not destroyed. The solution lies in practice sessions that concentrate on passing options so that players can learn which ones go hand in hand with their natural instincts of positive thinking. Time spent on passing possibilities and understanding movement off the ball within the shape will help them to choose the right option in any situation. This is discussed more fully below.

UNDERSTANDING ATTACKING OPTIONS

Knowing the law and the way you can position yourself in relation to defenders is vital to attacking play. Fig 85 shows the vulnerable positions of the back unit when confronted by an opponent. The skills of passing and movement, and an understanding of these vulnerabilities, form the basis of attacking play. Knowing how and where to pass the ball is essential when playing against any team.

There are two major skills involved in making forward progress with the ball. The first of these is the ability to move constructively as a team (shape

unit) in support of play/ball. The second skill is the team's ability to pass the ball in various technical ways. Such skills go together to achieve the ultimate aim, which is to keep possession of the ball, though this aim naturally has further team applications including the creation of 'goal-scoring opportunities'.

The skill of passing to feet can help your players to hold their positions, or alternatively, can help your team to take opponents out of their entrenched positions, which should help you to open up further forward attacking possibilities. Drawing opponents towards the ball may open up spaces behind them, which allows your team in turn to play the ball into holes rather than to feet. This enables your team to attack behind defenders into advanced forward positions.

Such passing and movement skills can destroy any offside tactic or defensive shape; for example, when the back unit attempts to squeeze up on play, the new offside law helps attacking midfield players to break through from midfield positions. The flat defence line-up is vulnerable to the ball played over the top, through or diagonally to the back of the defence. Remember that the attacking player comes onto the forward/diagonal ball whereas the defender is facing the wrong way and has to turn with the ball in order to play it in the right direction.

Even if the defending player were to win possession of this ball, in this situation his options are limited and still favour the attacking side: for example, when acquiring possession of the ball in these circumstances, the defender may be forced to play out for a throw-in, play the ball out for a corner kick, or play the ball back to the keeper, which forces the keeper to kick it up-field. In certain game situations this is not a problem for the keeper, but the safety and accuracy of his kick still depend on the amount of time he has to clear his lines.

The Pass to the Feet
(Fig 144)

The ball to the feet forms the basis of any number of passing and team movement combinations. The following scenarios describe the issues involved in this seemingly simple passing move.

Consider a set-up as shown. The defender D1 has man-to-man marking responsibilities, and his position marking attacking player A2 can deter other attacking players from passing the ball to him (A2). However, you may be surprised to know that this man-to-man marking situation can be turned around to favour attacking play.

To counter attack, player A2 has to hold his ground, aiming to keep himself between the opposing defender and the ball. This counter tactical ploy will create holes to the sides, front and back of the defender, if he is without cover. These holes can be filled by attacking players (for example A3) who will receive the ball.

Checking Out
(Fig 145)

In this scenario, the attacking player A2 stands his ground waiting for the right moment to act, and then suddenly 'checks out' towards player A1, who has possession of the ball. This is a bluff move, where a player tries to fool his marker into thinking he is going one way, and then suddenly heads off into another direction (*see* Fig 142). The defender (D1), sticking to his task, responds by going after player A2; so A2's tactical move has opened up areas of play behind the defender.

The situation is then further exploited by another attacking player, A3, who is able to move into this vacated space. A3's move into this space is made to coincide with D1's run, and A1's pass into the space.

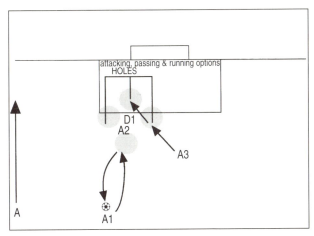

Fig 144   Creating holes.

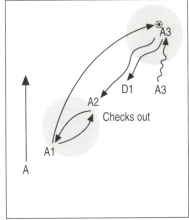

Fig 145   Checking out.

143

The Pass into Space
(Fig 146)
There are times when the ball cannot be played to the feet, as there might be a chance of interception. In these situations, the pass must be played in such a way that the opposing defender is last to reach the ball.

Here the pass by player A1 is made to the side of the receiving player A2 (away from the defender). The co-ordination of this pass and A2's move involves player A2 signalling to show where the ball should be played, then checking out from his marker; he signals to go left, but in fact goes to the right. The signal can be made in a number of ways, for example, it could be made with the hand or head, or be a call. A1 times the pass and direction in accordance with A2's run and signal.

The Overlapping Run (Fig 147)
If the receiving player A2 (in Fig 146) has the skill to lose his marker (D1) long enough to be able to turn with the ball and take him on, there is a way to help him to get the ball past the defender. This involves creating one of the most classic moves of all time – the overlap. Even in today's modern game, this tactic can still be employed.

The overlap is a classic example of playing the ball to space. In Fig 147, player A2 (in the middle) times his pass to coincide with the overlapping player (who could be A1 or another player) coming up on his blind side. The pass is made into space, behind the defender and into a forward position. The overlapping player picks up the ball in his stride on his way into a forward position.

Cross-Over Plays (Fig 148)
The nature of the game is such that the defending principles of being goal side of the ball can sometimes get in the way of an effective defence. If an opponent marks you closely goal side of the ball, it is possible to tie him up with his own defenders, preventing them from doing an effective defensive job.

In the photograph the player in possession has screened the ball away from his marker and has worked his way across the face of this defence. The player who was trying to keep close to him (on the right of the picture) has been forced to move across his own defence,

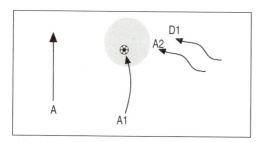

Fig 146   Passing into space.

Fig 147   The overlapping run.

Fig 148   The cross-over run.

and as a result has collided with one of his own co-defenders, who was also concerned with marking his opponent. Both defenders have been blocked by this cross-field tactical run. The player in possession has kept the ball on his outside, away from defenders. It is now picked up by his working partner (on the left of the picture). Swapping possession of the ball in this way at an appropriate moment leaves the incoming attacking player enough time and space to put himself into a goal-scoring position.

THE CHANGES IN THE LAW

The first sign of change within the game came with the outlawing of the back pass to the goalkeeper. Some people inside the game considered the change was like using a sledgehammer to crack a nut. However, I was quietly confident it this was the first meaningful change in the law for some time, and represented the step in the right direction.

Prior to this change in the law, the pass back to the keeper was used to control play. This tactic became one of the

game's dominating features, taking away the strikers' opportunities to play a more effective role. Clearly, if the situation had been left unchallenged, the game would have become a second-rate sporting event.

Thankfully this change in the law, reinforced by further changes to the offside rules, has transformed the game to one of the most exciting club sports in the world, by laying new emphasis on attacking play. Attacking play requires skill, skill equals entertainment, and entertainment equals revenue. The future of the game lies in new play systems that adhere to the new laws, and these by implication must have a strong attacking element.

The New Offside Law and the Flat Back Four
(Figs 149 & 150)
The new offside law still applies only in the opponents' half of the field. Fig 149 shows the players' attacking positions, now possible under the new law. The exception is the position of attacking player A11, who is technically in an offside position. However, in this example striker A7's goal stands because player A11 is not interfering with play. This interpretation of the spirit of the law is left in the hands of the referee.

Fig 150 shows the weak points of the flat back four defensive unit, brought about as a direct result of the changes to the offside law. Let us analyse the picture more closely. The ball is played into the practice by the player nearest the centre circle, wearing a dark strip, and wings its way towards the two dark-strip strikers on the left side of the picture. The striker

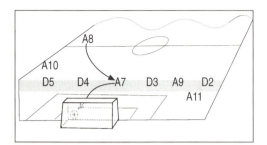

Fig149   The spirit of the law.

Fig 150   The flat back four.

nearest to the edge of the penalty area has timed his run correctly and has managed to be in line with one defender on his far left, a position which makes him on side.

The four light-strip defenders are positioned according to their own defensive responsibilities on the field of play. This defence was not manipulated in any way for the photograph, and the defending players did not receive any specific instructions. Their reaction to the play is natural, and according to what they thought was the right thing to do at the time. The numbers attacking this back four line-up – two strikers supported by two midfielders – are not unusual, nor is this practice picture

unrealistic, because this play scenario can now often happen during play. From a coaching point of view, the same set-up can be used for almost any team attacking coaching topic.

In order to break down any defensive system, the first priority is to understand what is going on in the main defensive unit. The defensive system in Fig 150 is clearly split up into three separate sections, which should work together – the two central defenders concerned with central defensive areas, and the right back and left back, who are left isolated by the close positioning of the two central defenders.

This type of defence creates defending problems. When the two central defenders keep to this formation, they open up holes to either side of their position. This leaves the two full backs to cope with opponents on their own without cover, resulting in a lack of depth to the front and back of the defensive unit. The attacking side can therefore easily take advantage of such defensive positions.

In the past, you could not line yourself up alongside the last defender because to be on side, the attacking player was required to have two opposing defenders between himself and goal. Now the law allows the attacking team/player to stand in line with the last defender, and still be in an on-side position. This redefinition of the offside law has created today's attacking possibilities. Look at Fig 149 and see the advantage the attacking players have in taking up position alongside the defenders. Compare this with Fig 150, where the attacking dark-strip players have managed to cut inside the full backs on the right and left of the picture. These attacking positions have left the full backs stranded on the wrong side of their opponents/the goal. The fact that the strikers can position themselves inside and alongside defenders in this way means that it is now possible for them to be first to the ball, especially when it is played into holes as is attempted by this long ball pass shown.

THE APPLICATION OF SKILLS

The arena for the application of the skills taught in this chapter is the full game part of your training session, but the acquisition of these skills can be worked on throughout this book, using the various cone formats. The modern player needs to be skilled in all aspects of play: the striker who is knowledge-able in defensive responsibilities will also learn how to attack against defensive positions, and will in time learn the weak points of any defence. Players also need to know the passing options and how to play the long and short passing combinations.

In playing against any shape, players need to learn how to construct the shape in order to understand how the passing options work. If you have difficulty in understanding this topic, the best solution is to work with such routines as the 'keeping shape format'; the positioning of the players in this exercise will help you to work out how and where to pass the ball against defensive positions. The passing can be restricted to a short and long passing option, or if you are advanced, you may be able to play to a much higher number of passing combinations.

13 BALL CONTROL AND POSSESSION

BALL CONTROL SKILLS

In addition to knowing how to take opponents on in certain game situations, there are times when the player needs to display special skills in order to retain possession of the ball. These skills have an in-built element of surprise and disguise, especially when performed to high standards. Modern attacking play is based on such skills.

The Foot on the Ball Drag Back
(Figs 151–153)

This movement changes the direction of the run. The ideal way to perform this turn is to make sure that the ball is kept well away from the opponent. The right foot is the forward foot and is placed to the right of the ball. The next stride positions the left heel firmly on top of the ball, a position giving plenty of 'foot base' room to roll back the ball one whole turn. It can then be transferred from the base of the foot to the instep, and push-turned into a forward direction in one movement. Fig 153 shows the end result – the left foot has played the ball forwards and the player is now well on his way. He should be able to perform this move equally well with both feet.

The Heel Turn
(Figs 154–156)

The starting position for this move is as shown in Fig 154. The player moves in

Fig 151   Place the right foot to the side of the ball...

Fig 152   ...put the left foot on the top, drag back and turn...

Fig 153   ...and follow through with the ball.

*Fig 154   Run through with
the right foot past the ball...*

*Fig 155   ... the left foot
heels the ball backwards.
Twist and turn...*

*Fig 156   ...and follow
through.*

front of the ball with his right leg, and while his upper body starts turning to the right he flicks the ball with his left heel, so it moves backwards and to his right. The turn is completed when the player has turned and picked up the ball in his stride.

What is vital to remember is that on completing this movement, the next stride, which takes the ball forwards, also needs to accelerate the body away quickly from this turn position. This change of pace helps the player to get away from his opponent. These movements are closely related to the checking out sequence.

The Teaser
(Figs 157–159)

There are times when the opponent is not that impressed with the player's skill movements. When this happens, there are ways of creating uncertainty in the opponent's mind, as shown in this next skill routine which is designed to play the ball in a teasing way. Although the ball does not go anywhere in particular on this move, perhaps on the next move it will – but the opponent may make the mistake of going for *this* ball. When he 'bites', he may be surprised to find that the attacking player has introduced a new technique at that moment, leaving him – the opponent – swiping at fresh air.

The player starts the technique by running in a forward direction. The tease comes in when he drags his foot across the top of the ball (Fig 158), then leaving it to follow his run; when he turns, the ball is in a welcoming position, still close enough for him to get to, yet far enough away to give him the chance to look up and assess the situation, his body being ready poised for the next bit of action.

Fig 157   Run forwards...

Fig 158   ...drag foot across the top of the ball...

Fig 159   ...look up.

The Flick Backwards
(Figs 160–163)

I include this skill in the working examples because all players should have the right to use their imagination. That is what attacking skills are about. This particular skill requires good foot co-ordination – *see* Figs 161 and 162.

The feet come astride to the ball, then the right foot presses the ball against the left foot. This enables the left foot to roll the ball up and onto the back heel of the right foot. Once the ball is in place the right foot flicks it into the air.

Fig 160   Straddle the ball ...

Fig 161   ...push onto the left foot ...

This technique can also be used to start off keep-ups, as shown in Fig 163, where the player must endeavour to keep the ball in the air as long as possible. Every practice exercise comes in handy in developing foot co-ordination.

PASSING TECHNIQUES

The shape of the foot is ideal for ball skills, although the actual skill of

Fig 162   ...flick up...

Fig 163   ...keep up.

striking the ball depends on a number of factors – the balance of the player, and the position of the foot, head and arms are all crucial to the successful outcome of any skill used. These factors will be worked on in the following passing and ball-skill techniques, which are the bread and butter of passing.

Striking with the Laces
(Figs 164 & 165)

The first pass concentrates on striking the ball with the laces part of the boot, although the starting position in Fig 164 is used for many techniques. The picture sequence does not show the actual impact with the ball because it is more important to study the follow-through foot position, and the position of the head and the leading hand, which balance the body in relation to the force of the kick.

You can see what must have occurred by looking at the position of the player. Note that the toes point towards the intended target. On impact with the ball, the toes must have been pointing to the ground, and the ball struck with the laces part of the boot. Moreover the position of the ball supports this theory: it must have been struck mid-centre on because there is no lift or deviation from the straight line. Compare this body follow-through position to that in Fig 168.

Striking with the Outside of the Foot
(Fig 166)

When the ball is played with the outside of the foot, it ends up to the side of the body. The body in this position is weakened by the force required to propel the ball forward, which pushes the body away from the ball. To counter this effect, you must lean towards the ball, as shown in Fig 164.

The Push Pass Technique
(Figs 167 & 168)

This is probably the most comfortable passing technique from the point of

Fig 164   Prepare...

Fig 165   ...strike.

Fig 166   Pass with the outside of the foot.

151

Fig 167   Using the inside instep...

Fig 168   Pass off the laces.

view of weight/impact resistance and the position of the body in relation to the ball. The body position, especially the head, tends to be over the ball.

However, the accuracy of the pass depends on the correct position of the foot on impact. If this is not adhered to, the ball could end up heading away from its intended target. Any deviation from the full sideways on foot position will impart spin on the ball; unintended or intended spin comes from the foot being turned to varying degrees. In general terms the spin comes from the front part of the foot, which is the first part to make contact with the side of the ball. Fig 168 shows the perfect follow-through and head position (over the ball).

Height of Flight

To make the ball fly through the air, revert back to the 'striking with the laces' technique. The height of the flight of the ball depends on how much of the foot goes underneath the ball – the more foot underneath, the higher the ball will go (see Figs 37 and 38). Leaning the body backwards and sideways away from the ball also helps you to lift the ball high into the air. Varying the body movement helps your feet to create a range of different passes.

LINKING INDIVIDUAL AND TEAM SKILLS

The circle training routines described here can become the link between individual training and competitive team environments, and they can be used for many of the skills discussed in these chapters. The circle format is flexible in that it can accommodate a variable number of players, and the skill being practised can be changed instantly. The work can concentrate on the individual, but it can also be changed to a more competitive game situation by introducing an opponent.

Individual Skills Practice
(Fig 169)

Fig 169 shows a number of players positioned in a circle round a central player, to whom they will serve the ball. Most but not all of the players in the circle have a ball; it is up to the coach to determine the precise distribution.

In this example the player has received the ball from one of the outside players and has controlled it with his chest. Once he has performed a set task such as this, he returns the ball to he circle by passing it to another player who has not got a ball. The middle player then has to turn and face someone else in possession of the ball to continue the practice. He receives the ball and repeats the skill practice, continuing until the coach says otherwise. Once again, skills such as

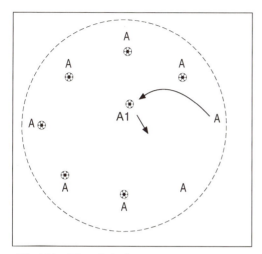

Fig 169   The circle format.

looking up to signal 'I want the ball' come into play – *see* Vision, Chapter 12.

Practice with a Defender
(Fig 170)
This exercise introduces a defending player into the circle. Attacking player A1 receives the ball from a co-partner in the circle, and with them, keeps possession away from the oncoming defender (D1). If the latter wins possession, as a reward he can take a rest by becoming a passing player in the circle and someone else (nominated by the coach) takes over his defending role. Alternatively, a passing player from the circle who makes a mistake in passing the ball to the player in the middle can become the defending player as a penalty. The coach can also simply nominate players for both roles as he sees fit.

The first touch on the ball by player A1 is vital, because if it is correctly played away from the defender, it helps the player to retain possession during play. Once A1 has possession of the ball,

the nature of the practice changes; he now has to introduce movement (on the ball and off the ball) to his work. The players in possession of the ball have to work very hard in order to keep the ball from defender D1.

The size of the circle can be reduced, as shown by the inner circle in the diagram: this has the effect of reducing time on the ball, which in turn puts pressure on the player in possession to work more quickly.

A Game-Like Format
(Fig 171)
Circle 3 shows the possibilities of introducing a game-like element into the circle routines. Again the players keep possession of the ball through passing, but this time further skills come into play. The circle needs to be expanded to cope with a two-on-two situation. Attacking players A1 and A2 keep

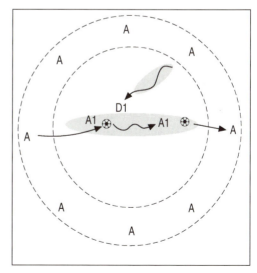

Fig 170   To put more pressure on A1 make a smaller circle.

153

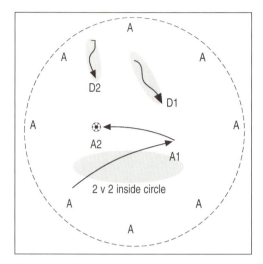

Fig 171   The possession circle.

possession of the ball by passing to each other with assistance from the players in the circle. If the defenders (players D1 and D2) win possession of the ball, the same rules apply as described for the exercise above.

Checking Out

Checking out is a special skill used to open up a receiving pass possibility, or to get away from your marker on corners, free kicks, throw-ins and so on. It can be performed to virtually any direction. The idea is to bluff your opponent into thinking that you are going one way (by moving off in that direction), then suddenly interrupting your run, and moving off at speed in a completely different direction. This hopefully leaves your marker wrong-footed, and still moving in the original direction; by the time he readjusts his position in relation to you, you will have been free of him long enough to interact with your own players.

This training routine simulates checking-out movements in man-to-man marking situations. The work involves checking out from your opponent, changing the pace of your run, coming short to the ball, receiving the ball and one-touch return passing play.

How It Works (Fig 172)

Set up the practice area as shown. The starting position of practising player A1 is between zone positions A and B. In the diagram, A1 starts by approaching one of the check-out zones B from the central starting position. When he enters the zone he checks out towards cone position 2. It is vital that player A1 works on changing his pace at the checking out moment.

This practice also concentrates on achieving the correct foot and body movement technique. On reaching cone 2, the body should be kept low and sideways on; the player does not turn around at the checking-out points. (The correct running angles and turns are described in The Skills of Turning in Chapter 3.)

When A1 checks out from cone 2 he automatically faces coach/service 2. He then looks up – the signal to receive the ball – and the coach plays the ball early to his feet. A1 knocks the ball back with one touch to the coach. Once this move has been completed, the player changes his speed from fast to almost walking pace, taking his time to walk across from zone B to zone A. When entering zone A he suddenly changes his pace again, checking out towards cone 1 this time. A1's body position is sideways on at each turning point; he uses the foot nearest to the cone to push himself

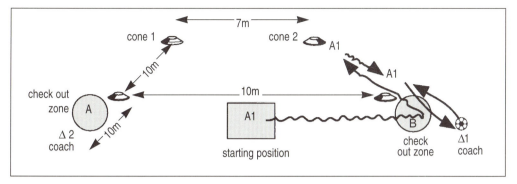

Fig 172   Checking out.

away, back in the direction of the coach. He again looks up to receive the ball, passes it back with one touch, and begins the practice again.

Player A1 continues his work in this way to a set number of repetitions, say ten check-out movements. Alternatively the practice could be set to last 20 minutes.

WINNING POSSESSION

The Fifty-Fifty Ball

The fifty-fifty ball belongs to no one – it has to be won, and the quickest player to the ball wins. Winning possession of the ball in these circumstances can be dangerous, however, as it is very easy to lose it again straightaway; so you must learn to play the ball to the side, away from the oncoming opponent. The technique required to pick the ball up in this situation is the 'dink sideways touch', and you may even have to skip over the opponent's foot if you get that close to the competition.

Learning to retain possession of a fifty-fifty ball when the opponent is coming straight at you, then to control it away from the opponent, sending him the wrong way, will give you skills worth having. This training routine not only simulates game conditions, it has other benefits for the working players: they usually find it very enjoyable because it offers a safe way to practise winning possession of the fifty-fifty ball. The coach works with the players to teach them the correct movements and reactions to keep possession of the ball. This set-up allows the players to practise picking up the ball in full flow in a realistic game situation.

How It Works (Fig 173)

The actual size of the practice area is only 10m long by 10m wide. This square area is marked out with cones placed 2m apart, which also act as pace guidelines for the players. There are two practising players at any one time, starting from the positions shown, facing each other across the square. If you find that one player reaches the ball (placed in the centre of the square) so much before the other that no sensible practice can result, reposition the slower player 2m (one cone length) closer in; adjusting the speed of the players in this way will ensure that the timing of

155

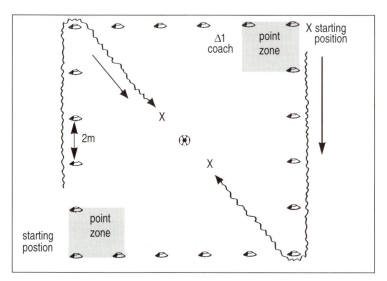

Fig 173   The fifty-fifty ball tackling format.

their arrival at the ball will be perfect for this practice.

The run of each player (on a given signal by the coach) is up one side of the square, rounding the last cone in the 10m line, and in towards the ball in the middle. The first man to the ball has to play it at an angle away from the other player and try to reach the nearest (in relation to his first touch of the ball) point scoring zone. Once he has made his touch on the ball, the other player is not allowed to compete for the ball any more.

Both players work on their pick-up touch in a competitive environment. Being first to the ball enables the player to score a point without further competition, which acts as an added incentive. The first player to ten (pick-up of the ball) points wins.

An Alternative Version

When the player picks the ball up with his first touch and plays the ball to, for example, his left, he cannot score by playing the ball to the point zone nearest to his first touch (on his left in this instance); he can only score if he manages to get the ball across to the opposite point zone. In this case the other player (who automatically becomes the defender) is allowed to compete for the ball until it reaches safety.

If the attacking player successfully reaches the opposite point zone, he receives double points because of the added difficulty of having to compete his way across to that scoring zone. Points can only be scored on a successful pick-up of the ball; if the defending player wins possession of the ball, the practice is simply restarted. Again, the first player to ten points wins.

FURTHER ATTACKING SKILLS

New attacking concepts are brought into being by appropriate training exercises as, for example, the one illustrated in Fig 209, which shows the difference between attacking and defensive thinking. Simplistically, the attacking shapes of the modern game are represented by the diamond, although the training routines in this book show exercises that in fact do not conform to the straight lines of this or any type of defence.

The attacking aspect of the game will involve the majority of players, who will support the man in possession of the ball from behind-the-ball positions. In fact, the most effective attacking methods will reflect on the need to drop off defenders, picking up play with the ball from deep positions, with the shape moving forwards in support of the ball. This means that the attack can develop at speed from depth, rather than from static positions.

In future players will need to be skilful on the ball and attacking minded – see the 1, 1, 4, 4, 1 shape discussed in Chapter 9 and below. This system is ideal for attacking concepts, and is explored in the following training formats. These work on skills which enable the team to attack opponents from deep positions, as the combined skills of the individual players will enable the players to work the ball from the back to the front of the shape. Every player should practise using these routines in order to acquire the necessary skills, not only to work the shape, but to keep the shape in support of the player in possession of the ball.

A NEW APPROACH TO TRAINING

Conventional training exercises do not cater for the development of ball control skills. This has never been accepted or understood by players or coaches. The easy option for all concerned is to allow the players to dictate the format of training, but when this happens most sessions end up with the players playing small-sided games, which are in fact nothing short of a waste of time. When young players are brought up in a small-sided game environment they lose the ability and the will to practise.

Small-sided games represent a short movement environment where the ability to acquire skills is greatly reduced, and it is vital to the future of the game that this disadvantage is understood. Conventional exercise formats may simulate fragments of the real game, but in most cases they do not provide the right environment to acquire skills and are merely forums for skills already learnt. In other words, the players use their existing capabilities to take part in a given task, rather than to help develop new skills in an effort to widen their playing repertoire.

157

Enclosed working environments such as indoor gymnasiums produce similar effects to five-a-side games. Such conditions restrict the development of skills because of the close proximity of the opponents, which always forces the player in possession to work quickly to get rid of the ball. When the development of skills is further restricted by conditioning the player always to play the ball on his first or second touch, the player's touch options are reduced to a minimum. As explained before, there are many skills involved in the game of soccer, and many of the touch play options required go far beyond the two-touch formats imposed by many who wrongly believe that these develop the player's skills.

DEALING WITH FATIGUE

One of the most important considerations in training is the onset of fatigue in the working player. The exercises are therefore designed to deal with such problems. Each working session is conducted in such a way that the player has plenty of opportunities to work on the skills required, but because the work is divided into sets of repetitions the player has time in between sets to recover his physical strength. His welfare can be further safeguarded by rotating the practising players.

The whole point of the exercises is to practise all the skill elements that make up a particular coaching objective, and the way each one is arranged makes it possible to practise one or more parts of a particular skill as required. The skill in question can be broken down into minute details, worked on in isolation, then reincorpo-rated in the main theme of the exercise.

Soccer training has two major requirements: the player needs to work on his fitness and on skills, and these exercises cater for both requirements. There are times when the fitness aspects are not clearly visible during practice, as the emphasis on skills seems to preclude fitness training. However, closer examination of the exercises will reveal that this initial assessment can be misleading. For example, there are different running skills in soccer play, and where some of the exercises require short, sharp runs and movements (anaerobic exercise) which result in oxygen debt, promoting the process of quick heart recovery rates, others impose longer running distances where the player has the opportunity to take in lots of oxygen. This type of running (aerobic) promotes strength, endurance and stamina, which again are valuable for soccer in a different way; for example there are important moments in play when the player needs to call on his strength and stamina in order to perform the requisite skills in a given task – as is the case in the following exercise.

TOUCH PLAY SKILLS

The list below includes all the touch play skills a player should have to maximize his options on the field of play:

1. The first touch play option.
2. The control touch (includes a wide range of options).
3. The set-up touch (includes a wide range of possibilities).
4. The passing touch (includes a wide range of skills in passing possibilities).

5. The forward movement touch.
6. The change of direction touch (includes a wider range of skills).
7. The reverse direction touch.
8. The finishing touch (includes a wide range of options).

This list gives some idea of the wide range of skills players need to master, and it is why the cone formats in this chapter are so important to the future of the game. They provide an environment where players can progress beyond the two-touch skills and the conditioned games built round them. They need to have the chance to practise and learn other skill touches of the ball, and to use five, six, seven, in fact any number of skills combinations if they are to acquire the skills required for success in the modern game.

Any player who is restricted to the two-touch formats may be useful in running off the ball, catering to the running and passing game, but he will be scared to use the ball when it matters most. Yet the strength and battling characteristics do not disappear simply because the player becomes more skilful on the ball; on the contrary, combine these characteristics with an improvement in his skills repertoire and you have a formidable player who would easily grace any company in the world of soccer.

THE FOUR-CONE FORMATS
There are serious reasons for using the cone exercises. The most important of these is the fact that the player receives the ball many times in a short space of time and has to deal with it in a very specific way when he does receive it.

These exercise formats therefore give him the opportunity to practise his touch play in a very relevant way for soccer because he has to play the ball to a designated length and direction.

To practise any skill, the player needs to repeat the movements many times in order to establish that skill for his playing repertoire. The proper way to practise his skills is to work on realistic movements. The four-cone format explained below combines the practice of several base skills by simulating real playing movements.

If you look closely at Fig 174, you will see that there are three separate skill areas in play. The shaded area depicts where the first touch will be worked on, where the player works on getting the ball away to a specific direction. This working simulation caters for moments during play when your first touch of the ball takes it away from a defender.

Cones 5 and 6 are deliberately angled to the back of the player because turning with the ball must include a change of angle in avoiding opponents. There are different ways of turning with the ball, some of which have already been demonstrated in other exercises. The skill of your first touch will decide whether or not you retain possession of the ball. The first touch has to be positive, and to the correct distance. There is nothing worse than to bring the ball under control only to see your opponent take it away from under your nose, which is what happens when the first touch is not good enough.

The four cones in the foreground are there to simulate forward directional movements. They are not numbered

159

because the choice of dribbling skills and the working directions around or through these cones will at this stage of training be up to the player. Use the cones to make positive changes of direction, making sure that when you implement your skills you are using the outside of your boot or the inside/instep. The first touch should be at least 1m in length, and sideways on in relation to the cone/s. The player must be in control of the ball. Do not let the ball touch any of the cones during your angled touch play attempts: if it does, this is equivalent to playing too close to opponents' feet.

Work to realistic end products; in this example player A1 has completed his skills routine by playing the ball to the coach. Instructions on using this format as a skills test are given below.

Touch Skills Test
(Fig 174)
The cone working environment can also be used for assessing the player's ball technique/skills. If the player lacks in skills he will not be able to perform the basic touch play requirements. A test is then useful because technical faults will show up in his movements.

The four-cone format shown in Fig 174 is very good at detecting such faults. If, for example, the player cannot kick with his left foot, he will reveal this fault by always playing the ball with his right foot even when clearly the ball was nicely set up to be played by his left foot. The working sequence can begin from any direction determined by the coach, and this in itself can force the player to use his so-called bad leg. The sequence of work set by the

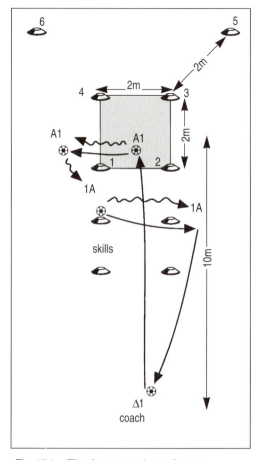

Fig 174   The four-cone base format.

coach ensures that the player has many opportunities to demonstrate and to acquire different skills.

Player A1 is positioned in the centre of the square marked out by cones 1 to 4. Other cones are specially placed in front and behind this square, as explained above. The distance between each cone is 2m. The numbered cones are specifically referred to by number in the exercise: when the coach shouts out a number on playing the ball to A1, A1 knows his first touch must send the ball in to that cone, and he must carry out the appropriate skill as described below.

The cone position explanations are an outline of the working objectives, and in addition the coach may emphasize other skill requirements – for example tackling, when a defending player could be positioned to take on the working player, as well as the working cones 1 to 6. This opponent can also come into play instead of the unnumbered forward cone placement/s.

Cone 1

The player uses the inside/instep part of his left foot to play the ball to his left, playing the ball and striding off in the same direction in one movement. With his next move he changes angle to approach the nearest (unnumbered) front cone, which represents an opposing player; the arrow on the diagram shows the angle of approach for this attacking move. He takes up the ball with his right instep, striding off towards the cone.

On reaching the cone he again drops his shoulder and changes his direction of run, this time turning into the inside of this front four-cone formation. He now uses the outside of his left foot to effect yet another change in direction before playing the ball back to the coach. He then jogs back to the starting position, inside the numbered cone square.

Cone 2

When cone 2 is specified, the first touch should be a dink touch, the ball sent flying over the cone with the top of the foot. The player speeds off after it, and gets it under control as quickly as poss-

ible. He then changes direction, practising going in and out of the cone placements, using skills such as turning with the outside and with the inside of the foot, manipulating the ball to change direction, and changing the pace of his work. When this sequence has been completed he plays the short pass to the coach, then jogs back to the starting position.

Cones 3 and 4

The skill sequences at cones 1 and 2 are alike in that the player moves forwards with the ball each time; cones 3 and 4, on the other hand, represent moments during the game when the ball arrives at the player's feet and he needs to turn with it, being unable to play it the way he is facing. It is surprising how often a player receives the ball with his back to his intended attacking direction.

Cones 3 and 4 are positioned to allow the player to practise the skills of taking the ball with the instep and controlling it on the turn. The first body movement turns the body sideways on to the direction of the player's run. The foot closest to the intended run direction controls the pass from the coach with the instep, cushioning the ball; then the other foot comes into play, picking the ball up on the turn and taking it and the player in the intended direction (towards cone 5 or 6).

Practising Touch Skills
(Fig 175)

The special set-up of the cones in the exercises is designed to give the player the right type of practice options so that he can improve his skills on the ball. The exercises adhere to the require-

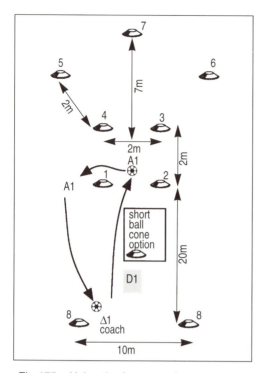

Fig 175 Using the four-cone format to practise touch skills.

ments of the modern game, and the cone positions simulate the first touch directions, followed by other relevant touches of the ball. The positions of the cones will teach the player to move his body in a co-ordinated and balanced way (the most important single factor in ball control) and to work with the ball to specific lengths of touch. They will also allow him plenty of practice at changing his direction of play.

This first touch distance and direction is crucial to the skills of retaining possession of the ball.

Fig 175 is the starting practice formation, thereafter the cones can be positioned differently to simulate other play options. For example, the routine

described next (Fig 176) has four stages, including one where the player deals with taking on an opponent, and finishing with a shot on target.

Set up the cones as shown in Fig 175. As in the previous exercise/test, the player starts in the middle of the four cones numbered 1 to 4, facing the coach. The coach shouts a number as he passes the ball, and A1 passes the ball to the designated cone and carries out one of the following skills routines.

Cone 1

The ball is played with the inside/instep of the left foot across the player's body position. The ball travels close to cone 1 in a sideways-on direction. The player quickly follows the ball, controls it, then plays it back to the coach with his second and third touches of the ball.

Cone 2

The player dinks the ball over the top of cone 2; it is played with the inside of the right foot, getting the foot under the ball and using just the right amount of pace/touch so that it lands behind cone 2. The player dinks and moves in that direction at the same time. He controls the ball, then plays it back to the coach.

Cone 3

The ball is played with the outside of the left foot towards cone 3. The player gets an extra touch on it, turns, controls the ball, turns again, alters its angle in relation to himself, sets it up to strike it with the top of his foot, and plays it back to the coach.

Cone 4

The player plays the ball with the

inside of his left foot towards cone 4, at the same time moving off in that direction. He picks it up with the outside of his right foot, changing the angle of run to the right, towards cone 5. He controls the ball by performing a turning skill, ending up facing the coach; he now knocks it long to the coach. Again it is struck with the laces part of the boot, getting the foot slightly underneath with a good follow-through onto target.

Cone 5

The first touch of the ball to cone 5 is strong and positive and should land at least halfway between cones 4 and 5. The player plays the ball with the instep of his left foot, turning and going after it at the same time (touch and move), accelerating as he catches up with it. With his next touch he plays the ball away at a different angle using the outside of his left foot. He controls it, turns with it using a turning skill of his own choice, and plays it low along the ground with his next touch to the coach's feet. To do this he uses the laces part of the boot; the non-kicking foot is planted firmly alongside the ball, and the head is down on impact.

Cone 6

The ball is played with the instep of the right foot, the player controlling it as he strides off to cone 6. He now works at changing angles before playing a long pass back to the coach – performing skills on the ball, playing the ball with the outside of the foot, the inside of the foot, turning and so on.

Cone 7

The player receives the ball with his back to cone 7. He takes it up on his right foot, then drags the foot back, allowing the ball's own pace to bring it through and under his body. He now turns his body almost on the spot. This technique and body movement allow him to pick the ball up with the other foot as he turns. Now he sprints with the ball to cone 7 where he will perform a turning skill before playing the ball back to the coach with a lofted pass.

Come Short – Cones 8

The ball is played short to the player, who comes forwards and positions himself and the ball at an angle to the coach (defender). He works on dribbling skills, taking on the coach to dribble the ball through to the gate position marked by cones 8.

The above reference points are the starting requirements of this exercise. In addition, each player has the freedom to demonstrate other skills while carrying out any of the numbered routines. However, his touch and movement must be realistic, and there are times when too many touches of the ball are unrealistic; for example, when turning with the ball and when it is nicely set up for a pass, it would be foolish to play one more touch: if the ball is in the right place, strike it to the intended target.

Having said that, it is vital to understand that in order to develop the player's skills on the ball, you must in general allow him to take as many touches as he wishes, even if in your opinion this is somewhat unrealistic. Only limit the number of touches in clear-cut cases. The value to the player of this working format cannot be overstated. Always make sure that the player works the ball in and out of the cones to a good length of touch each time.

Taking up the Pass
(Fig 176)

In this coaching topic the player uses the basic four-cone format to work out ways of receiving the ball, then moves on to implement relevant skills in game situations. This time the cones are placed ahead of his actual starting position, because they now represent the movements required to deal with the first challenger. The cone positions need to be avoided by using appropriate touch skills with the instep of the foot to change the angle of approach.

The player must make sure that when inside the cone formation, he plays the ball out at an angle. Alternatively, the way the touch work is carried out through the cones can be left up to the player, but stipulate that he must vary the angles and direction of his work on the ball.

Remember to use the different touches on the ball: the first touch implements a change of angle, which should take the player away from any immediate opponent; the second touch changes direction, usually taking the player into forward positions; the third touch can simply be used to play the ball forwards.

This exercise has everything to do with what happens after using such skills in play. It deals with picking up the ball from a pass in different ways, and shows how your own body can be of great help in retaining possession of the ball. (Further ways of dealing with defenders are explored in the screening

techniques exercise, Fig 178). It is obviously important to work out ways of dealing with different 'receiving the ball' situations during play. This four-cone format begins by allowing the player to work out ways of receiving the ball without interference.

The cones are arranged as shown. The coach acts as left back and has the ball close to the halfway line. Ahead of him, to his left, is his midfield team player, A1. The left back has seen him and wants to pass him the ball. In this exercise we concentrate on the kind of problems associated with this.

Note For younger players the distances and cone positions can be altered to suit the coaching requirements for different age groups.

Cone 1 – Receiving the Pass

How often have you seen the ball strike

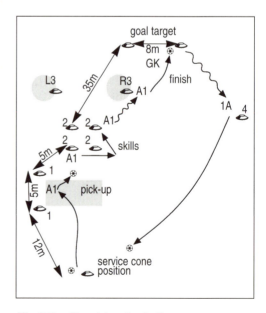

Fig 176   Receiving the ball.

164

the player's back or his feet when it should have been neatly played for him to collect? When this happens, both players are at fault – the receiving player because of his incorrect body position (usually with his back turned to the ball at an inappropriate moment), the passing player because he did not read the situation correctly, and so played the ball at the wrong time.

In the first part of this practice, player A1 works on receiving and dealing with the ball correctly. This section of the practice fosters a greater awareness of body language: the receiving player should never turn his back on the player in possession of the ball, and the player in possession should only pass the ball if he knows that the target player is ready to receive it.

The receiving player should be aware of where he is on the field of play in relation to his opponents. If there are no opponents in his vicinity he should position himself sideways on in relation to the player in possession, because it allows him to keep an eye on the ball while observing what is happening ahead of his position. This body position also allows the player to receive the ball with his back foot, which puts him in a position to sprint off with the ball.

The technique of receiving the ball is as follows. The ball is played to the inside of the receiving player, and he cushions it with the instep of his back foot (in relation to the passing player). Once he has taken the pace off the ball in this way, he uses his other foot (the right foot in this case) to pick it up in his stride, again using the instep. The body turns on this leg in action, and the player moves off with the ball to cone 2.

Cones 2 and 3 – Changing the Angle

At cones 2 the player performs a sequence of dribbling skills going through the cones. The object here is to move the ball out of the straight line of run and to practise positive touches in changing direction.

The player uses his skills to change direction towards either cone L3 or R3. These represent the left- and right-foot approach angle and finish – the left cone represents the player going down the line, while the right cone represents the inside route to goal. Striking the ball from alongside cone L3 towards the goalkeeper represents a left-foot finish, and from cone R3 a right-foot finish.

Cone 4 – Target Practice

Once the player has accomplished all the stages of the working format, he receives the ball back from the goalkeeper and takes it to cone 4. Here he works on the skills of striking the ball.

The first skill option is striking the ball with the laces part of the boot. This should result in a low shot to the coach, with the player following through on target with his kicking foot. Some players get into the habit of cutting across the ball, and this section of the exercise can help to counter this problem simply because it practises the correct follow-through technique on striking the ball. The correction process is further helped by the player having to nominate the type of shot he is about to play.

The second option is to get the foot under the ball to make it fly high. The player should play the two types of shot alternately. After the shot is played the player returns to cone 1 and the practice begins again.

Scoring

There are four skill practice areas in this exercise, and each area can be assessed separately, giving marks for effort and excellence. There are two ways of marking points: one is to give a mark out of a total of forty points, based on an overall assessment of the work. Alternatively, you can mark each area separately out of a possible ten points per section. When the player works really well on a skill station, he can hit a perfect ten; otherwise he will be marked down accordingly, for example for bad touches or poor ball control. The practice should last 40 minutes.

THE L AND M FORMAT

This two-part exercise is for the player to practise dealing with second and third challengers for the ball: the attacking player A1 receives the ball with his back to the defender/cone positions 3 and 4, and the exercise works on the skills of turning and the movements involved in dealing with the second challenger. The positions of the defenders are 'zone-orientated' and not based on man-to-man marking.

How It Works
(Fig 177)

Set up the cones as shown. Cone positions L and M are very important to this working scenario. When a player receives the ball with his back to play, and turns to take on a defender or to go into a forward run position, he could encounter an immediate second challenge for the ball. Moreover in tight

game situations opponents can come at you fast and furious. The secondary cone positions of L and M simulate the need for evasive actions, allowing the player to implement different touch skills on the ball.

Phase 1

The scenario begins with player A1 having to deal with an opponent who has taken up a goal-side position, represented by the first set of cones numbered 1 to 4. In this first part of the exercise player A1 works on his first touch technique, playing the ball to the side of the cone placements, well away from cones 3 and 4. In the diagram A1 has received the ball from the coach and has started his sequence of movements by playing the ball with his right instep to the left of cone 2.

Phase 2

The player practises changing angle and direction through the cones in either the L or the M formation to simulate taking on a second challenger. When it comes to finishing the exercise, there are a great many options open to the coach; for example, instead of having A1 pass the ball to player A3 as is the case in this example, the coach can replace the short and long play passing options of players A3, 4 and 5 with a portable goal, in which case A1 will be asked to finish his sequence of skills on the ball by striking the ball on target. Taking on the keeper/defender can also be an option as an end product to this working format.

Kicking Technique

The player can work to very late

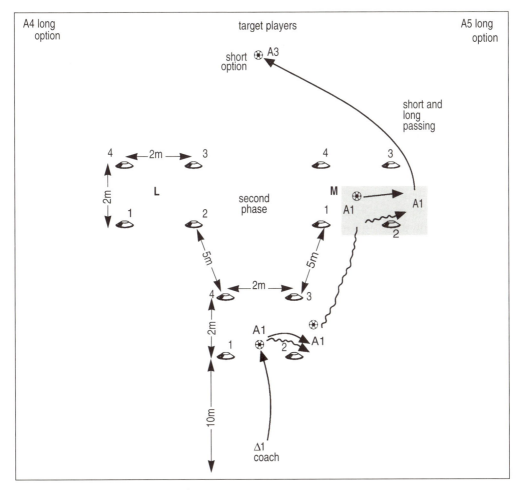

Fig 177   The L and M working format.

instructions, which puts him under pressure to deliver the right pass technique quickly. When the coach plays the ball to A1, he watches the player's movements on the ball; when he sees A1 coming up to cone positions L or M (depending on whether he has gone to the right or left on his first touch of the ball) he can command A1 to play the ball long or short. The short pass needs to go to feet, so the ball has to stay low, parallel to the ground, whereas the long ball will have to fly high.

The technique of kicking the ball high is as follows. The player needs to get his laces under the ball, and he needs to lean slightly away to the left or right of the ball (depending on which foot he is using), which will help him to send the ball into the air. The non-kicking foot comes alongside the ball, the head is down and the eyes are firmly on the ball; the kicking foot is firm on impact, and there is a slight follow-through.

SCREENING THE BALL

In this exercise the player is taught to deal with tight man-to-man marking problems. There are times when your opponent has marked you so tightly that you feel he has climbed all over you; when this happens use his body position to your advantage. Thus instead of trying to get away from him, get as close as you can to him to restrict his movement.

How It Works
(Fig 178)

Position two cones and the attacking players (A1 to A4) and defender (D1) as shown. A1 has his back to player D1. A1's left hand is held outstretched to the back and left side of the defender, with the body almost ready to turn sideways on him. When the players are in place the coach will play the ball to the side of A1.

A1 screens the ball by keeping as much of his body as he can between the ball and the defender. He works at repositioning his body into a half-turn position, so that he can turn the defender and clear the way for passing the ball to the strikers A2, A3 or A4, who start the practice positioned behind the defender.

The players can spend 20 minutes swapping roles to practise screening the ball in this way. To extend the exercise there are various options available.

Option 1 – Taking the Defender on
If the defending player D1 stays off player A1 rather than crowding him on

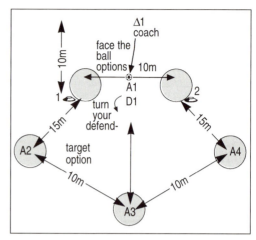

Fig 178   Target options: turn your defender.

A1's first touch of the ball, this will create the space A1 needs to turn and face D1. He is then also facing players, A2, A3 and A4, and can pass the ball to one of them.

Option 2 – The Return Pass
A1 can play the ball back to coach with his first touch. He would then have to move to either cone 1 or 2 to ensure that he does not turn away from the coach – remember you should not turn your back on the player in possession of the ball. This run creates an angle between A1 and the coach which opens up receiving/passing possibilities, and the coach can work together with A1 to create an opportunity for A1 to receive the ball and take on opponent D1.

Option 3 – Alternative Return Pass
If D1 follows A1 into a wide position his run will create a hole behind him, allowing the coach to play the ball direct to players A2, A3 or A4. These players then

join player A1 in keeping the ball with the attacking side, while D1 tries to win possession. The attacking players should try to keep possession of the ball for three consecutive passes, after which the exercise is restarted. The practice should last 25 minutes.

RUNNING, CROSSING AND FINISHING

This topic considers the different skills required when the player wins or receives possession of the ball. The exercise concentrates mainly on the situation where the attacking player is in possession of the ball just inside the opponents' half of the field and now has the opportunity to attack free space ahead of his position. Attacking this space includes the possibility of finishing his run with a shot on target. Another option is to cross the ball under pressure, for example if the attacking player is confronted by a defender. Both these situations are considered below.

How It Works
(Fig 179)
Arrange the cones as shown. Player A1 starts in the middle of the four central cones, where he receives the ball from the coach. The coach calls out a cone number (1, 2 or 3), and A1 carries out the appropriate pre-arranged skill sequence as described below.

In each training routine the cones actually represent opposing players, and therefore have to be avoided by the use of an appropriate skill. Some cone positions have clearly defined routines associated with them while others represent areas of improvisation; this is deliberate – the exercise is designed in

this way to achieve both conditioned and improvised aspects of training. This combination brings about the highest possible transfer of skills to the player.

Cone 1
On receiving the ball from the coach, A1 controls it with his right instep; he plays the ball to his left, moving off in the direction of his first touch. At this point he changes his pace to move as fast as he can, keeping the ball in close control on his right foot, to the left of cone 1.

On reaching cone 1 he turns with the ball, using his left foot to go round to the right of the cone so that he faces the coach. He then looks up at the coach, puts his head down again to look

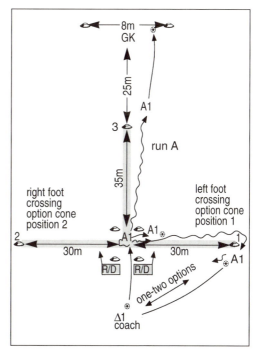

Fig 179   Running, crossing and finishing.

at the ball and knocks a long pass back to him. The coach controls the ball then plays it back to the player, who brings the ball under control and returns it to him again with an appropriate pass. The player now plays a passing sequence of one-twos with the coach all the way back to the vicinity of the four-cone starting position. At an appropriate point in the working sequence the coach allows the player time to reposition himself in the starting position.

Cone 2

The practice objectives at cone 2 are similar to those at cone 1, but it is possible to change the routine as required. For example, at cone 1 the player plays a long ball back to the coach. At cone 2 he could be made to wait till he looks up (immediately before making the pass) before he is told what pass to play. Other options could include the target (coach) being on the move and the ball having to find it accurately.

Additional pressure can also be applied by introducing a defending chasing player, who will come into play (from the R/D position) just as the player moves off with the ball towards cone 2. This chasing player must catch A1 before he reaches cone 2. If he fails, A1 is allowed to continue the practice as described. What happens if the chasing player catches A1 is left up to the coach. The players could work to ten set attempts, where the first to ten wins.

Cone 3

In this option the player works hard at getting away from his marker. A1 should stand almost sideways on to the coach before receiving the ball; when

the coach passes the ball to him it is vital that A1's first touch is with his back foot. This way, the first touch of the ball can be quickly supported by the other foot, which can put a touch on the ball just as the upper part of the body turns to go towards cone 3. This saves time on the turn and can give the player in possession a couple of metres advantage over the defending chasing player, who is now released from the R/D position.

A1 plays the ball with his right foot up to cone 3, and finishes with a shot on goal/target. The chasing defender can make it hard for A1 to finish well, and may even stop him from scoring. Once again the players can take turns at being the attacking player, and can work to set repetitions or to the first to score ten goals.

The distance of the chasing player can be adjusted as desired. Remember, the general aim of the defending player is to put pressure on the practising player without affecting his scoring opportunity, thus keeping to the working theme of practising ball skills and finishing during a running work sequence.

CLOSE BALL CONTROL AND DRIBBLING

In this training routine the player is introduced to a sequence of work that places his practised skills in a game-like setting. He works on his first touch, followed by close ball control, then takes on a defender to practise his dribbling skills.

There are several important reasons for bringing in this exercise at this stage of the book. For one thing, the player is introduced to a competitive environment where he can combine all sorts of skills in a practical way. Also, the way he moved with the ball from cones 1 to 3 in the previous exercise is completely different from the way he needs to move in a confrontational situation. The skills required to take on the defender in this exercise can only be practised by using the four-cone base formats shown previously (*see* Figs 174 and 175).

This training routine is a classic example of the differences between running with the ball and dribbling skills as it practises both. When the player simply runs with the ball, the ball can be played forward of his run or it can be kept in close control by touch playing the ball forwards with either foot. When it comes to dribbling, different body movements and touch skills are involved, and the player must use changes of pace and direction which are not used when simply running with the ball. If your training routines do not distinguish between running with the ball and ball control skills, then this will contribute to a lack of skills in the players.

There is one other very important point, namely no matter what you are practising, there should always be a starting point which will decide the first touch of the ball. The work in this exercise begins with the correct first touch by player A1, which *must* send the ball towards zone 1 for the exercise to work effectively. The first touch in this instance must also be accompanied by the player moving in the direction of his first touch.

How It Works
(Fig 180)
Set up the practice area as shown. The exercise is in two parts, with an against-the-clock element in each.

Stage 1
The skills to be practised in zones 1, 2 and 3 are pre-arranged by the coach, and the player must complete them all as quickly as possible, as he is competing against the clock. The coach starts the exercise by passing the ball to player A1, who controls the ball and sets off running to zone 1. On entering zone position 1 he performs a turning skill, changing his run direction. He now continues to run with the ball to zone 2, performs an appropriate skill and runs on to zone 3. He has now completed the first part of the practice.

When performing the above run, the practising player has to run with the ball against the clock. The total points of the three running zones is six. This total is doubled up on completion of the run if the run is completed within 3 seconds of the total points, that is within 9 seconds. The points are carried over to the second stage of the exercise. Most players should not take more than 8 seconds to complete the sequence. This is within 3 seconds of the total points (six) and so the player is entitled to double points (twelve). However, the number of seconds taken above 6 – in this case 2 – is deducted from the total of twelve, leaving ten in this example. This gives player A1 a total of 10 seconds to complete the next stage of the exercise – taking on opponent D1 and winning through to zone 4. Obviously, the more quickly the player completes

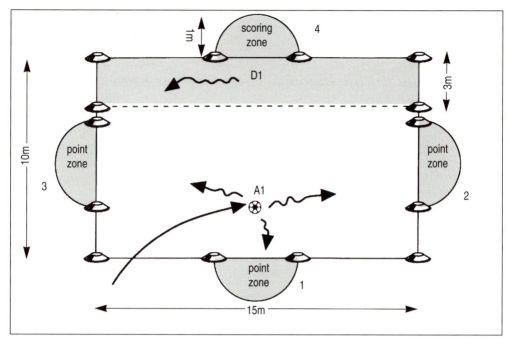

Fig 180   Ball control and dribbling – beat the clock.

the first half of the exercise, the more time he has bought for himself to complete the second, and harder part.

Stage 2

A1's objective in the second stage is to touch place the ball in zone 4 – this is the only way he can finish. The defender is not allowed to come out of the shaded area, and he must not take up a steady position in front of zone 4. His job is to try to knock the ball out of play, and if he succeeds, A1 has to start the second part of the exercise again. If the defender manages to hold up A1 so that he runs out of time, the attempt is void and A1 has to start all over again.

Each player receives ten point-scoring attempts. The difficulty of the exercise can be altered to suit different levels of play; for example, the base score can be increased from six to eight to allow the player more time in the second stage of the exercise, or the dribbling zone can be increased in depth from 3m to 6m.

Keeping Possession
(Fig 181)

In this exercise cones are positioned to mark out a central 'keep possession' zone. In this zone are two 'keep possession' players (A1 and A2) working against one defender (D1). Four other attacking players (A3, A4, A5 and A6) are positioned round the 'possession zone', each in a 2m-square box on each side; players A1 and A2 pass the ball to each other and must keep possession for three consecutive passes before one

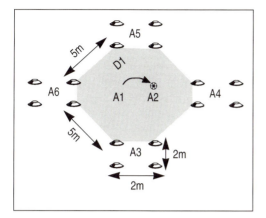

Fig 181   Playing in – striker format.

of them is entitled to swap (in rotation) with one of the outside players. The player who is on next must signal this to the players in possession of the ball; this encourages the players to talk to each other.

The defender does not actually need to win possession of the ball; all he has to do is to get a touch on the ball, which allows him to take the place of the player who has let him in (made the mistake of allowing him a touch on the ball).

Playing Someone In

The next man 'in' (when the attackers have achieved three consecutive passes) is determined by number, so A3 would be first, then A4 and so on. Although the possession zone is inside the cone format, the first touch of the ball by the outside player in any of the boxes must be towards the next box along on the outside; thus, if A3 was being played in, his first touch would send the ball towards A4, not into the box to his new partner. After this first touch the new player has to work out a way of getting the ball and himself into the possession

zone. The easiest way is to pass the ball to his new working partner, but if he was closed down, then the new player would have to dribble the ball into the possession zone. Once inside the zone, play is continued as before.

You can add a scoring incentive by pairing the players off: the first pair to achieve three successful link-ups (that is, they are the two attacking players in the possession zone), wins.

PLAYER INTERACTION

The exercise below – Look up– Assess –Play – is designed to promote the player's individual skills in a passing and moving environment, by encouraging him to look up, assess the situation and select the right skill option in relation to his own position on the field of play.

Remember that there should be four working stages in any training session; this exercise could come in the third stage – small game formats. Fig 182 shows the link between the four-cone base of the individual formats and the third stage interaction with team players. The first challenger is represented by the four-cone formation; the second challenger is for real, and makes his appearance in the second phase of the working format.

The exercise is set up so that A1, on going past the initial four-cone arrangement, suddenly needs to look up and assess his passing options. This teaches him to read the game in front of him quickly, which is important because his choice of action will be based on this; his reading of the game must therefore be accurate, too.

Look Up–Assess–Play
(Fig 182)

When the player has possession of the ball he needs to practise working out ways of doing something constructive, depending of course on his situation on the field of play; in this respect, this exercise is very versatile as it can be redesigned to deal with any scenario you wish. This particular example concentrates on giving the player plenty of opportunities to develop his all-round awareness.

Arrange the practice area as shown, divided into three sections to reflect the different themes of this practice.

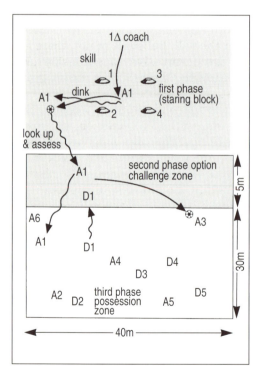

Fig 182   Look up and assess.

Phase 1
Player A1 receives the ball from the coach, and dinks it away on the turn to his left with his right instep.

The first phase of the practice concentrates on improving the first touch away from the oncoming challenger (who is represented by the position of the first set of cones); we have dealt with this topic previously, but in a slightly different way. The theme of this format, although closely related to the first-touch skills, concentrates mainly on what happens after the working player goes past the first challenger and has to decide what to do next.

Phase 2
Player A1 now moves forwards with the ball into the challenge zone, where he has to get past a real defender who will come out to challenge for the ball on the outside of the main possession zone, timing his entry into the play to co-incide with player A1 rounding cone 2. A1 must look up to assess the situation, and make a quick decision about his next action. He may wish to pass the ball long, to someone appropriately placed inside the possession zone; alternatively he may feel that he can outwit his opponent, taking him on and using some deft dribbling skills. In this case A1 will need to work hard at getting the ball to an appropriately positioned team mate-inside the possession zone.

Assessing the situation inside the possession zone while at the same time keeping possession of the ball is not a simple task; A1 needs to work fast and incorporate plenty of changes of pace and direction in order to lose his marker. He must work out a passing move that makes sure of retaining possession of the ball inside the possession zone. If he fails to pass the ball, he may be asked to swap places with another player and become involved in some other way. Alternatively, he may be asked to repeat this sequence of work up to this point.

Phase 3

After practising how to deal with the second challenger, the player continues to work out further play options. These will be simulated by allowing him to enter the possession zone and interact with his team players, keeping possession through passing. In Fig 182, A1 passes the ball to player A3, who now instigates possession play. Team D will now try to win possession, while team A have to try to keep possession of the ball for three consecutive passes. This emphasizes the need for moving off the ball in order to support the player in possession, and maintaining possession through passing.

The two teams in the possession zone could be colour coded, with half the players wearing one colour and half another; on emerging successfully from the second phase, the player can receive last-minute instructions telling him what colour to play the ball to, in order to retain possession. A1 will thus practise keeping possession of the ball with a particular team colour in the final stage of this.

Alternatively, the coach can simply allow possession play to continue until he changes the exercise format. Play in the possession zone is performed by two teams of unequal sides (six attackers against five defenders). This is arranged deliberately so that the work can be focused on the keep possession theme. Team A are more or less guaranteed possession by strength of numbers. The defending team is only in place to put pressure on the player in possession of the ball, simulating game requirements. The duration of the practice can be left up to the coach.

Do not think that the introduction of a live challenger in the second phase of this work makes it any way superior to practising with cones. As far as skills are concerned the second part of the work does not make the practice any more or less realistic, as the skills of moving the ball to the correct width and length of touch cannot be simulated by bringing on a real person to challenge for the ball. Believe it or not, there is no better alternative to practising skills than using the cone placements, simply because they allow a player to develop his touch skills without having to concentrate on anything except his touches on the ball.

When you introduce a live defender to the working sequence, you introduce a completely different aspect to the training format. When taking on a live opponent the player tends to use skills he already has, and most of his work in keeping possession of the ball is performed in an improvised way. He will not learn new skills in such situations. A successful outcome comes from work done previously, outside this type of environment. The exercises in this chapter draw together the skills learnt previously and practises them in a realistic environment. Only once the player has mastered the skills individually can he hope to combine them effectively in play, using the skills of vision and assessment worked on here.

THE FOUR BOX FORMAT

The following exercise simulates the different skills and situations of game conditions using a standard 4, 4, 2 configuration. Opponents do not like positional changes so this exercise concentrates on allowing the players to create movement within the shape. The two centre backs are left out of the practice session (they would stand between A1 and A2 in Fig 183) because in most free play scenarios they keep to a key central defensive position, only occasionally moving outside this role. Apart from them, technically speaking, all the other players may change positions during play.

In practical terms the team is divided into three sections: in this exercise the possession zone represents what happens in midfield and is used to practise midfield skills. The midfield player is different from a striker and defender because he must be able to break down his opponent's movements and create scoring opportunities for himself and others; therefore this position calls for all-round capability.

The positions on the outside of the practice area – the directional touch boxes – are designed to give practice in appreciation of movement within the shape. When a player in one of the boxes receives the ball his first touch must send it towards a specified cone in the box before he can bring it into the possession zone. This simulates the game condition of running with the ball into forward positions while interacting

with other team players. In soccer this practice of movement is of paramount importance.

How It Works
(Fig 183)

Set up the practice area as shown, with four players from team A and four from team B in the possession zone, and four team A players in the directional touch boxes round the outside. The practice is started by the coach playing the ball to one of the A team, who then try to put three consecutive passes together. When they have done this, they are entitled to swap one player (A7 in the diagram) with one of the players waiting in an outside box (A3). The third consecutive pass is the signal for the swap. The players on the outside signal this with a shout 'third pass!', and at this point the player with the ball plays the next man in, swapping places with him.

The player being swapped in must perform a pre-arranged skill movement before he can move with the ball into the possession zone. Here player A3 dinks the ball on his first touch to cone 1 of his box format then changes his direction to go forwards into the possession zone, dribbling the ball across the no man's land. He then interacts with team A, keeping possession of the ball through a passing sequence, as requested by the rules of the exercise.

The outside players can be swapped in order (from box 1 to 4), the A team scoring a 'goal' once they have completed a sequence (swapped in one outside player).

The practice is always restarted by the coach playing the first pass to team A. The defenders (team B) inside the

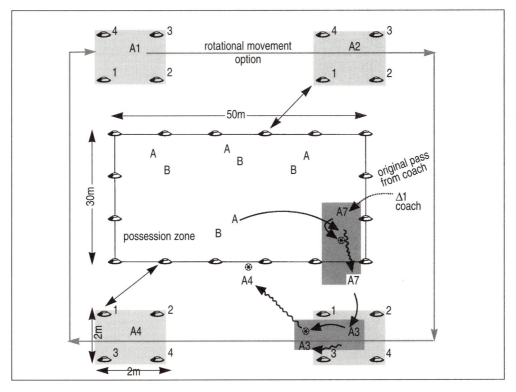

Fig 183   Possession and rotation of players format; if required, raise the number of passes in order to achieve rotational change.

possession zone are replaced after three goals have been played, always by the players in the outside boxes. As an alternative to the above format the team in the possession zone that keeps possession of the ball can outnumber the defenders by at least two. The practice should last 45 minutes.

The outside boxes can serve a number of useful purposes; for example, the working players defending inside the possession zone need a rest. If they can stop the A team from playing a three-pass sequence, they are rewarded with a position in an outside box where they can have a rest. Going to work in the boxes also gives them the opportunity to get involved in other ways. The position of the boxes simulates certain reaction and concentration skills. Mental alertness and concentration can also be brought into consideration.

Variation – The Rotation Format

In this variation, once the practice has started in the possession zone, the coach shouts 'Change!' and the players on the outside must rotate clockwise, each moving to the next box up; for example, A1 must run to box 2, A2 to box 3 and so on. While this is happening team A must keep hold of the ball in the possession zone; if they succeed they are awarded one point. If the defending players (team B) win possession of the ball before the outside players have finished rotating, the outside players become the defenders for failing to rotate in time and team B take up their positions.

This practice format is highly flexible, as you can adapt the set-up and exercise rules to suit your training requirements. The important point is that movement off the ball practices must be designed to make it difficult for any opponent to pick up players: this tactic makes the job of marking strikers almost impossible, forcing opponents to rely on a zone form of defence. Zone forms of defence create holes, and where there are holes, there are attacking possibilities.

THE CHANGE OF DIRECTION PASS

This practice routine creates a completely new working and thinking environment. It considers the direction of passing options. If any team has several passing options in play, the players also have several running combinations in play – the two skills always go together. You will find that when the standards of play are on the low side, then the game becomes more predictable. Put simply, most teams only recognize one directional play option at any one time, and mostly play the ball to the right side of the soccer field. This does not happen by design, it simply happens because most young players can only kick the ball with the right foot.

This phenomenon has taken its toll

on the skills of many, and many hours of skill-improving play are lost in this working environment. This drive always to play the ball forwards is so predictable that opponents automatically position themselves to deal with it, so that poorer players constantly find themselves intercepted by defending players. The constant forward movement with the ball does not create space in which to play, especially if opponents get behind the ball which they often do. When this happens there are few opportunities to hold on to the ball.

It is important to approach possession play in a balanced way, so do not rush in with a constant diet of reverse passes. Instead use different forms of practice and make sure that all your selected topics complement each other in order to practise all sorts of skill options.

To be effective in attacking play, the player's passing and movement has to be unpredictable; he must be able to switch play or play the ball backwards in order to create space and be effective in controlling play. This exercise has been developed to counteract constant one-directional play options. It makes players aware of other possibilities, teaching them to work out passing movements which draw defenders out of defensive positions. The players practise a different approach to possession play, learning to mix the direction of passing and movement.

Working to the theme of this exercise allows the players to develop the ability to change the pace of work, giving the team options not only in controlling play, but also in developing counter-attacking moves in working the

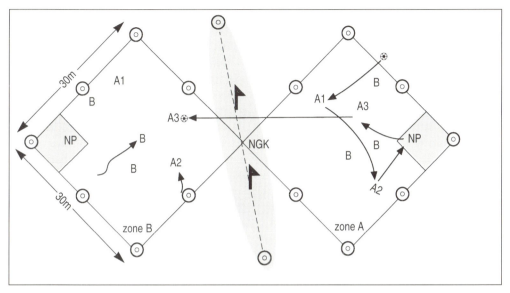

Fig 184   The change of pace and direction format.

ball from the back into forward positions. When the ball is played forwards in this exercise, the pace of the game changes on the forward pass, and the pass and movement combination creates a finishing/scoring opportunity.

How It Works
(Fig 184)
The practice area consists of two separate diamonds joined together in the middle by two sets of flags, which represent the goal target. The object of the exercise is to play the ball to the back then reverse the direction of play with a forward pass in order to counter attack, then set up a strike on goal. The habit of having to start the practice by working the ball back, starting with a pass to the neutral player (NP), brings about an understanding of the theme of this topic as discussed above.

There are two teams of six players

(A and B) each split into two, and half in each diamond; keeping the numbers down gives each player more time on the ball. The practice starts in the right-hand zone with the coach playing the ball to a team A player; A1 in the diagram.

For simplicity's sake the players may not move from one zone to the other in order to support play. However, it is possible to implement play conditions where additional defensive or attacking responsibilities are allocated to one or two of the players. When this is the case, the relevant players join their respective teams in opposite zones. For example, in this scenario the B team are defending so one of the B team players in the left-hand zone may be allowed to go across and help with defending duties in the right-hand zone.

Of course, you must remember to

179

maintain the bias of the training exercise. If the bias is on attacking play, then if you were to release an additional defender, you would also have to release an attacking player to keep the numbers at least even. On the other hand if you wanted to help the team in possession, you could go one step further and allow two A players to move across and help to retain possession of the ball. The choice of working formats is up to you.

One major game condition must be made in order to bring about the right simulation of the passing theme – namely, the player receiving the ball from the coach has to play the ball to one of his own players in order to work out a passing sequence that will retain possession of the ball. The A team cannot just keep possession of the ball, but must work out a passing sequence so that the ball is played to the neutral player, who is to be found in the neutral box (NP) in the furthest corner of each diamond. This neutral player must always play the ball back to the team that has played him the pass. Although in this example the A team have the advantage of possession because they have received the ball from the coach, both teams have the same rights in play and both teams must make use of the neutral player.

The practice format allows the ball to be in play almost all of the time, but there are always moments in play when the ball will be miskicked and leave the areas of play. When this happens, normal throw-in rules apply, but if the ball is kicked far afield, the coach will start the practice again, this time playing the ball to the other team.

Once the initial objective of passing the ball to the neutral player has been achieved, the second team objective comes into play: the players in possession must work out a scoring opportunity. In the centrally positioned goal is a neutral goalkeeper, whose job is to face the next strike on goal. There is only one ball in action at any one time. If the keeper wins possession of the ball through a save, he turns around with the ball and throws it up in the air to the next zone, to start off the practice sequence there; this fifty-fifty ball is competed for by both sets of players. If, on the other hand, the ball has been struck so that the keeper has no chance of saving the shot, the shape of the working format is such that the ball will travel past him to the other zone. Again, both sets of players compete for the ball, and normal fifty-fifty rules apply. The team that wins possession starts the practice over again, working the ball back to the neutral player before playing a counter pass to a forward goal-scoring position. The practice should last 45 minutes.

About the Shape

The object of the shape is to create a psychological feeling of depth in play. This fosters an attacking-minded attitude by making sure that the angles of work are multi-directional. If you were to take a throw-in, for example, at no time would your position be limited by a square touch line, a shape which makes it hard to open up play in support of the throw-in.

The rules of this exercise reinforce the concept of shape by making the players play the ball back as well as forwards. They also allow the players time to recover physically because after a team from one half has had a go at scoring a goal, the ball passes to the other side. This stop and start format is precisely the right type of working environment to help develop good recovery rates, so playing in these conditions gives players an all-round development programme not achievable through conventional practice formats. A training session based on running will leave players tired and vulnerable to injuries.

As you can see, the exercises in this chapter are made up of different sections. None of them adhere to the two-touch mentality, because in the real world of soccer you need to apply a different skill almost every second of the game. What is so important to this issue is that in the game there is a need to play different touches of the ball *and* different lengths of touch. In the two-touch format, if you receive two touches of the ball and you happen to make a mistake with your first touch, what then? In the real world of soccer, if your first touch lets you down you correct it with your next touch and keep on play-ing the ball until it is in an appropriate position to do something constructive. There is absolutely nothing wrong with this approach. When the player needs to dig out a pass from under his body it is better for him to take one more touch than to try and play the ball from a bad position. Just as long as the extra touch is played away from an opponent, it will be successful in setting up the next play option.

The skills of ball control, dribbling and keeping possession of the ball are all interrelated, but when the game moves into the possession zone there are again different skills required. The players are in fact encouraged to perform all types of skills, remembering that getting hold of the ball is a priority, while getting rid of it is not! All players are required to play in a sensible way, which means that the ball is retained by any positive legal means. A player should pass the ball when it is feasible to do so, rather than hanging on to it selfishly. Dribbling skills are encouraged, but so is playing the right type of ball at the right time. The players should learn not to give the ball away for nothing; it is as simple as that.

15 PLAY WITHIN THE SHAPE

A major failing in today's game is the inability of the players to keep the shape, and this can be vital to your team's success. The team that can play very well within a team shape formation is able to use all its players at one point or another during play. Conversely, if players do not learn to keep the shape, they will not know when to move forwards in support of play, and worse still, they will be unable to defend properly. Good coaching encourages players to play in a balanced way, which means that the game is not just about playing the ball down the right-hand side of the soccer pitch: when a player has possession of the ball, he should have various options open to him and be quickly supported by other players.

If a team is unable to play to a given shape it loses up to 35 per cent of its playing options. Other weaknesses in the team could push this percentage rate up by another 10 per cent, so this is not something to be taken lightly. Most people are not even aware of this lack of playing options, especially if the team has just won and everyone has gone home happy. However, any coach worth his salt would not settle just for the result. There are no excuses for not teaching players how to play the game properly, and a good coach will teach them to pass the ball to each other,

encouraging each one to use the skills at his disposal in order to support the working shape.

There are three major areas of play in the exercise below: the first section deals with defensive play, the middle section with the midfield and the remaining section with attacking skills. The way the shape itself behaves in the game has already been described. Young players tend to play with their head down and cannot see anything once they take control of the ball; yet nothing could be easier than to correct this tendency using this zone format exercise. It is very important to separate players who have tunnel vision and related problems. Some tend to look for their mates in order to pass the ball to them, and do not see any other passing possibilities; others simply have no awareness of what is going on at the time.

Explaining how to keep the shape in words just does not work. Players need to experience what is involved. By positioning each player according to his function, you are in fact teaching him how to keep the shape in play, thus developing his playing options. So the strikers are positioned in zone A, the midfielders in zone B and the defenders in zone C, and the area of practice can be extended or reduced according to the age of the participants. Normal soccer rules apply during the practice.

KEEPING THE SHAPE

Beginners' Version

Set up the practice area as shown in Fig 185, using two teams. Strikers go in zone 1, midfielders in zone 2 and defenders in zone 3; it follows that what is zone 1 for team A will be zone 3 for team B. The players are not allowed to move from one zone to the next, nor must they move to the right or left encroaching on other players' space in the same zone. The only way forwards with the ball is by passing it to a team-mate in the next forward zone. By staying in their allocated positions the players learn to appreciate their position on the field of play in relation to others.

The coach starts the practice by playing the ball to a defender, who must try to play the ball forwards into zone 2.

His team continue to play the ball forwards from one zone to the next until it ends up in the finishing zone, where a possible shot on target can be worked out. Alternatively, the practice can be played according to normal soccer rules, although the players must still keep to their allocated zones.

Movement within the Shape (Fig 185)

Keeping the shape as described above is for beginners, and you would expect to soon move on from this very basic understanding of shapes in play. The shape is kept as before, but certain players are allowed to move out of their allocated zones – both full backs for example can go into attacking forward positions. In this example the midfield player A7 has also moved in support of

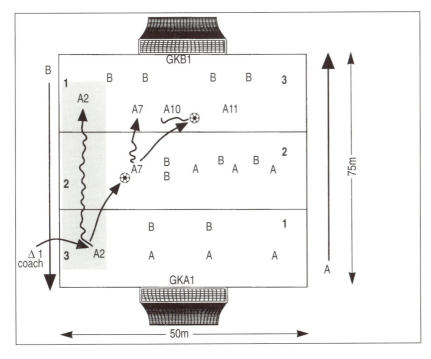

Fig 185
Keeping the
shape format.

the ball (remember the numbers have no meaning, they are simply used for describing events).

The shaded area in the diagram shows a channel on the left side of the area, where the left full back (A2) makes an overlapping run; he must stay in this shaded area. In my system of play, the player A2 has a special function, but for tactical reasons his position on the field of play can easily be changed and his role could be different; for example, he may be given such functions as a defensive screen in front of the back four (*see* Chapter 14).

Advanced Formats

Whether you allocate your players to a channel position (where they must stay at all times) role or a free role is up to you, but remember that there are times in play when it would be almost unfair to ask your players to stay in allocated zones. Attacking play must and does include improvisation, so the players should work at moves that surprise opponents. You cannot in all seriousness expect players to create advanced movements by asking them to stay in rigid channel positions when in possession of the ball.

It is of course understood that there is a need to keep to the shape in play especially when defending. Managers who advocate channel positioning should realize that the shape does not fall apart just because the players improvise in attacking play. In practical terms the shape changes in and around the ball but is kept intact elsewhere by all the players moving out together in support of attacking/defensive play. For example, in Fig 185 player A2 has sup-

ported attacking play by going all the way forwards into an attacking position and is now in the old-fashioned outside left role in advance of the ball. All his co-defenders on the other hand have stayed back, thus keeping the shape intact. This type of movement is considered a tactical running option.

TACTICAL AWARENESS FOR EXPERIENCED PLAYERS

This practice format can give your players the opportunity to practise such tactical running options. They are not difficult to implement – all you need to do is to allocate players to their respective positions as before, then select one or two to go into forward zones in support of the ball.

Diagonal Support
(Fig 186)

In this example player A2 will keep to a diagonal running pattern throughout the game. He starts to the right of the opponents' goal and moves into a wide position, but as the ball moves ever closer to his goal he takes on a more central defensive role. In attacking play, he again moves forwards ever wider until he reaches the halfway line, giving his team a wide play option, before coming back in diagonally as shown on the diagram. It is difficult for opponents to deal with such runs if they use a zone defensive system.

Working in Pairs
(Fig 187)

The working-in-pairs tactic can be very useful in certain winning-of-the-ball situations, for example when a long ball

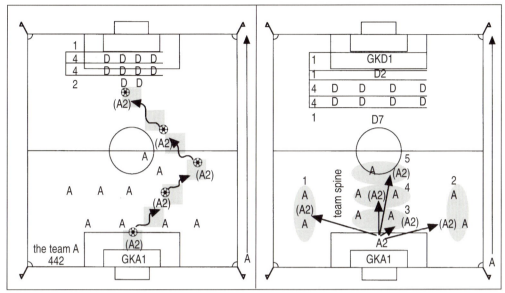

Fig 186   Making the diagonal run.   Fig 187   Working in pairs.

is played forwards from the back positions; in that instance one player shapes up to control the ball, while the other player is prepared to do something constructive with it when it is passed to him. It is also handy sometimes to back up a player in certain crucial attacking or defensive positions, to strengthen him. The most common usage of this tactic, and the one most readily recognized by the members of the public, is the partnership up front, usually two attacking players working together to create goal-scoring opportunities.

PASSING AND MOVEMENT COMBINATIONS

When players are brought up on a diet of one-directional play, they do not learn how to create passing and movement options. Keeping the shape helps players to work out passing movements, as is taught by the following exercises.

As far as passing is concerned, there are not that many techniques of passing the ball, but these can be used in a phenomenal number of ways. As a great simplification it is possible to say that basically the ball needs to travel either on the ground or in the air. However, within these parameters it can travel to almost any length or height.

The team structure as shown in Fig 185 demonstrates that the players have starting positions that do create playing shapes. This means that in general terms there are specific distances between each player, and it is true to say therefore that the basic passing skills can be categorized as the short and the long pass options.

These options are used in accordance with the position of the players on the field of play. The team is split up into three main sections, linked by passing combinations; for example, if

185

your position on the field of play is right back in defence and you are in possession of the ball, you could start the passing sequence by playing the ball to the middle section of the shape, probably using a short pass because the midfield is so close to you. The player you pass to may then return the ball to you, and you use the momentum of this pass to strike the ball long, bypassing the midfielder. The two passing options combined are known as the 'short and long passing combination'.

Such combinations are central to your play so start your practice session by using this combination, and consider it as your base combination in play. Remember that this skill is only the foundation and not your only option in passing, as all the exercises concerned with passing skills in this book will show you. Even the simplest of passing options such as passing the ball to feet can be profitably used in play.

The Short and Long Passing Combination

In this training routine the right back (player D1) works out passing movements with his coach and a helper (coach 2), who represent the midfield section of the team. In a game situation, for example, the coach's initial pass backwards to D1 could be used by D1 to play a long ball forwards to coach 2. In this exercise, however, he will work on passing the ball back accurately on his first touch.

Most players need to develop confidence in using the non-kicking foot to at least a competent level. There is often a need to play the ball quickly, and in such situations there is no time to switch the ball from one foot to the other without the risk of losing a good passing or scoring opportunity. The following exercise can eliminate the bad habit of transferring the ball from the so-called weaker foot to the good foot (the habit of taking one more touch than necessary in order to pass or strike the ball).

This exercise also helps players to react correctly to passes made during play; for example, there are times when the pass has to be played short rather than directly to the feet. When receiving this type of pass the receiving player needs to go towards the ball, and if he is slow to react an opposing defender could nip in front of him and regain possession.

How It Works (Fig 188)

Set up the practice area as shown. Cone 1 represents the right foot (long) return pass, cone 2 represents the left foot (long) return pass and cone 3 represents coming short to the ball and returning the pass with either foot. The practising player (D1) starts in the shaded box in the middle before each serve. The coach and service player stand directly in line with cones 1 and 2, 20m apart and 20m away from cones 1 and 2.

The ball is passed along the ground to one of the cones and D1 must run to the target cone and make an appropriate return pass. For example, if the ball is played to the left side of cone 1, D1 should return it with his right foot. The return pass should be of good quality – its pace and accuracy should cause no problems for the coach/service player. The main techniques of passing in this exercise use the instep and the laces part of the boot.

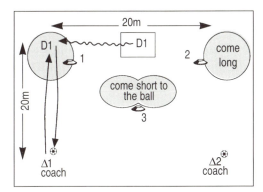

Fig 188 *Working the shape: come short – play long.*

After performing the return pass D1 walks back to the starting position and prepares to receive another ball from the other side. If the short pass is played to cone 3, D1 responds by coming to the ball short and knocking it back with either his right or left foot depending on which side the ball came from. The practice should last 20 minutes.

Because the player always has to start from a central starting position, he has the opportunity to practise dealing with the ball when it is played into space as well as to feet. The shaded area behind cone 3 represents a checking out movement where the player comes short to the ball. The shaded areas round cones 1 and 2 represent receiving the ball in space to the side of the defending player; this type of pass within the shape favours the attacking player because the ball is played away from any defending position into free space. Working the ball in this way is known as playing the ball into holes.

Passing Combination Codes
(Fig 189)

The players can prepare a number of passing sequences and remember them using a number code. For example:

1 Short pass forwards–short pass return–the long ball.
2 Long ball forwards–short pass return–the short pass forwards.
3 Square pass–reverse pass–short forward pass–return pass–long ball forwards.

There is no point at this stage to create any more passing sequence codes as there are far too many possibilities to be encompassed in one book. The point is that in theory you could develop a working base of specific passing and

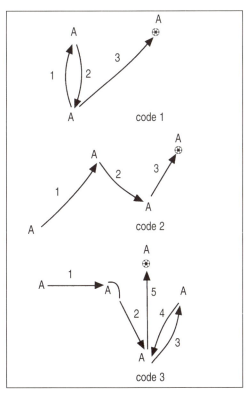

Fig 189 *Passing combinations.*

187

movement combinations that could come in handy in your team-playing repertoire. Remember, however, that all this work could come to nothing if one of the players in your planned sequence was injured and could not link up with the others in any of the passing combinations.

Having said that, working out these combinations is still a useful skill for players to learn. In time they will have a playing repertoire and will recognize some of these basic movements automatically. Team play can be left to spontaneous reactions, and sometimes this is desirable, but if your players could learn an unpredictable passing and movement sequence and put it into practice in front of your opponents' goal, it could take the opponents by surprise and open up goal-scoring opportunities, especially if performed at speed.

The H-Format

Set up the practice area as shown with the players positioned in an H-shape, which is highly adaptable and can easily be related to many topics in this book. The players work on passing techniques, practising the long pass, short pass, chipping and using passing shapes (swerves) – generally playing the ball with many skill variations. Unlike some formats, this introduction shape can be altered to resemble any shape you want; for example, the position of players can easily be adjusted to a circle format. To avoid tiredness, each player performs for a number of minutes then swaps places with another player in the shape and has a rest. The return pass to the practising player is always along the ground.

How It Works (Fig 190)

A1 plays the first pass, which is a short pass to player A2. A2 returns the ball to A1, who then plays a long pass to A3, who plays a long pass back. The practice continues in this way with A1 passing the ball to each player in turn until the coach says stop and player A1 swaps places with another player in the H. Each player should have approximately 4 minutes as A1.

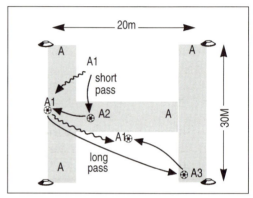

Fig 190   The H-format.

THE SHORT AND LONG PASSING GAME
(Figs 191 & 192)

It is possible to position the players to carry out a particular passing sequence within the shape, and this can be practised and implemented as part of your playing repertoire.

Fig 191 illustrates the short passing game. This type of passing can be used tactically to draw opponents to the ball. When this passing objective has been achieved the ball can be played long to change the direction of attack.

Fig 192 shows the long passing game. Hitting the second player in the

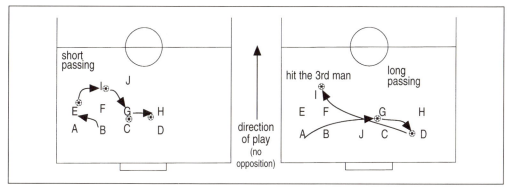

Figs 191 & 192   Long and short team passing formats.

shape (G) makes it difficult for opponents to close him down and try to take the ball off him.

The team should be able to pass the ball in a variety of ways, as keeping to the same style of play can be predictable and easy for the opposition to cope with defensively. Remember that the long passing game has to be extremely accurate because more often than not the long flight of the ball allows the opponents time to position themselves where they are most likely to win possession. There are many ways of practising passing and movement.

How It Works
(Fig 193)

This sample exercise uses two teams of six men and a practice area divided into two halves, only one of which is in use at a time. It puts together the short and long passing game in a keep-possession format: keeping possession of the ball is assured by playing the short passing game; to set up the long pass option each team takes turns to leave one player in the zone not currently being used.

The two opposing teams (only five are shown in each team in the diagram for clarity) compete against each other under normal soccer rules in one half of the practice area to keep possession of the ball, while one player from one team waits in the other half. The objective during possession play is for the team with the waiting player to retain the ball for four consecutive passes without giving away possession. When this is achieved the team is entitled to knock a long ball into the opposite zone to the waiting player. Successfully achieving the four successful passes and the long

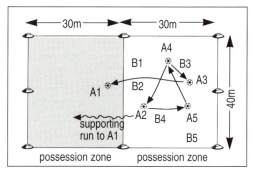

Fig 193   The support and possession format.

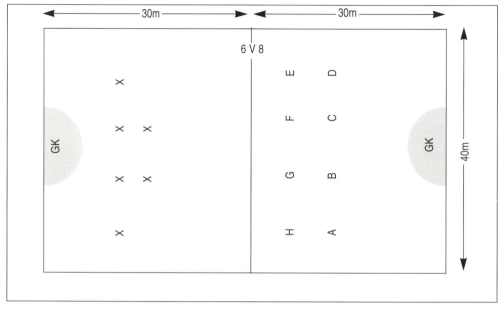

Fig 194   *The chip pass format set-up.*

ball link-up is rewarded with a point, which is the equivalent to a goal scored. After the long pass all the players move into the other zone to continue the practice, and the other team leaves a player behind in the vacated half.

If the team with the man waiting fails to string four passes together it cannot score a point and so the practice is void; it then starts again from scratch with the other team leaving a player behind, giving them an opportunity to score a point. In short, one team is always trying to win a point while the other is competing for the right to leave a player behind. The first team to ten points wins the game, or the practice can simply be timed to last 30 minutes.

THE CHIP PASS FORMAT *(Fig 194)*

When playing against any team shape, players must be able to use different passing skills. The positioning of opponents may be such that playing the ball over the top of opposing players will open up attacking opportunities, and one way to do this is with a chip pass. This simple exercise practises 'chipping' the ball – lifting it into the air, lobbing and shaping it – and is performed in a small-sided game setting. The chip passing technique will ensure that the length and flight of the ball will vary. The players play an ordinary game of soccer adhering to normal rules, except that to score, the team has to chip pass the ball to the keeper's hands.

FINISHING 16

Scoring goals is a great pleasure, everyone knows that – it is the end product of all the work that goes into soccer training. From a coaching point of view bringing about this end product takes a long time, and the learning process involves a wide range of skills.

There are all sorts of skill combinations for finishing, so you cannot approach the scoring training session with only one finishing method, especially the one where the players simply strike the ball on target. Things are not that simple. The exercises have to work at movements, techniques of finishing and often dribbling skills which are used to open up just that little bit of room in order to strike the ball on target. It often amazes me how a little movement with the hips can send defenders packing.

In most finishing situations it is very difficult to think of anything other than striking the ball. The chances of a free strike on goal are limited and sometimes there is little or no time to dwell on the shot or target; it is therefore not unusual for the player to pull or snatch at a striking opportunity.

In these exercises the ball is struck mainly with the laces part of the boot. This helps the player to develop a calm and correct attitude to finishing, so that in time he learns to put his chances away without snatching or pulling.

PROBLEMS ASSOCIATED WITH FINISHING

Firstly, the weather affects the way the ball travels in the air. If it is cold it is difficult to make the ball fly at great speeds, and when it is warm the opposite is true.

Less obvious problems include a lack of confidence, or over-confidence and greed on the ball. Sometimes goal-scoring opportunities can be lost for quite selfish reasons that have nothing to do with soccer: for example, strikers at the very top of their profession sometimes expect everyone to pass them the ball rather than take the opportunity to finish themselves – strange, but true – and remonstrations by older players will sometimes shake the confidence of a younger player to have a go. To avoid such problems, there should be a golden rule for everyone: if you are on the edge of your opponents' penalty area or inside it, there should be two things on your mind – if there is an opening on goal, strike the ball on target, if not, attack the nearest defender and create an opening that way for a strike on target.

If players tend to walk the ball into the net, this is probably due to incorrect coaching. If they work to a constant diet of possession play without an end product in view, then they will keep to this possession format in play and try to walk the ball into the opponents' goal.

Finishing is about attitudes, and attitudes are a result of training concepts. The possession format, working in co-operation with the two-touch restriction, teaches the habit of 'head down', which leads to lack of 'vision'. Where there is a lack of vision there is a lack of finishing opportunities.

As already said, other implications of incorrect training include the inability of the player to create passing options. This is why each of my coaching formats requires the player to work to three different stages: the first touch, the second (implementation) touch, and the end product touch (choosing the right finishing/passing option). Such an approach creates the right frame of mind and attitude to given tasks.

Here I have selected a wide range of finishing exercises, taking into account a number of playing considerations. The skills of finishing routine is a good introduction: it simulates taking care of the first challenger, then any immediate covering player, and finishes with the actual strike on target.

THE SKILLS OF FINISHING

Most of the time when a player is in a position to finish, the ball either comes to him direct and he strikes it first time, or he takes a couple of touches on it and works out a finishing opportunity, usually by taking players on just after picking up the ball from a pass. This exercise deals with both scenarios.

How It Works
(Fig 195)
Set up the practice area as shown, with two movable nets and two diagonal cone shapes. The practising player (A1) starts in the middle of the format and receives the ball from both sides of the practice area, from coach 1 or 2. When the coach serves the ball to the player's blind side he shouts a signal, which has a pre-arranged meaning and tells A1 exactly how he should play the ball. The instruction consists of a direction (right or left) and a cone number; for example, if the coach shouts 'turn right 1' A1 controls the pass and on his first touch sends the ball to the side of the right-

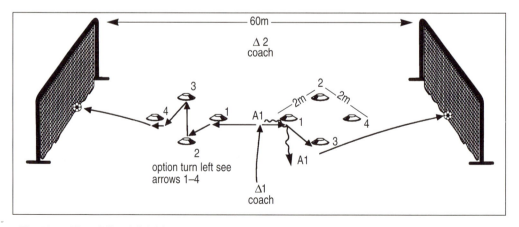

Fig 195   The skills of finishing.

hand cone 1; from here he strikes the ball on target.

The right-hand half of the diagram shows A1 responding to a call of 'turn right 3'. The ball has been played to A1, who controls it and plays it with the instep of his right foot, taking it to the cone formation to the right of coach 1. A1's first touch is made in such a way that his body moves in the direction of his first touch; now he has to deal with the cone formation. The first cone is positioned directly in his way, so he plays the ball to the side of it, quickly gets it under control with his next touch, sends it to the right of cone 3, and then strikes it on target. A1 then goes back to the starting position and begins again, this time receiving the serve from the other side.

Cone 4 is slightly different. The left-hand half of the diagram shows the player responding to a shout of 'turn left 4'. He touch controls the ball and plays it to the left cone formation. His next touch takes the ball towards cone 1, and he then plays the second touch towards cone 2. With his left foot he drags the ball across and inside to cone 3; then with an extra touch on it with the outside of his left boot he drags it left of cone 4, before going on to finish with a strike on target from alongside cone 4.

The player needs to perform these skills very quickly and to interpret the shouted signal correctly. He also needs to learn how to look up in between touches of the ball, at least once in a two-cone movement sequence. The touches of the ball should come naturally when using the side and instep of the foot to change directions.

Alternatively this format can also be used by playing the ball directly to the practising player, who simply strikes the ball on target with his first touch.

THE FOUR-NET FORMAT
(Figs 196 & 197)

This is one of the best individual finishing routines. A 40m square practice area is set up as shown, with a net in the centre of each side. The practising player (A1) starts in the middle of the practice area and the coach plays the ball to him at varying heights. A1 must not move away from the centre excepting to adjust his position in relation to the service of the ball. He strikes the ball with his first touch, trying to use the laces part of the boot. He tries hard to keep the ball down and hit any one of the target nets.

The striking techniques include finishing on the turn with either foot, depending on how the ball arrives at the player. The angle and height of the service is varied in order to simulate all sorts of game finishing opportunities. The player tries to keep the striking

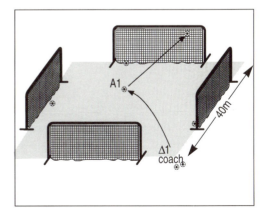

Fig 196 Power play.

Fig 197 *Poised to strike.*

foot over the ball, to be positive and to keep his eyes firmly locked on the ball.

TAKING ON THE KEEPER
(Fig 198)
This is probably the simplest of possible exercises. All you need is half a football field, some practising players (who are numbered) and a goalkeeper. Each player is in possession of a ball, and practises his skills on the ball in

between the penalty box and the halfway line. In this example there are ten players numbered 1 to 10.

The coach shouts out a number, and the relevant player attacks the goalkeeper with the ball. He has three options:

Option 1   Take the keeper on using dribbling skills.
Option 2   Strike on target – finish with power.
Option 3   Chip the keeper – finish with skills.

THE VOLLEY SEQUENCE
The finishing volley/half volley in this exercise is the end product of a passing set-up sequence which culminates in a strike on goal; players A3 and A6 (in Fig 202) are responsible for finishing although players can be rotated to work on finishing. The exercise is set up to simulate shapes in play.

Fig 198
Finishing
options.

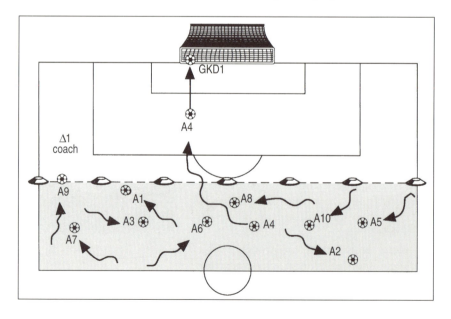

How It Works
(Figs 199–204)

The players are arranged round two central cones (the goal) as shown. The goal is 40m away from each finishing player (A3 and A6). The other players are positioned to enable short and long passing combinations to be played.

Player A2 begins the practice by playing a short pass with the instep of his right boot to player A1. A1 then plays a long pass with the laces part of his boot, getting his foot under the ball to make it fly through the air to player A6. This puts momentum on the ball to help A6 with his volley. A6 watches this ball coming to him, adjusts his position according to its flight and strikes it before it lands with his first touch, using the laces part of his left boot.

This sends the ball to and through the goal target to player A3, who brings the ball under control and plays a long pass with the laces part of his right boot to player A5. A5 half volleys the ball to A4, who controls the ball with the instep of his right boot, setting it up for himself to play the long ball to A6. Keeping his

Fig 199
Move to inter-
cept the ball
but keep your
eye on it.

Fig 200
Draw back
the striking
leg as the
ball drops.

Fig 201
Push the
striking leg
through and
strike. Arm
raised to
maintain
balance.

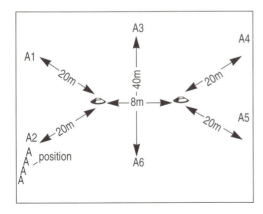

Fig 202   The volley sequence.

Fig 203   The volley technique – follow
through.

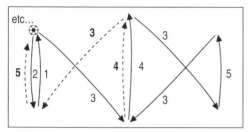

Fig 204   The short and long passing option.

eye on the ball, A6 adjusts his position according to the flight of the ball, then volleys the ball through the goal again to A3. A3 once again controls the ball, then plays it long to A2. Player A2 plays the ball with a half volley to A1 who in turn manages to play the long ball (with his first touch) back to A6. A6 volleys the ball to A3, and so on.

This passing sequence is shown using numbered codes in Fig 204. There are any number of passing sequence options available to the players, however. A change of direction can be implemented and the order of finishing can be changed at will.

Variation – Clockwise Movement of Players

Alternatively the players can move round the practice formation so that more of them can participate in the exercise, moving one place following the ball in the working pattern. A particular skills sequence could be performed at each position. The practice begins with six players in position. A2 plays a short pass to A1. When A1 has controlled the pass in this working format and has performed the skill requirements of this first position, he moves on to the next position, A6 and all the other players move on one place (in the

order described above – A2, A1, A6, A3, A5, A4) and the player at A4 drops out. A2 moves to A1's position and a new player comes in at position X, beginning the exercise again.

A possible passing sequence could be (using the codes given in Fig 207) 1, 3, 4, 3, 5, 3, 4, 3, 2, but of course you can devise your own and include what ball control skills you like.

CROSSING THE BALL

This competitive crossing-of-the-ball exercise is especially useful when you want to practise various finishing techniques including heading.

How It Works
(Fig 205)

Set up the practice area as shown, with half of team A's players and half of team B's in each zone, so that each half has a team trying to finish and a team trying to defend. There are two separate 'crossing-of-the-ball' players in special crossing channels at the sides of the practice area. Each team have their crossing player (A1/B1) on their right. He receives the ball from his goalkeeper and crosses it into his team's attacking zone, where his team compete for the ball and try to finish with an appropriate finishing skill.

At the outset all players stick to their allocated zones and functions. If any team finds this working format too hard to cope with, simply reduce the number of defenders. When a goalkeeper catches the ball or saves the shot he throws the ball out to his team's crossing player.

If the crossing player wants, he can play the early ball into the box from

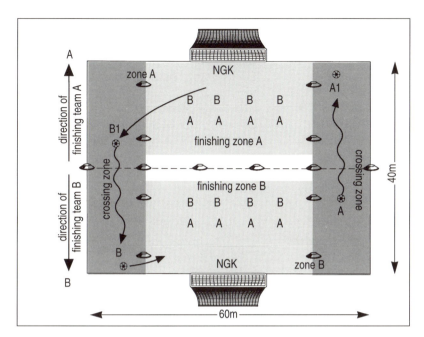

Fig 205   The crossing format.

inside his own half, or leave the service of the ball late, in which case he needs to go on a run to the attacking zone and cut the ball back from the goal line across the face of the finishing area (*see* B1 in the diagram); this type of cross will be ideal for practising heading the ball.

This exercise can become almost as complicated as any team game format, but keeping it simple ensures that the play concentrates on the theme of the practice and the players are not side-tracked into practising other skills. For example, the service of the ball is performed from inside an isolated channel, without interruptions, which ensures that there are plenty of crosses coming into the finishing zones.

The exercise can be adapted as required. To reduce the competition inside the finishing area remove the opposition; to make things difficult for the finishing players, simply bring it

back. Alternatively, when the service of the ball comes in from the wide position the players can bring it under control and play can continue by one team taking on the other in a small game format, which can end with a set-up move and finish. The practice should last 30 minutes.

PRESSURE FINISHING
(Fig 206)

There are two teams in this exercise, A and B, each with ten players. Each team has six strikers and four defenders, the strikers going in one half and the defenders in the other, so that in each half the defenders are outnumbered. Players must keep to their allocated zones and functions throughout.

Normal soccer rules apply, except that only attacking players can score goals. If the defenders win possession of the ball they play it across to the other

197

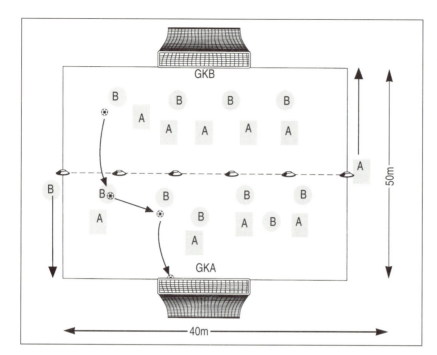

Fig 206
Competitive
finishing.

zone to their own attackers. The attacking players may not pass the ball back to their defenders. When the goalkeeper wins the ball he simply plays it to one of his own players. The bias of the exercise, with four defenders coping with six strikers, reinforces the attacking finishing theme of the practice.

This is an intense finishing exercise which can put players under pressure; this can be counterproductive because it can affect the physical and psychological well-being of any player, and so it must be used sparingly. The intensity comes from the small size of the working area. It stands to reason that if you cram players into a small area, they will have less time on the ball, and so this exercise cannot produce skills other than finishing. The practice should last at least 20 minutes.

USING A WALL

This training exercise is deliberately chosen for its community use potential. It is very difficult for local authorities to find and designate land for soccer, so perhaps this piece of equipment can solve some of the problems. Children will kick a ball against any wall that is suitable, but they often get into trouble if they do because the wall is most likely to be someone's property. The children in my area have been provided by the community parks department with a climbing fence, which they seem to have adapted for playing one of the finest fun games in the world, called Wembley. By using this equipment for this purpose they have inadvertently proved my point about the potential use for such a wall in the community.

Non-Competitive Wembley

This passing game in front of a wall concentrates on setting someone up for a shot on target. It is an unselfish format where anyone can finish off the moves by striking the target (a goal drawn on the wall) after a passing sequence. The finishing strike comes naturally, when someone feels that it is time in the passing sequence to show their skills in finishing and have a go at trying to score a goal. The timing of the shot or header on target sometimes depends on how the ball arrives at the participant's feet.

There are few set rules; everyone just enjoys themselves passing the ball around using various skills, and finishing techniques when they want to. There is a neutral goalkeeper, who saves all goal-scoring attempts without bias. To start the practice after each goal attempt, the keeper simply kicks the ball out from his hands, and anyone can begin another passing and movement sequence to set up a finishing touch.

Competitive Wembley

In this competitive version of the game there are as many rounds in the competition as there are participants, in this example ten. Each player competes against the rest in order to try to work out a goal-scoring opportunity. When one of the players is successful in scoring a goal, he automatically steps out of the arena for the time being. The game continues in this way until there is only one player left, who has not managed to score. This player is now out of the competition.

The game is restarted for its second round by the remaining nine players who again compete against each other

exactly as before. The winner of this Wembley competition is the player who manages to score a goal in every round and therefore is never knocked out of the competition.

Again, there is a neutral goalkeeper who protects the goal, and who on every save or goal scored, restarts the play by kicking the ball out from his hands into the playing arena where the players compete for possession of the ball.

The Wall in a Club Environment
(Fig 207)

This exercise requires the wall to have different sized and shaped holes in it, numbered 1 to 6; if this is not possible, just draw the targets on the wall. Instead of an arena, four cones (numbered 1 to 4) are placed as shown 20–30m out from the base of the wall, and the practising player (A1) stands inside them. The coach plays the ball to A1 and calls out a number between 1 and 4, referring to one of the cones. A1's first touch must send the ball in that cone direction, using an appropriate skill such as the side foot touch/turn on the ball. The player then controls the ball with his next touch, looks up and strikes it on target. The cone number called by the coach can also be the target number on the wall itself, or else the coach can call out another number for the target. Alternatively you could use a six-cone formation to match the number of targets.

This exercise can help the player in many ways. For example, on turning with the ball he works on the skill of looking up and assessing his target option. He then needs to work out

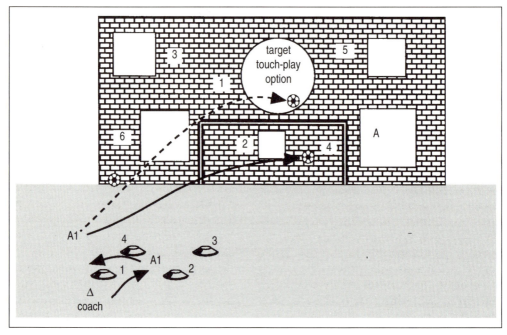

Fig 207   The target wall.

appropriate moves in order to hit the designated target. The holes in the wall are there for the purpose of developing the player's touch rather than his power; he may use different techniques, such as chipping the ball, swerving it or place touching it on target.

If you have a wall with holes, it is also possible to add a reaction training element by positioning a player on the other side of the wall. The ball is struck by the finishing player through a hole in the wall, and the player on the other side has to control it and play it back, either over the top of the wall (optional) or again through a hole. Both players continue to play the ball back and forth to each other in this way, reacting quickly as they don't know through which hole it will come. Failure to play the ball through the wall costs points. The winner is the first player to hit ten balls through the wall.

OFFSIDES AND THE HALF-FIELD FORMAT

When you come to think about all the different skills and the different psychological effects of training, you will soon realize that the full game format is very special in many respects. There is clearly a distinction between the game of soccer and specially designed soccer training routines. When players are put in a proper game environment to practise certain skills, and the game stops every two or three minutes while the coach explains something, the players soon become bored and agitated, and in this working environment learn less than you think. They often do not hear what the coach is saying if the weather is bad or if they are too far away or still trying to get their breath back. Nor will they give their best if there is a chance of picking up an injury, which is obviously more likely in a full game format than in individual or small game practices.

These are important reasons for using alternative practice formats. The full game format is not the right environment for practising skills, tactical or otherwise. The half-field format, on the other hand, is good because it avoids all sorts of unwanted coaching problems. It is accepted by the players for what it is, and will therefore be treated by them as a practice environment. This gives the coach greater control and information exchange possibilities as most of his players are within his reach.

The half-field format is as close as you need to get to the real thing. Other complementary exercises such as 'keeping the shape' and 'crossing the ball' can supplement the half-field format, allowing the coach to work with the players in an acceptable low-risk, high-value environment. This means he can leave the proper game of soccer well alone, using it only at appropriate times to complement all the work and training sessions. When you add the cone working formats to the equation, you will have the right ingredients for the development and progress of any player.

Before looking at the half-field format, here is an example of a training routine that complements other working routines: beating the offside trap. You would not be able to practise cheating the offside trap as effectively if you were to rely on the full game format. This version gives your players plenty of opportunities to practise the passing and movements required in dealing with the offside trap.

PLAYING AGAINST OFFSIDES

With the new law in place, the attacking players are permitted to be in line with the last defender. Playing against offsides can therefore be reconsidered.

How It Works
(Fig 208)
There are two opposing teams with six

men in each, and the game is a possession play format (with an end product, I hasten to add) played in two halves of a specially marked out area. Each half measures 40m wide and 30m long. The two halves of the field are separated by a line of cones, which also represents the offside line.

The game is started by the coach playing the ball into zone A. There are two practice objectives: to retain possession of the ball, and to play the ball out of zone A from an onside position, through the mid-line in this set-up. The theme of the practice is ensured by the keep possession format. The team that wins possession must keep the ball for four consecutive passes before it can work on playing it out into zone B and the way it plays it is conditioned as follows way. The ball cannot be dribbled out of the zone. It can be passed diagonally to a runner from an onside position, as shown in the diagram.

Alternatively it can be played over the top from an onside position, also to a runner.

The opponents are entitled to defend in any way they see fit in order to win possession for their side. If the team in possession is successful in playing the ball past the offside trap/line (getting someone into the other zone from an onside position) they must then support the runner and the ball by moving into zone B. Play is continued in this zone, with the defending team also moving across. Each successful four-pass sequence by any team, followed by a successful play of the ball through the offside trap into the other zone, is awarded one point, the equivalent of a goal scored. The first team to ten points wins.

THE HALF-FIELD FORMAT IN DEFENCE

The first topic using the half-field

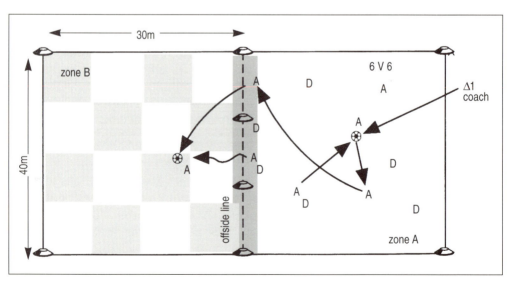

Fig 208   The offside trap.

format deals with defensive considerations. There are many schools of thought on this issue, some advocating playing in channels, others man-to-man marking. In truth there is no such thing as a perfect defence system. The best system of all is a mixture of defensive ideas put together in a collective defensive shape – that is, everyone contributes to the defence of their own goal. This mix is presented in my defensive system, here practised in the half-field format.

If you want to work with your right side of defence, stand as shown in Fig 209. If you wanted to work with the left side of your defence you would position yourself on the other side. In these positions the coach should be able to work on the following team-work topics: attacking and defending considerations, the system of play, keeping the shape, adjusting the shape according to play requirements and functions in play. The details of these topics can be broken down further.

How It Works
(Fig 209)
The diamond shapes in Fig 209 represent attacking play. The half-field is divided into seven channels 10m wide, which represent the defensive topics. When you position your players in channels, it is easier to explain to them their defensive roles. The remaining figures illustrate the possible defensive situations, using player numbers that relate to the codes below to explain defensive roles.

Defensive Function Codes

Code 1	Man-to-man marking

Defending Considerations

1	Man-to-man marking
6	Send inside
2	Man-to-man marking – cover
7	Defensive screening
3	Man-to-man marking – cover zone
8	Sweeper – cover
4	Zone defence
9	Body positions
5	Send outside
10	Control of movements – stand up

System of Play

1	Channel positions
2	Moving the shape
3	Adjust according to ball
4	Keeping the shape
5	The three-plus anchor positions plus zone

Code +1	Man-to-man marking plus jockeying
Code 2	Cover
Code 3	Zone
Code 4	Zone defence
Code 5	Tuck-in

Attacker in a Wide Position
(Fig 210)
The attacking player A9 has the ball in a wide position, so defender 1 starts his job of closing him down from a defensive channel position; when he goes forward towards player A9 he vacates his own channel, so the rest of his defence move across the channels to close the gap between each other's positions. The process is known as 'tucking in'. The channels keep everything in order defensively. The defensive players are numbered according to function: player 1 is the first challenger, the two players

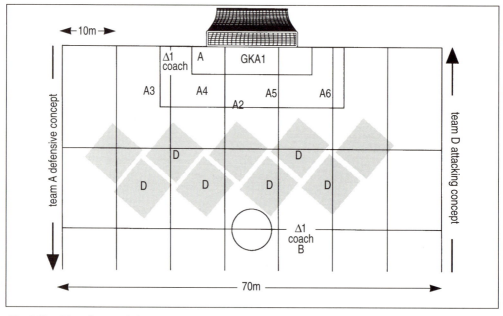

Fig 209   The diamond shapes represent positive thinking play options. The coach starts the practice by serving the ball.

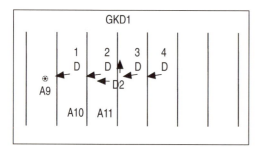

Fig 210   Giving cover.

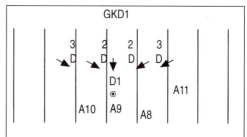

Fig 211   Tucking in.

numbered 2 give cover, player 3 establishes zone security in an anchor position and player 4 tucks in at the far side.

Attacker in a Central Position (Fig 211)

In this defensive shape the tuck-in happens to both sides of the first challenger as he moves forwards to challenge the

central attacker. Player D1 is again the first challenger, the two number 2s to the back of the first challenger give cover, and the two number 3s tuck in on either side of play.

Sending the Attacker Wide (Fig 212)

This is a mixture of the three main defensive positions. Player D1 is the

204

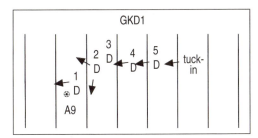

Fig 212   Sending the attacker wide.

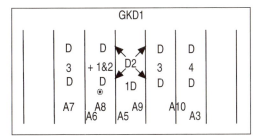

Fig 213   The double bank defensive system.

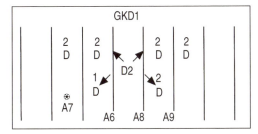

Fig 214   Setting a trap.

first challenger, who sends the opponent A9 into a wide position. Player D2 gives cover. Player D3 is the anchor, establishing the back shape in play. Player D4 is the first base in relation to the anchor holding the shape and line of defence. Player D5 tucks in at the far side.

Pulling the Attackers Inside (Fig 213)

The defenders form a double base line with one player (D2) holding a screening/diagonal cover position. The shape is designed in this way to encourage the opponents to come inside. Player +1 'opens the door' inside the shape for opponent A8; he and player 2 position themselves outfield to let A8 come in – this is a jockeying function. Player 2, the screening player, also provides cover for the front of the defence. The number 3s on either side hold firmly to baseline positions. Player 4 holds a line position to the front part of the shape; this is a special function and responsibility. This shape is designed to help the defenders win possession of the ball.

Luring Attackers into Holes (Fig 214)

The defensive shape is held in such a way that the opponents are forced to go into specific areas of play. The defensive screen is poised to give diagonal cover while the rest of the shape holds firm. The whole secret of this defending shape lies in the way the two players to the front and either side of player D2 function in this defensive system.

Player 1's job is to send opponent A7 outside into a wide position as shown; alternatively, he could just as easily position himself on the outside of his present position to send A7 inside. This position protects the full back and the nearest central defender (number 2s). The three work together to deal with any attacking move by players down that side of the field.

Apart from player 1, the first challenger, the rest of the player functions in this instance fall into code 2 – giving cover. This is because the tactic here is to give cover to the defensive screens at the front; all players in front of the back shape work to jockeying principles.

These functions are similar to the 'Venus trap' principle. Defensive screens at the front of the defence lure attacking players into holes where the back defenders deal with the actual challenge for the ball.

SUMMARY

Soccer is about playing the right numbers in all areas of play. If you are working to defensive principles, then you will try to get the shape to work in the way described above. You must create a defensive shape, which is held in relation to the ball. The depth or position of your defence depends on your play circumstances – for example, if you are caught short of numbers at the back and you cannot possibly position to the full range of defensive roles, the best solution is to hold vital areas in front of goal, outside the penalty box, for as long as you can, without committing yourself to challenge for the ball unless you really have to. This should buy your team time to establish the right numbers to build an effective defensive shape. The different positions and skills in support of the first challenger will give your team the best possible defensive system.

The whole point of any defensive system is to minimize losses. It is in fact the team which knows how to combine defensive principles with high standards of attacking play that stands the best chance of winning.

THE GOALKEEPER 18

Goalkeeping is not placed at the end of this book because it comes last in order of merit on the coaching list of priorities, but because it is a completely different skill from any other. The goalkeeper interacts with the other players in a unique way: on the one hand he has to dominate his immediate area of play, being independent of other players; on the other there are parts of his game that cannot be performed without the co-operation of his team-mates.

His role has also changed because of changes to the laws of the game. Before the changes to the back pass rule the keeper was able to pick the ball up if any of his outfield players kicked it to him. This tactic was used in the past to slow the game down or to retain possession of the ball, and was so effective that it had become the dominant tactic in defence before the rule change. The ball would be played back to the keeper, arriving at his feet, but he would not pick it up instantly unless he had to. The opponents would send an attacking player towards the ball, the keeper would wait till he got close to it, then he would pick it up. All of this would take time, allowing the rest of his team to move up-field – which of course was what this was all about.

The keeper would then kick the ball out of his hands so that it would end up well into the opponents' half of the field. If the keeper's team then pressed further, the opponents would end up passing the ball to their own keeper's hands, and exactly the same thing would happen at the other end of the field. In other words the defensive game totally dominated the proceedings. The attacking players were frustrated, and so were the members of the public, as there were times during the game when, with the ball flying backwards and forwards, they thought they were watching a game of tennis.

Thankfully this is no longer possible, as the new laws of the game have changed all of that. The players can still play the ball back to the keeper, but the keeper can only pick it up with his hands if it is headed to him. Otherwise he must kick it.

This has had a profound influence on the keeper's role. He now has to possess some outfield skills such as the ability to pass the ball with his feet. He is in effect the last defender, and in this position he needs to become more skilful in passing the ball out from back positions. He needs to be good at holding his nerve, especially when his opponents are putting him under pressure to deal with the ball.

The goalkeeper's position should never be underestimated – a good goalkeeper can save a team as much as twelve points in a season. If the goalkeeper is not confident in his own performance his team will fall apart; if he is good at his job then the team will grow in stature. The best goalkeepers will always help the outfield players to perform with confidence, because by their own brilliant performance they can inspire others. If they can keep the opponents from scoring, this gives the rest of the players a chance and raises team morale. In holding the team together the keeper is like the striker, who boosts team confidence through scoring, and the great midfield generals who can make others play with confidence; these positions can literally make the difference between success and failure.

POSITIONING

The first important topic to work on is goalkeeping angles. It would not do for the goalkeeper simply to stay on his goal line and defend his goal from there; he should come out and take command of the whole of his penalty area.

The Four Points of Reference
(Fig 215)

The goalkeeper must learn to position his body to take into account four important points of reference:

1 The near post
2 The far post
3 The ball
4 The distance to the ball

By drawing an imaginary line from each post to the ball, the keeper finds his central position in relation to the first three points of reference. The keeper's positioning himself in this way is called 'narrowing the angles' and will make the goal a smaller target. When he is profi-

cient at judging his position in relation to these reference points he will be in a better position to protect his goal.

The 'No Man's Land'
(Fig 216)

Next, the goalkeeper needs to acquire an appreciation of his position in goal in relation to the outfield opponents. There are areas of play which are his blind spots, called the 'no man's land', and knowing the shape of this zone is of paramount importance because if he finds himself trapped in this area, he will not be in a position to defend his goal. The greatest danger comes from an opponent chipping the ball over his head when it is too high for him to reach but not so high that it goes over the bar.

Another dangerous shot is the swerve shot, which is practically impossible to save; failure to save it cannot always blamed on the keeper because the ball will come in from outside the normal angles in play. This is a different type of no man's land. It is not unusual for a striker to look up and see that the keeper is out of position, too far forward off his goal line (in the no man's land), and take the opportunity to strike the ball from well outside his area.

When saving a penalty there is a no man's area in the top and bottom corners of each goal post, and if the ball is struck with swerve (right to left or left to right) to the top and bottom corners of the goal there is nothing the keeper can do about it.

Angles
(Fig 217)

Knowing all the angles in relation to

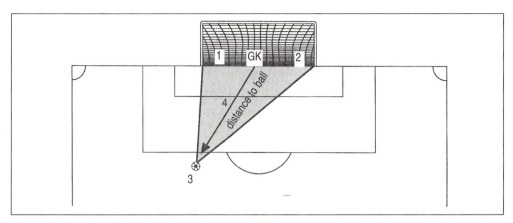

Fig 215   The four reference points.

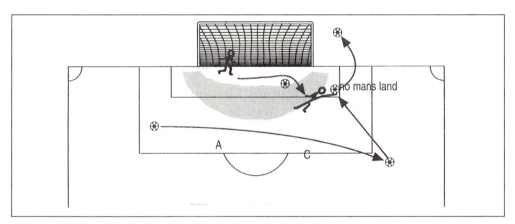

Fig 216   The no man's land.

shot stopping is obviously vital, as narrowing the angles makes the target as small as possible; it can also help the keeper to deal with one-on-one situations. This knowledge is vital when the keeper comes out and confronts the striker; how fast he comes out is governed by his ability to assess the situation.

To help you understand the relationship of angles and how to approach your opponent I have constructed a stage-by-stage shot-stopping chart which will help you to understand how to handle some of the goal-threatening situations in play. Use the chart as a guide to coping with a one-on-one situation.

The Shot-Stopping Chart (Fig 218)

In this scenario, player A1 moves within a metre of the box to position 2 and still has his head down. On seeing this, the goalkeeper moves slowly towards him. At position 3 he has the ball at his feet and his head is still down. The

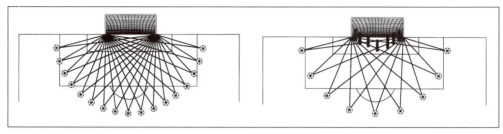

Fig 217(a)   Myriads of angles.   *(b)   Body position in relation to angles.*

goalkeeper moves into top gear, coming out very fast to position B as A1 reaches point 4; once on the edge of no man's land the goalkeeper slows down, and this momentary check-out movement serves him well in terms of controlling the situation.

At this point the striker could be forced by the keeper's action to make a decision. If he carries on advancing to point 5, the goalkeeper accelerates through no man's land to position C and pounces at A1's feet at position 5. As long as the striker keeps moving towards the goalkeeper, the goalkeeper is in with a chance, but how fast he approaches the striker is a different matter. The variations in the speed of coming out by the keeper are vital in order to give him some chance of protecting his goal. If he uses a constant speed of approach he is much more predictable and the striker can bypass him much more easily. There are times to move fast and there are times to stand up and hold your nerve.

The Wrong Angle of Approach (*Fig 219*)

This topic covers what to do when the ball is switched by the opponents from

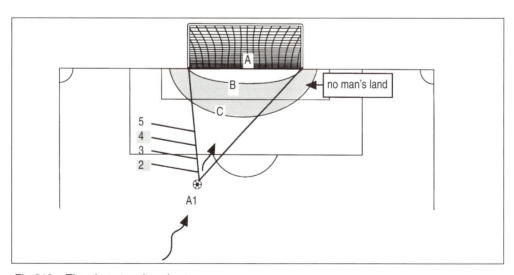

Fig 218   The shot-stopping chart.

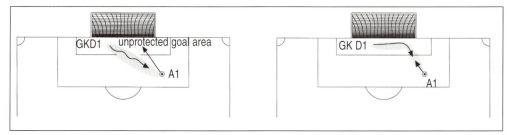

Fig 219 (a)   The wrong angle of approach.   (b)   The correct angle of approach.

one side of the penalty area to the other. This can happen in free play or during a corner kick, and if the keeper's position is on the wrong side of the ball, he will need to make his way across the goal area in order to make the goal target as small as possible again. Remember that as keeper your first priority is to get as quickly as possible across your goal line to the appropriate place in goal, then to reassess this position in relation to the three points of reference. This is not an easy task, because there is so much that you need to remember and act upon – you need to assess the distance from your line, the position of the ball, and your own posi-

tion in relation to your goal, which is a lot of information to deal with on the run; nevertheless this is what you have to do to protect your goal. Fig 219 illustrates these positioning problems, showing a correct and an incorrect approach.

How It Works (Fig 220)

For this exercise the keeper's starting position is at the far post. When attacking player A1 passes the ball to A2, the keeper moves across his goal line during the flight of the ball. He keeps as close to his goal line as possible, checking out at an appropriate position in relation to opponent A2. When he has

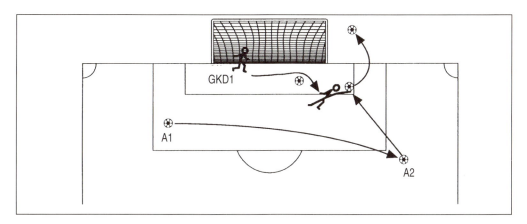

Fig 220   The working format.

reached the right position, he changes angle and comes towards player A2 and the ball. Going down the line makes the target as small as possible. In this example the goalkeeper has managed to play the ball out for a corner.

When the keeper has to come down the line to confront an opponent, things are never going to be easy for him, especially if he is dealing with a skilful striker; but there are things that could help him deal with the situation. He could look out for possible mistakes made by the striker A2. For example, A2's first touch of the ball could be too strong and carry the ball too far forwards; when this happens the keeper can time his movements easily to intercept the ball and smother it quickly. Saving at the feet of opponents without fouling them is of paramount importance in today's game.

THE SKILLS OF HANDLING AND PASSING

You do not need an elaborate practice format to practise catching the high ball. This technique will be used in co-operation with defenders in an appropriate setting. There is nothing mysterious about this topic; the keeper has to learn the basics just like anyone else.

The High Ball
(Fig 221)

Here the keeper works on catching the high ball, which deals with crosses of the ball into the box. Make sure that the hands take the ball at the highest point, and that the leading leg is bent on take-off to protect the body.

Fig 221   Take the ball at the highest point.

Taking the Pace Out of the Ball
(Fig 222)

When the ball is coming fast at the keeper, he should present the palms of his hands to the ball to take the sting out of the strike and make the ball safe; however, rather than allowing the ball to drop to the floor, try to catch it, because if the ball is dropped the opponents can sometimes pounce on it and score.

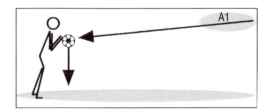

Fig 222   Take the pace out of the ball.

The Waistline Catch
(Fig 223)

The keeper can use his body to cup the ball into his waistline. The hands are presented to the ball in such a way that the backs of the hands are towards the ground, while the palms face the oncoming ball. The keeper's backside tucks away from the impact area and hands. Once the ball strikes the palms, the hands bring the ball up towards the mid-diaphragm area, with the elbows now curling around the ball. The elbows tuck in, keeping together and pointing towards the origin of strike.

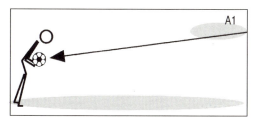

Fig 223   Tuck in on impact.

Closing the Gap
(Fig 224)

To pick up a rolling ball, the palms are presented to the ball, as shown. The feet have to be positioned in such a way that the ball does not slip through them if the hands miss the ball. The leading leg bends at the knee, tucking the knee in towards the other leg, and the back leg also bends slightly inwards. The body stoops to cup the ball up into the hands, the hands curl around the ball and bring it up to the diaphragm where again the elbows will protect it. This all happens as the keeper rises to his feet, though sometimes he has to skip-jump out of this position in order to avoid an

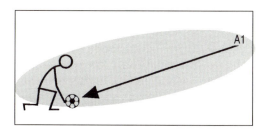

Fig 224   Close the gap, scoop and lift.

incoming striker. In the diagram the left leg knee should be tucked in more to close the gap between the legs.

The Javelin Throw
(Fig 225)

When it comes to passing the ball back into play, you are most likely to use the overarm technique (javelin throw), which can send the ball almost any distance you want. However, the technique is not without risk and there are not that many keepers prepared to throw the ball in this way. The technique is similar to throwing the javelin. The ball sits in the palm of the hand and is pushed or driven forwards with a long follow-through to the target.

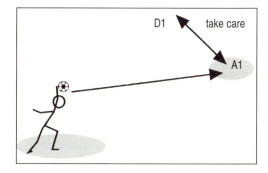

Fig 225   The javelin throw.

Kicking the Ball Away
(Figs 226 & 227)

The keeper needs to work on kicking the ball out of his penalty area, because under the rules he cannot pick up the ball from his players in many game situations. In this example the coach serves the ball along the ground to the keeper, and the keeper practises volleying the ball or striking it along the ground to a designated team-mate on

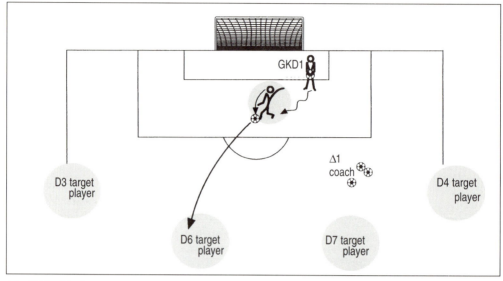

Fig 226   Find your target.

Fig 227   The defence's last resort – the keeper boots the ball upfield.

his first touch. Dealing with the ball in this situation is not as simple as you might imagine; for example it is quite easy for the keeper to slice his shot (skim the ball with the outside of his boot) by mistake.

In this example the keeper has received a low pass back from the coach and has kicked the ball to target player D6.

Diving for the Ball
(Figs 228–230)

There are many occasions now when the keeper will be left in this position, as the laws of the game are such that the break through any defence is not that infrequent. Therefore the keeper needs to be able to dive for the ball.

This topic can easily be practised as follows. Two strikers are positioned on the edge of the box: player A1 sets the ball up for a strike on target, and player A2 performs the strike – in this example to the left of the keeper.

In Fig 229, you can see the correct left knee and elbow position in relation to the ground. The keeper must also keep his head steady, his eyes firmly on the ball and the palms of his hands presented to the ball. In Fig 230 the keeper finishes up curled round the ball so that the feet and knees protect the head against any oncoming opponent – more

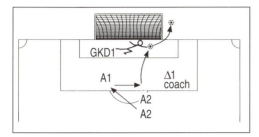

Fig 228 Shot-stopping

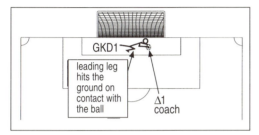

Fig 229   Landing position.

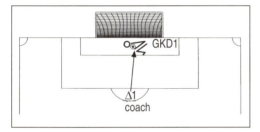

Fig 230   Protect your head.

so than it is possible to show in this diagram.

COMMUNICATION
(Figs 231 & 232)
The keeper's instructions should always be carried out to the letter. Standard instructions are listed below; some of these are informative, others are commands and yet others are warnings. Which are which? Good communication means that instructions should be clear and precise, and, of course, must keep to the laws of the game. The keeper is the boss of his area, and can see all the dangers in front of his goal, so the players need to listen to him carefully. In Fig 235 the keeper has seen an unmarked opponent (A9) in a free play situation. He instantly shouts 'pick him up' to his midfield player D7. D7 knows what the keeper wants and obliges by quickly coming goal side of A9.

Keeper's Instructions
The following are common instructions used by keepers. Make sure that everyone on the team knows exactly what they mean.

Man on	Covers on
Time	Touch
First time	Safe hands
Turn	Push up
Pick him up	Stand up
Man to man	Send right
Tight	Send left
Keeper's ball	Help him
Away	Played
Cover	Jockey

Away
There are times when the keeper decides that he cannot come out to a cross because his players are better

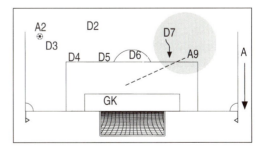

Fig 231   Pick him up.

215

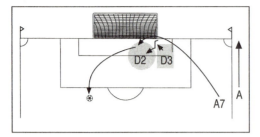

Fig 232   Away.

positioned than he is to deal with the danger. In this situation he uses the 'away' command. On hearing this command the defenders deal with the ball in the appropriate way; in Fig 232 player D2 heads the ball to gain distance. In these situations the defender's touch on the ball must be meaningful.

The Keeper's Ball

(Figs 233 & 234)

Not all circumstances are so clearly defined, and sometimes the keeper may choose to punch the ball to clear his lines. In this situation the defenders help him by standing out of his way as soon as they hear his signal 'keeper's ball'.

The best keepers in the world do not hang around too long. They make quick decisions and keep control of the situation. Fig 234 shows the keeper coming

out to deal competently with the ball after a shout of 'keeper's ball'.

The keeper needs to work on his handling and passing because these are his bread-and-butter skills. These training routines are his skill foundations, and once he is competent at this level he will become an integral part of the team. The training routines in this book which relate to the work with strikers and defenders are his domain, as the end product of many of these exercises can be organized to include strikes on target so the keeper can profitably participate.

FREE KICKS AND CORNERS
(Figs 235–240)

The diagrams opposite show the position the keeper should take up for free kicks and corners.

STAMINA AND FITNESS TRAINING

There are stamina training routines and reaction training routines that help the keeper with his physical and mental fitness. The first two examples are fitness-orientated, but have an end product. The keeper works on diving to his right and left side (saving shots). The timing

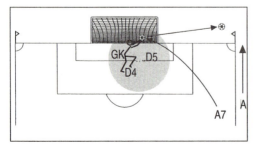

Fig 233   Punch!

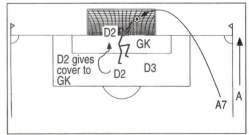

Fig 234   Keeper's ball!

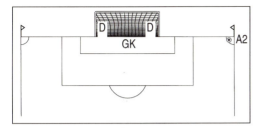

Fig 235   Corner kick position.

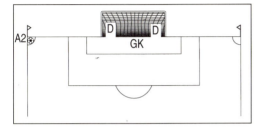

Fig 236   Corner kick position.

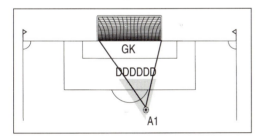

Fig 237   Positioning the wall.

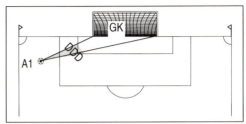

Fig 238   Covering the near post.

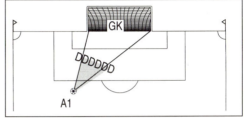

Fig 239   Watching the far post.

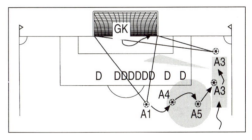

Fig 240   Protecting direct and switch play angles.

of the service of the ball coincides with the running patterns, which relate to what happens in game situations.

Coming Out to the Opponent (Fig 241)

This run simulates coming out to an opponent. The keeper starts at the front of the cone formation and runs to the back cone, then back to go forwards through gate A. Just as he goes past gate A the ball is served to cone B or C in such a way that it is possible for him

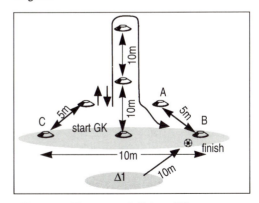

Fig 241   Fitness and diving skills.

217

to reach it. The run ends with the keeper diving for the ball to prevent it hitting cone B or C.

The Figure-of-Eight Run
(Fig 247)

The exercise simulates the game situation where the keeper comes across his goal area to dive and save the ball at the far post. The keeper runs round the two cones in a figure-of-eight pattern and the coach plays the ball low to either cone just as the keeper rounds the back of the cone. In this example the keeper will dive to his left and catch the ball in his hands.

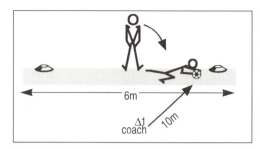

Fig 243   Penalty saves.

The Working Clock
(Fig 244)

This sort of training routine is designed to help the keeper make reaction saves. The reaction save is usually made when the keeper is unsighted or the shot strikes someone *en route* to goal. This working format is called the working clock because the keeper dives from a standing position to the time positions 3, 6, 9 and 12 o'clock.

There is a soccer ball placed on the ground in each time slot. The coach throws or plays the ball to the side of any time slot and the keeper must dive over the top of the ball. In doing so he is not allowed to touch any of the balls on the ground.

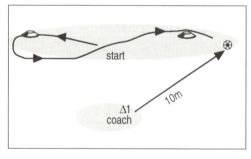

Fig 242   The figure-of-eight run.

Penalty Saves
(Fig 243)

Penalties are now more frequent than ever before, so this simple exercise will prove very useful. The keeper stands in the centre of the 'goal', which is marked out by two cones. The coach plays the ball to one side of him and he works on his feet co-ordination: the dive to the ball is made by pushing off with the leg furthest from the ball.

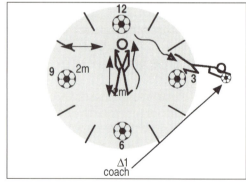

Fig 244   The working clock.

Simulated Game Situations

In a game situation you never know what will happen next, so the keeper has to be mentally and physically fit enough to cope with whatever may happen. He may have just been involved in a magnificent save where he has just parried the ball to the left of his goal, only to see the ball picked up by an opponent; even if the opponent is closed down by his co-defenders, the job of the keeper is to get up quickly, reassess his position, and reposition himself to protect his goal.

The next two exercises put the keeper through his paces. They are very intensive working formats, the intention being to develop the keeper's strength, stamina and speed of physical reaction, and to develop his ability to command his area.

The A and B Format (Fig 245)

Here the keeper has just dived on the near post and has to get up quickly to deal with a high ball (position A); he is beaten to this high ball and the ball wings its way to the far post as shown. The keeper has to readjust his position and dive to the far post at position B. The coach/service players must time the passes of the ball accurately.

The A, B and C Format (Fig 246)

I have never seen a more intensive training exercise than this, which is almost the ultimate in reaction training exercises. The keeper has to move and save the shots through three different positions in quick succession: the high ball (position A), the low dive (position B) and the parry at position C. Again, the service of the ball must be timed to coincide with the keeper's actions.

BODY PROTECTION

The keeper's position is always going to be vulnerable in today's game, when competing for the ball is at its fiercest. The penalty box is not a place for

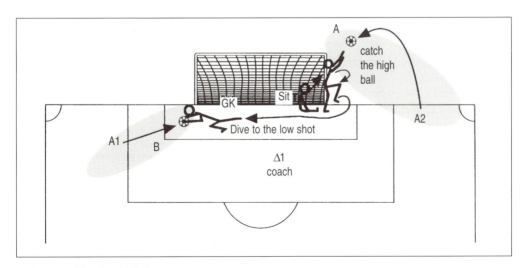

Fig 245   The A and B format.

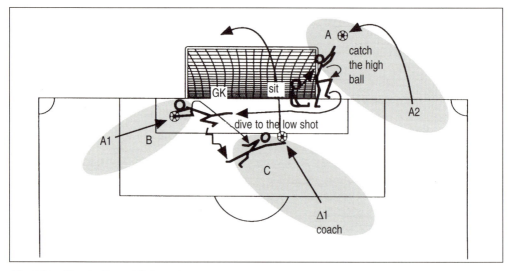

Fig 246   The A, B, and C format.

dilly-dallying, but for being positive in dealing with the ball; decisive action can save the keeper from being hurt as well as help him to protect his goal. The goalkeeper has the right to use his body, but not in a violent way; he is not allowed to punch or kick his opponents. He does have the right to use his knees and his elbows to protect himself, however, when holding onto the ball. On crosses he needs to jump up to get to the ball at the highest point. To do this he needs to take off using the one foot take-off technique, allowing the other knee to come up to the mid-part of his body. The knee comes up to protect his groin region, not to dish out any punishment to oncoming opponents. The same applies when the keeper is on the ground; his knees and elbows are his only protection, so he needs to get these parts of the body wrapped around the ball and himself in order to protect him-

self from other challenging players.

It is up to the strikers to know when to challenge for the ball and when to withhold their challenge. The worst possible scenario is the fifty-fifty ball when the striker is committed to getting to the ball ahead of the keeper; the momentum of both players coming into a head-on confrontation can result in a serious injury. There are times when this is possibly acceptable, however, because this type of ball has to be dealt with.

Finally, there is protective clothing available, which the keeper should wear to minimize the risk of injury. The fact that the keeper has such protection will also help to protect the striker. The most important areas are the hips, knees, groin/kidneys, heart, and shoulders. Gloves are essential, as the finger bones can be broken on impact with the ball, or in a collision with other players.

CONCLUSION

Thank you for reading this book. I hope that many of the exercises will become part of your training repertoire. Remember that the most significant coaching point in any ball control exercise is to practise specific length of movements on the ball. In dribbling skills, no one takes on an opponent without ever changing direction, or runs with the ball in a straight line unless he wants to lose possession of the ball!

As far as training sessions are concerned, stick to the four-stage planner which automatically creates the right working sequence. The choice of exercises within the training sessions is left up to you, now that you have read about conventional formats and more advanced concepts. The first coaching topic I would choose would be the four-cone format described in Chapter 14. This provides a solid base for acquiring technical skills on the ball.

The four-cone formats do not adhere to the two-touch concepts and are limited only by your own imagination; the beauty about them is that they have no limitations with regard to their potential use. These formats will test you whoever you are and however good, and if needs be they will go with you all the way to the top. And if you think you are already there, then they will make you think again.

Good luck in your endeavours.

INDEX